THE SALT PATH

RAYNOR WINN

ISIS
LARGE
PRINT

First published in Great Britain 2018
by
Michael Joseph
an imprint of Penguin Books

First Isis Edition
published 2019
by arrangement with
Penguin Random House UK

A catalogue record for this book is available
from the British Library.

ISBN 978–1–78541–803–7 (hb)
ISBN 978–1–78541–809–9 (pb)

Published by
F. A. Thorpe (Publishing)
Anstey, Leicestershire

Set by Words & Graphics Ltd.
Anstey, Leicestershire
Printed and bound in Great Britain by
T. J. International Ltd., Padstow, Cornwall

This book is printed on acid-free paper

For the team

Contents

ix

South West Coast Path

B r i s t o l   C h a n n e l

Combe Martin

Westward Ho!

Hartland

Bude

Tintagel

Padstow

Newquay

St Ives

Polruan

Plymouth

Gorran Haven

Falmouth

Penzance

Land's End

Kynance Cove

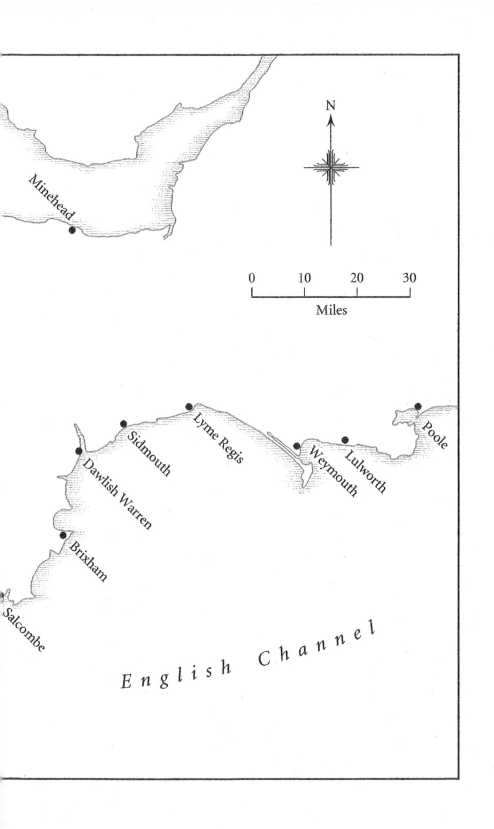

N

0   10   20   30

Miles

Minehead

Lyme Regis

Sidmouth

Dawlish Warren

Brixham

Salcombe

Weymouth

Lulworth

Poole

E n g l i s h   C h a n n e l

Prologue

There's a sound to breaking waves when they're close, a sound like nothing else. The background roar is unmistakable, overlaid by the swash of the landing wave and then the sucking noise of the backwash as it retreats. It was dark, barely a speck of light, but even without seeing it I recognized the strength of the swash and knew it must be close. I tried to be logical. We'd camped well above the high-tide line; the beach shelved away below us and beyond that was the water level: it couldn't reach us; we were fine. I put my head back on the rolled-up jumper and thought about sleep. No, we weren't fine, we were far from fine. The swash and suck wasn't coming from below, it was right outside.

Scrambling through the green-black light in the tent, I tore open the flaps. Moonlight cut across the cliff tops leaving the beach in complete darkness, but lit the waves as they broke into a mess of foam, the swash already running over the sand shelf ending only a metre from the tent. I shook the sleeping bag next to me.

"Moth, Moth, the water, it's coming."

Throwing everything that was heavy into our rucksacks, shoving feet into boots, we pulled out the steel pegs and picked the tent up whole, still erected with our sleeping bags and clothes inside, the groundsheet sagging down to the sand. We scuttled across the beach like a giant green crab, to what had the night before been a small trickle of fresh water running towards the sea, but was now a metre-deep channel of sea water running towards the cliff.

"I can't hold it high enough. It's going to soak the sleeping bags."

"Well, do something, or it won't be just the slee . . ."

We raced back to where we started from. As the backwash headed out I could see the channel flattened to a wide stretch of water only a foot deep. We ran back down the beach, the swash landing far above the shelf and rushing over the sand towards us.

"Wait for the backwash then run to the other side of the channel and up the beach."

I was in awe. This man, who only two months earlier had struggled to put on his coat without help, was standing on a beach in his underpants holding an erected tent above his head with a rucksack on his back saying, run.

"Run, run, run!"

We splashed through the water with the tent held high and climbed desperately up the beach as the swash pushed at our heels and the backwash tried to draw us out to sea. Stumbling through the soft sand, our boots brimming with salt water, we dropped the tent down at the foot of the cliff.

"You know, I don't think these cliffs are stable. We should move further along the beach."

What? How could he be so careful at three in the morning?

"No."

We'd walked 243 miles, slept wild for thirty-six nights, eating dried rations for most of that time. The South West Coast Path guidebook stated that we would reach this point in eighteen days, and directed us towards delicious food and places to stay with soft beds and hot water. The timescale and comforts were all out of our reach, but I didn't care. Moth ran up the beach in the moonlight in a ripped pair of underpants that he'd been wearing for five days straight, holding a fully erected tent above his head. It was a miracle. It was as good as it gets.

The light started to break over Portheras Cove as we packed our rucksacks and made tea. Another day ahead. Just another day walking. Only 387 miles to go.

PART ONE

Into the Light

Tell me about a complicated man.
Muse, tell me how he wandered and was lost . . .

Homer, *The Odyssey*

CHAPTER
ONE

Dust of Life

I was under the stairs when I decided to walk. In that moment, I hadn't carefully considered walking 630 miles with a rucksack on my back, I hadn't thought about how I could afford to do it, or that I'd be wild camping for nearly one hundred nights, or what I'd do afterwards. I hadn't told my partner of thirty-two years that he was coming with me.

Only minutes earlier hiding under the stairs had seemed a good option. The men in black began hammering on the door at 9 a.m., but we weren't ready. We weren't ready to let go. I needed more time: just another hour, another week, another lifetime. There would never be enough time. So we crouched together under the stairs, pressed together, whispering like scared mice, like naughty children, waiting to be found.

The bailiffs moved to the back of the house, banging on the windows, trying all the catches, looking for a way in. I could hear one of them climbing on to the garden bench, pushing at the kitchen skylight, shouting. It was then that I spotted the book in a packing box. I'd read *Five Hundred Mile Walkies* in my twenties, the story of a man who walked the South West Coast Path with his dog. Moth was squeezed in next to me, his head on his knees, his arms wrapped around in self-defence, and pain, and fear, and anger. Above all anger. Life had picked up every piece of ammunition possible and hurled it at him full force, in what had been three years of endless battle. He was exhausted with anger. I put my hand on his hair. I'd stroked that hair when it was long and blond, full of sea salt, heather and youth; brown and shorter, full of building plaster and the kids' play dough; and now silver, thinner, full of the dust of our life.

I'd met this man when I was eighteen; I was now fifty. We'd rebuilt this ruined farm together, restoring every wall, every stone, growing vegetables and hens and two children, creating a barn for visitors to share our lives and pay the bills. And now, when we walked out of that door, it would all be behind us, everything behind us, over, finished, done.

"We could just walk."

It was a ridiculous thing to say, but I said it anyway.

"Walk?"

"Yeah, just walk."

Could Moth walk it? It was just a coastal path after all; it couldn't be that hard and we could walk slowly, put one foot in front of the other and just follow the map. I desperately needed a map, something to show me the way. So why not? It couldn't be that difficult.

The possibility of walking the whole coastline from Minehead in Somerset, through north Devon, Cornwall and south Devon to Poole in Dorset seemed just about feasible. Yet, in that moment, the idea of walking over hills, beaches, rivers and moorland was as remote and unlikely to happen as us getting out from under the stairs and opening the door. Something that could be done by someone else, not us.

But we'd already rebuilt a ruin, taught ourselves plumbing, brought up two children, defended ourselves against judges and highly paid barristers, so why not?

Because we lost. Lost the case, lost the house, and lost ourselves.

I reached out my hand to lift the book from its box, and looked at the cover: *Five Hundred Mile Walkies*. It seemed such an idyllic prospect. I didn't realize then that the South West Coast Path was relentless, that it would mean climbing the equivalent of Mount Everest nearly four times, walking 630 miles on a path often no more than a foot wide, sleeping wild, living wild, working our way through every painful action that had brought us here, to this moment, hiding. I just knew we should walk. And now we had no choice. I'd reached out my hand towards the box and now they knew we were in the house, they'd seen me, there was no way back, we had to go. As we crawled from the darkness beneath the stairs, Moth turned back.

"Together?"

"Always."

We stood at the front door, the bailiffs on the other side waiting to change the locks, to bar us from our old lives. We were about to leave the dimly lit, centuries-old house that had held us cocooned for twenty years.

When we walked through the door we could never ever come back.

We held hands and walked into the light.

CHAPTER
TWO

Losing

Did we begin our walk that day under the stairs, or the day we got out of a friend's van in Taunton, to be left in the rain on the side of the road with our rucksacks on the tarmac? Or had the walk been coming for years, waiting on our horizon to be unleashed on us only when there was absolutely nothing left to lose?

That day in the court building was the end of a three-year battle, but things never end the way you expect them to. When we moved to the farm in Wales the sun was shining, the children were running around our feet and life was spreading out ahead of us. A derelict pile of stones in an isolated spot at the foot of the mountains. We put every ounce of ourselves into its restoration, working on it through every spare moment while the children grew around us. It was our home, our business, our sanctuary, so I didn't expect it to end in a dingy grey courtroom next to an amusement arcade. I didn't expect it to end while I stood in front of a judge and told him he'd got it wrong. I didn't expect to be wearing the leather jacket the kids had bought me for my fiftieth birthday. I didn't expect it to end.

Sitting in the courtroom, I watched as Moth picked at a white fleck on the black table in front of him. I knew what he was thinking: how had it come to this? He'd been close friends with the man who was making the financial claim against us. They'd grown up together, part of a group of friends; riding their trikes, playing football, sharing teenage years. How *had* it come to this? They'd stayed close even when others had fallen away. As they grew into adults and their lives took them in different directions, Cooper moved into financial circles that few of us understood. But Moth kept in touch regardless, remaining friends. Trusting enough that when an opportunity arose to make an investment in one of his companies we took it, putting in a substantial sum. The company with which the investment was made eventually failed, leaving a number of unpaid debts. The suggestion that we owed money had crept in insidiously. At first we ignored it, but over time Cooper became insistent that, owing to the structure of the agreement, we were liable to make payment towards those debts. Initially, Moth was more devastated by the breakdown in a friendship than by the financial claim, and the dispute rumbled between them for years. We were convinced that we had no liability for the debts as it was not specifically indicated in the wording, and Moth firmly believed that they would eventually work it out between themselves. Until the day when a court summons for payment arrived in the post.

Our savings quickly ran out, eaten up by solicitors' fees. From then on we became litigants in person, just a number amongst the unrepresented masses, something the government had created in their thousands when they announced the recent legal aid reforms, leaving us with no right to free representation as our case was classed as "too complex" to qualify for legal aid. The reform may have saved £350 million a year, but left vulnerable people with no access to justice.

The only tactic we were able to employ was to stall, and stall and stall again, playing for time, while all the time in the background contacting lawyers and accountants, trying to find some written evidence that would convince the judge of the truth: that our interpretation of the original agreement was correct, and we had no liability for the debts. Without a barrister on our side we were constantly outmanoeuvred and a charge was registered against the farm as security for payment of Cooper's claim. We held our breath, and then it came: a claim for possession of our home, of the house and the land, of every stone we had carefully placed, the tree where the children played, the hole in the wall where the blue tits nested, the loose piece of lead by the chimney where the bats lived. A claim to take it all. We continued to stall, making applications, requesting adjournments, until we finally thought we had it, the shining white light of a piece of paper that proved that Cooper had no right to make the claim, as we didn't owe anything. After three years and ten court appearances, we had the evidence that could save our home. We'd sent copies to the judge and the claimant's barrister. We were ready. I wore my leather jacket, I was so kick-ass confident.

The judge shuffled his papers as if we weren't there. I glanced at Moth, needing some flicker of reassurance, but he stared straight ahead. The last few years had taken their toll; his thick hair was thinning and white and his skin had taken on a waxy, ashen appearance. It was as if a hole had been cut through him; a trusting, honest, generous man, this betrayal by such a close friend had shaken him to the core. A constant pain in his shoulder and arm ate at his strength and distracted his thoughts. We just needed this to be over, to get on with normal life, and then I felt sure he'd get better. But our life would never be that kind of normal again.

I stood up, my legs loose, as if they were underwater. I held the piece of paper like an anchor in my hand. I could hear seagulls squabbling outside with agitated distracting calls.

"Good morning, sir. I hope you received the new evidence which was supplied to you on Monday."

"I have."

"If I can refer you to that evidence —"

Cooper's barrister rose to his feet, straightening his tie as he always did when he was about to address the judge. Confident. In control. Everything that we weren't. I was desperate for a lawyer, begging for one.

"Sir, this information which you and I have both received is new evidence."

The judge looked at me accusingly.

"Is this new evidence?"

"Well, yes, we only received it four days ago."

"New evidence cannot be proffered at this late stage. I cannot accept it."

14

"But it proves everything we've said for the last three years. It proves that we don't owe the claimant anything. It's the truth."

I knew what was coming. I wanted to freeze time, stop it there, never let the next words come. I wanted to take Moth's hand, to get up and leave the courtroom, never to think of it again, to go home and light the fire, to run my hands across the stone walls as the cat curled into the warmth. To breathe again without my chest tightening, to think of home without fear of losing it.

"You can't produce evidence without the correct judicial procedure. No, I'm going to proceed to judgement. I will give possession to the claimant. You will have vacated the property in seven days' time, by nine a.m. on that day. Right, we'll move on to costs. Is there anything you wish to say about costs?"

"Yes, you've made a complete mistake, this is all wrong. And no, I don't want to talk about costs, we've got no money anyway, you're taking our home, our business, our income, what more do you want?" I gripped the table as the floor fell away. Don't cry, don't cry, don't cry.

"I'm taking that into consideration and dismissing the claim for costs."

My thoughts were drifting, running for safety. As Moth moved in his chair I could almost touch the smell of hot dry gravel and fresh-cut boxwood as it whispered from his jacket. The kids had grazed their knees on that gravel learning to ride their bikes, and skidded on it as they drove out on their way to university. The roses were in full flower, hanging over the box hedge like cotton-wool balls; I'd be dead-heading soon.

"I request the right to appeal."

"No, I'm denying the right to appeal. This case has gone on for far too long; you've had plenty of opportunities to supply evidence."

The room was shrinking, the walls closing in. It didn't matter that we had only just found this evidence, or that it contained the truth; it only mattered that I hadn't submitted it in the correct way, that I hadn't followed the correct procedure. What would I do, what would we do, what would I do with the hens, who would give the old sheep a slice of bread in the morning, how could we pack a farm in a week, how could we pay for a hire van, what about the families who had booked holidays, the cats, the kids? How could I tell the children we'd just lost their home? Our home. Lost, because I didn't understand the procedure. I'd made a simple, basic error: I hadn't made a request to submit further evidence. I didn't know I needed to. I'd been so happy, so sure, I just sent it in. Wasted my perfect piece of paper, with the perfect white truth. And now we had lost it all. Penniless, homeless.

We closed the courtroom door behind us and walked down the corridor, stiff, silent. I glanced at the barrister in the side room and kept walking, but Moth went in. No, Moth, no, Moth, don't hit him. I could feel all the anger, all the stress of the last three years. But he held out his hand to the barrister.

16

"It's all right, I know you're only doing your job, but it was the wrong decision, you do know that, don't you?"

He took Moth's hand and shook it.

"It's the judge's decision, not mine."

I still didn't cry, but a silent internal howl took hold and screwed me tight, making it hard to breathe.

I stood in the field behind the house, under the twisted ash tree, where the children built an igloo in the big snow of 'ninety-six. I broke a slice of white bread into six pieces, a ritual that had marked the start of the day for the last nineteen years. The old ewe snuffled at my hand and her soft lips took the bread: nineteen years old, no teeth, but still a great appetite. The children called her Smotyn, Welsh for spotty. Now she was a grumpy old ewe, with a scruffy black and white fleece and two wonky horns. Well, one now, she'd knocked the other off in her desperation to get into a feed bucket a few years before. Tom had kept the horn; it was in the treasure box he took with him when he left for university, along with his fossils and Pokémon cards. When Rowan was three I'd taken her on a forty-mile road trip in our tiny van. We bought three scatty, spotty little lambs from a farm on the side of a hill overlooking the sea. She howled with annoyance when I wouldn't let her sit with them, so I relented and drove home with all four of them together on the straw in the back of the van. They'd been part of our lives ever since, part of our family. They'd had many lambs over the years, but now

Smotyn was the only one left, her sisters had died and I'd sold all the rest to another breeder the year before, when the court case had reached a point where we thought it couldn't go any further and we were about to lose. I hadn't been able to let Smotyn go: at her age no one else would keep her; the average lifespan for a sheep is six to seven years before they're sent to make dog food or meatballs. The day after the court hearing I'd taken the hens to a friend, but there was no room for Smotyn. She wandered away down the field, clouds of dandelion seeds engulfing her, to below the beech trees where the grass was always dry. We both knew that field as if it was an extension of ourselves. How would either of us live without it?

We'd both be homeless in five days; then we'd know.

What I didn't know, what I couldn't know, was that it wouldn't take five days for my life to change forever, for everything that kept me stable to turn to quicksand beneath me. It would happen the next day.

We were in a consultant's room in a hospital in Liverpool. Finally, we would have the results of years of medical procrastination and we'd know the cause of Moth's shoulder pain. After a life of physical work he'd been told by one doctor: "Pain is normal, you should expect to suffer when you raise your arms and stumble a bit when you walk." Others had raised questions about a slight tremor in his hand and numbness in his face. But this doctor was the top dog, head of his field, the real deal. He was going to tell us that it was ligament damage or something similar and how it could be fixed; that it had happened when Moth fell through the barn roof years ago — maybe there'd been a hairline fracture. He was certainly going to tell us how it could be put right. He would sit authoritatively behind his desk and tell us this. Without a doubt.

We'd barely spoken during the long drive to Liverpool, each of us in our own mire of shock and exhaustion. The days since the court case were a blur of packing boxes and bonfires, endless fraught phone calls and despair. The realization had dawned that we had nowhere to go. The worst thing that could possibly happen had happened. This seven-hour round trip was something we didn't need. Every hour was precious, every hour to finish packing, every hour to still be held safe within those walls.

The endless trips to doctors' waiting rooms had begun six years previously. A debilitating pain in his shoulder and arm, and then a tremor beginning in his hand, had led to doctors believing he had Parkinson's disease, but when that was proved not to be the case, they felt maybe it was nerve damage. This consultant's room was like every other: a square, white, emotionless box overlooking the car park. But this doctor wasn't behind his desk; he came and sat on the corner of it next to Moth, put his hand on his arm and asked him how he was. It was wrong. Doctors don't do that. No doctor we'd seen, and we'd seen a fair few, had ever done that.

"The best thing I can do for you, Moth, is give you a diagnosis."

No, no, no, no, no. Don't say any more, don't speak, something awful is going to fall out of your smug, tight lips, don't open them, don't speak.

"I believe you have corticobasal degeneration, CBD. We can't be absolutely certain about the diagnosis. There is no test, so we'll only know at post-mortem."

"Post-mortem? When do you think that will be?" Moth's hands spread wide over his thighs, holding as much of himself as he could between his broad fingers.

"Well, I would normally say six to eight years from onset. But yours seems to be very slow progressing as it's already been six years since you first presented with a problem."

"That must mean you've got it wrong then. It's something else." I could feel my stomach rising into my throat and the room slipping out of focus.

The doctor looked at me as if I was a child; then he carried on trying to explain a rare degenerative brain disease that would take the beautiful man I'd loved since I was a teenager and destroy his body and then his mind as he fell into confusion and dementia, and end with him unable to swallow and probably choking to death on his own saliva. And there was nothing, absolutely nothing they could do about it. I could hardly breathe; the room was swimming. No, not Moth, don't take him, you can't take him, he's everything, he's all of it, all of me. No. I tried to keep a calm face, but inside I was screaming, panicking, like a bee against a glass pane. The real world was there, but suddenly out of reach.

"But you could have got it wrong."

20

What was he talking about? This wasn't how we would die. It wasn't Moth's life; it was our life. We were one, fused, enmeshed, molecular. Not his life, not my life: our life. We had a plan for how we would die. When we were ninety-five, on top of a mountain having watched the sun come up, we would simply go to sleep. Not choking to death in a hospital bed. Not separate, separated, alone.

"You've got it wrong."

We clung together in the van in the hospital car park, as if the simple act of pressing our bodies together would make this stop. If there was no light between us, then nothing could separate us, this wouldn't be real and we wouldn't have to face it. Silent tears rolled down Moth's face, but I didn't cry, couldn't cry. If I did, I'd give in to a river of pain that would wash me away. Our whole adult life had been lived together. Every dream, or plan, every success or failure, had been two halves of one whole life. Never separate, never alone, one.

There were no drugs to halt the progress, no therapies to keep the disease at bay. The only help that could be offered was a drug called Pregabalin to ease the pain, but Moth was already taking that. There was nothing else. I longed to be able to go to the chemist and collect a box of magic, anything that would stop the march of destruction burning through our life.

"Physiotherapy will help with the stiffness," the doctor had said. But Moth already had a physio routine that he did every day. Maybe he could do more; maybe if he did more we could stop it progressing. I clutched at every straw, any flimsy thread to drag me from this suffocating fog of shock. There were no threads, no hand reaching down to pull me to safety, no soothing voice to say it's all right, it's just a bad dream. Just the two of us holding on to reality, to each other, in a hospital car park.

"You can't be ill, I still love you."

As if just loving him was enough. It had always been enough, it had always been all I needed, but it wouldn't save us now. The first time Moth told me he loved me was the first time I'd ever heard those words said. No one had ever said they loved me before, not my parents or friends, no one ever before, and those words had lifted me up, shining, glowing, into the next thirty-two years of my life. But words had no strength against Moth's brain shifting into self-destruct, against a protein called tau sludging up the cells, blocking the connections.

"He's got it wrong. I just know it, he's wrong." He had to be wrong. The judge had got it wrong, so why not the doctor?

"I can't think, can't feel . . ."

"Then let's think he's wrong. If we refuse to believe him we can carry on and live like this isn't real." I couldn't let it in. Nothing made sense, nothing was real.

"Maybe he is wrong. But what if he's right? What if we get to the end stage he talked about? I can't think of that, don't want to think . . ."

"We won't get there; we'll fight this thing somehow."

22

I don't believe in God, in any higher force. We live, we die; the carbon cycle keeps running. But please, God, please don't let us get there. If He exists He had just grabbed the roots of my life and ripped them from the ground, turning my very existence upside down. We drove home with the CD player at full volume, hiding in the noise. The mountains falling away below and the sea crashing over my head, my world was upside down. By the time the van stopped I was walking on my hands.

Thoughts of choking plagued me. Night after night, for weeks after the diagnosis I woke in a cold sweat, head throbbing, panicking from nightmares of drowning in mucus. Visions of Moth's neck swelling, his jaw distorted, fighting to suck in air until he reached a suffocating end, while the children and I stood by and watched, helpless.

The swallows had arrived late, in ones and twos, finally finding their way home after an epic journey, to swoop through the beech trees and gorge on insects. If only I could be a swallow, free to fly, free to come home if I chose. I broke the bread for Smotyn and went out into the fresh June morning. The air was soft and light, brushing my face with the promise of a beautiful day ahead. I squeezed over the stile between the branches of the wild pear hedge. I'd bought the hedging in a sale at a tree nursery; it was supposed to be beech, but had grown into a small-leaved, spiky hedge with no pears and a bad attitude whenever I went over the stile. I rubbed at the scratches on my arm, new ones amongst the healed scars. It wasn't worth cutting it back now. The field was warm and honey-filled with the smell of clover coming into flower. The moles had been active again overnight, and mounds of finely tilled soil spread across the centre of the field. I kicked them flat, instinctively, still concerned about the wellbeing of the land, our land. Moth had reclaimed this field from an overgrown patch of weeds. Refusing to use pesticides and without any machinery at that stage, he had hand-scythed the two-acre patch. Raked away the debris and dug out nettles. He'd restored the boundary that surrounded it, carefully replacing hundreds of stones into walls that had been derelict for decades. It was the field where the children of visitors collected eggs, warm from the hens, and fed pet lambs in the spring. We'd played endless family cricket matches here and lain in long grass before it was cut for hay and watched shooting stars in dark summer skies. Our land.

Smotyn didn't come. She always came to the stile for her slice of bread. Always. As I looked around the fields for her, I already knew what I was going to find. In her favourite spot under the beech trees, her head laid out on the grass as if she was sleeping. She knew. She knew she couldn't leave her field, her place, and had simply died. Put her head on the grass, closed her eyes, and died. As I stroked her hairy face, passing my hand one last time over the bent horn, it came like a contraction. All-consuming and uncontrollable. I curled on the grass next to her and sobbed. Crying until my body stopped, spent, drained of tears, dried out by loss. The grass wrapped around my face and I lay under the beech trees and tried to die, to let go and be free with Smotyn, free to fly with the swallows and not have to face leaving this place, or the desiccation of Moth. Let me die now, let me be the one to go, don't let me be left alone, let me die.

I got the spade and started to dig, to bury Smotyn next to her sisters, in their field. Moth came out and we silently dug the hole together, refusing to speak, refusing to acknowledge the hole as it grew. The blackness that we had looked into the day before was still too shocking, too new for us to admit its existence, even as an idea. I covered her head with a tea towel; we couldn't look at her as the soil fell on her face. She was gone. It was all over. The dream that had been the farm was buried with her.

CHAPTER
THREE

Seismic Shift

After closing the door for the last time we had two weeks to put our few belongings into a friend's barn and try to work out what to do next. The children couldn't help: they were both students, living in shared accommodation, with barely enough money to keep themselves afloat. Moth's brother was on holiday so we could use his house, but we had just two weeks before he came back with his family, then there wouldn't be room for us all and we would have to leave. Only twenty miles away from home, just down the road, but we couldn't go back. It was agonizing. Reeling from the shock of leaving our house and trying to acknowledge what the doctor had told us, the first few days passed in a near catatonic haze.

Logic said we should work hard and find somewhere to rent. It wasn't just the house that had been taken from us, but our holiday-rental business too. Our income was gone. We'd need to find a job to enable us to reconstruct a life. But we were faced with the possibility that our life together was to be limited to a short time of moderately good health, followed by a decline into paralysis and death. I couldn't leave him and go to work — I needed to spend every minute of this precious semi-health with him. I had to save every memory to carry with me into a lonely future.

I hated the doctor, sitting on the edge of his desk delivering his diagnosis as if he was presenting a gift. *The best thing I can do for you, Moth, is give you a diagnosis.* It was the very worst thing he could do. I wished he could take it away, and let me live without knowing. I didn't want to see the black void of my future every time I looked at Moth. We stumbled through those days as if we had just come from a battlefield, scarred, shocked and lost.

Long-term camping was an option until we could find something better, but the best offer we had from a campsite was eighty pounds a week, far more than we could afford, and there was no housing benefit for campsite fees. No one we knew had a room to spare, or a garden they were willing to sacrifice for more than a few weeks. And we needed somewhere to settle our thoughts and come to terms with what had happened. No caravans were available in a holiday hot spot, where in midsummer every caravan is booked out for visitors who pay a lot more than housing benefit.

In an ideal world we'd have found a place to rent, but it was quickly apparent that when you've had your house repossessed it's close to impossible to get a rental property. Our credit rating was on the floor. The council could put us on their waiting list if we chose that, but we were low priority and the only accommodation they could offer at that moment was a room in a bed and breakfast that housed mainly those with drug and alcohol problems. A girl with dark hair pulled back into a tight ponytail sat behind a desk in the council offices, speaking to us in a strong Welsh accent: "Well, if you're not going to die soon, like in the next year, then you're not that ill, are you, so I can't call you a priority, can I?" That was the moment when we knew it for certain: we'd rather be in the tent.

Back in Moth's brother's house I gazed through the window, dazed, unable to think of a way forward.

"I'm glad really. I can't imagine living in a council house down the road from the farm. That would be just soul-destroying." Not only that, but in such a tight-knit rural community we would be the source of gossip for months.

"I know. At the farm we could shut ourselves away from everyone, couldn't we? On our island."

That's what the farm had been to us, in every way: an island. As soon as we left the road and drove into the forest, we left the rest of the world behind. Beyond the trees the views opened up as if we had entered another world. Old field systems on all sides, separated by hedge-topped banks. Mountains rising high in the west and stretching away to the east, a delicate, smooth cloud snaking between. A huge buzzard lifting its wings, circling into the sky and hanging in the blue air, somewhere between the tree tops and the mountains. The world of the road, the villages and all human noise left behind as the forest closed the door behind us. But now we were cast adrift, with no safe haven to return to, floating through fog on a raft of despair with no notion of where we would come ashore, or if there would be a shore at all.

Moth stood by the window, looking across the hillside of gorse and heather. Home but not home.

"I don't think I can bear to stay around here. I need to put some space between Wales and us; it's too painful to stay. I don't know about the longer term, don't know if I've got a longer term, but for now I need to be somewhere else. Need to look for somewhere else to call home."

I took a deep breath.

"Let's pack the rucksacks then, and make it up as we go along."

"The South West Coast Path it is then."

Packing a rucksack when you're fifty just isn't the same as when you're twenty. The last time our packs had been ready for a trail was before the children were born, Moth still had long hair and I was a stone lighter. Then we'd shoved in anything we thought we would need and carried it regardless, our young bodies springing back from strain and injuries. We'd backpacked in the Lake District and Scotland, walking miles every day but nearly always staying on a campsite, very rarely wild camping. Thirty years on and I had the aches of twenty years of manual labour, damage that never quite heals but stays malevolently in the background. Stiff from three years spent fighting a court case, hunched over the laptop trying to construct our defence and prone to muscle damage at every twist or turn. And Moth? How could he possibly carry the weight he had before? We packed the rucksack as we would have in the past and gingerly lifted it on to his back. A sixty-litre pack, stuffed with our old orange canvas tent and two slightly rusty billy cans. Twice around the room and he was on his knees in agony.

"Get this off me. I can't do it."

"Then we'll have to look at getting some different kit. Lighter tent for a start."

"We can't afford it." Most of what we'd earned over the last year had gone towards the court case, or just supporting us while we worked on it. That, and two children in university at the same time. I'd returned the payments to everyone who'd booked the barn for their holiday that summer, which left us with only £320. But we did get forty-eight pounds a week in tax credits; as Moth had become increasingly unable to work, our income had dropped down to only the barn rental, which made us eligible for a weekly payment from the government. Even this small benefit needed an address, which meant staying in the area. We couldn't stay, so we left the tax credits at the farm address and forwarded the post to Moth's brother. Forty-eight pounds a week. We could survive on that, surely.

I reread *Five Hundred Mile Walkies* and told myself again that we could do this. Mark Wallington had romped along the South West Coast Path with a borrowed rucksack and a scruffy dog. We could do this, no problem. But it was obvious that we would have to walk it the other way around, from Poole to Minehead. The early section from Minehead to Padstow seemed by far the hardest, and the latter stretch from Plymouth to Poole the easiest. So it made absolute sense to walk the other way around and give ourselves time to adjust before we hit the harder sections. We just needed a guidebook. It had to be a guide that covered the whole trail, but it quickly became apparent that there was no guidebook that followed the route from south to north, they all went from north to south. I scoured the shelves in Cotswold Outdoors, but their massive guidebook section didn't have a single volume going in the opposite direction. The poor skinny assistant got the full force of my disappointment.

"I have to walk the other way, don't you see, the start has to be easy for Moth. Mark Wallington was in his twenties and the biggest problem he had was popping rivets." Feeling red with anger and panic and self-pity, my rivets were about to pop.

"I'm really sorry, ma'am, but there isn't one." The assistant slipped away and I sat and sulked at the back of the store. If we had to start with the hard bit Moth might not be able to make it through the first week. What then? I wasn't ready to face "what then"; my brain was moving into self-defence mode. There was only the walk; it was all I could think of, I couldn't see beyond that. We looked at OS maps as an option, but to complete the path would take many more than we could afford, or carry.

"Ray, I'm not going to walk five hundred miles reading a guidebook backwards. We'll just start in Minehead and take it really, really slow." Moth was stroking my hair, but all I wanted was to get into a sleeping bag and cry. Don't crumble now. You're

31

supposed to be the strong one, you're not the one that's going to choke to death. Easily derailed, I was only just hanging on.

We had to choose a book and when we looked properly there was no choice. Paddy Dillon's little brown book, *The South West Coast Path: From Minehead to South Haven Point*, with its comforting waterproof cover and an Ordnance Survey map that covered the whole path, fitted so nicely in my hand and in Moth's pocket that it had to be the one. But when we flicked through it over a cup of tea it became obvious that when Mark was walking his dog, he had either lost count of the miles, or missed a bit, or there'd been some seismic shift in the decades between that book and now, stretching Cornwall further into the Atlantic. The path wasn't 500 miles long, but 630.

We had to buy some new bits of equipment; it couldn't be avoided. Moth's old rucksack had massive metal buckles that had rusted and seized and the lining of mine had disintegrated, letting the water pour through. The price of replacing them with anything of the same quality was horrifying. Two new rucksacks would leave us nearly £250 down. We searched for a cheaper option, finally choosing two packs from Mountain Warehouse, for less than half the price of one big-brand pack. They didn't have any of the bells and whistles, but they were functional enough. The rucksacks became the focus of the next few days. Filling, refilling, packing, unpacking and walking around the house wearing them. It wouldn't work. The stuff we wanted to take just wouldn't fit in the small packs.

"No, Ray, I can't carry a bigger one. Let's just treat it like leaving the farm. Let's repack with only what we absolutely need to survive. Nothing else. Then maybe I'll be able to manage it."

"The tent's too heavy. I can't fit it in and it's too heavy for your shoulder, but there's no way we can afford a decent tent, something that's going to stand up to being on a cliff top for months. We're stuffed."

"EBay?"

Waiting for an eBay auction to finish on what would be our home for the rest of the summer and maybe beyond was nerve-racking. Three seconds, two, one, and it was ours. A used-once Vango tent weighing three kilograms, a quarter of the weight of our old canvas Vango and a fraction of the size. We danced around the kitchen table; we had just bought our new home for thirty-eight pounds.

I rang our daughter, Rowan, desperately excited, needing to share this tiny scrap of good news, wanting to alleviate the atmosphere that had settled between us over the last two weeks of endless gloom. Wanting to be Mum and make everything okay. I had to get back to being that mum, but as soon as the phone began to ring I was regretting it. They might have grown up and left, but the home we'd lost was theirs too. Moth was their dad and his illness was as hard for them to accept as it was for me. These weeks were changing the core of my relationship with them. There were things happening that I couldn't protect them from. The balance was shifting, and I hated it. I wasn't ready. Yet they were two surprisingly well-adjusted adults — we'd done a great job — and they were ready. I was the one who still wanted to hold the world at bay and keep their lives in a perfect bubble. If I wasn't that protecting hand to them any more, then what was I? It was the last shred that, deep down, I recognized as being "me". Without that, what was left? Nothing.

"What are you thinking of, Mum, are you mad? What if he falls off the cliff?" Rowan's voice jolted me back to reality. "You've got no money, so how are you going to eat? Do you really think you're going to spend the rest of the summer in a tent? How can you? Dad can hardly get up off the chair some days; what happens if he seizes up on a cliff? Where will you camp? Do you know how much campsites cost? Have you told Tom?"

"I know, Row. It's completely crazy, but what else are we going to do? We can't just sit and wait for a council house, that's not us. We need this; as long as we're together we'll be okay, don't worry."

The line crackled in the silence.

"I'm sending you a new mobile, with a battery that lasts more than ten minutes. Call me every day, and don't ignore me when I call you. And tell Tom."

"Okay, Row, love you too."

"Hi, Tom. Me and Dad have decided to walk the South West Coast Path. It's probably going to take at least two months, maybe three."

"Right."

"It's six hundred and thirty miles and we'll have to camp all the way."

"That's so cool."

Our manic star-jumping toddler had become too chilled for his own good, while the disco-dancing glitter queen had turned into my mum.

But who was I now? Who was Moth? Would 630 miles be far enough to go to find the answer?

The tent arrived three days later and we erected it in the living room: a wide low green dome, spanning the floor like the moss cap on a granite rock. We unrolled our self-inflating mats and got into our super lightweight sleeping bags, bought for five pounds each from Tesco. I made a cup of tea on the tiny Campingaz stove, and we sat in the tent doorway to watch *Gardener's World* on the TV. When we tried to get out, Moth couldn't move. However hard he tried, he couldn't stand. I dragged him out in his sleeping bag and hauled him to his feet.

"Do you think Rowan's right? It's probably not the wisest thing we've ever done."

"But when have we ever taken the easy option?"

We packed the rucksacks for the final time, in the knowledge that if we'd forgotten something, or there were things that we couldn't fit in, then we would have to manage without them for the whole summer. Buying new kit was going to be out of the question; there would be no spare cash to replace equipment along the way. We'd be lucky if we could eat, especially having to buy our food on the south-west coast during the peak holiday season. The pile of things we wanted to take grew next to each pack. They obviously weren't going to fit, but we started cramming them in anyway. I put my spare clothes in first, bare minimum to last for a couple of months and the pack was already half full. Nothing else for it, this was where I could save space. Throwing them across the sofa, I started again with only what I absolutely couldn't manage without. Old cotton swimming costume, three pairs of knickers, one pair of socks, a cotton vest, a pair of leggings and a long-sleeved T-shirt to wear in the sleeping bag. Everything else I'd be wearing, so I put those to one side; another pair of cotton leggings, a short flowery viscose dress from a charity shop, cotton vest, red pair of walking socks and a cheap zip-up fleece. That was it.

I rolled the clothes into a ball in a small dry sack at the bottom of the pack. Then everything else. A self-inflating mat, the tiny gas stove, a gas canister, a stainless-steel pan with a handle that folded over to clip the lid shut, matches, an enamel plate and mug, teaspoon and a plastic spork, a way too small crushable pillow, the sleeping bag that squashed down with its compression straps to be small enough to fit into a side pocket, waterproof jacket and leggings. Then all the other trivia I felt I couldn't manage without, a three-inch torch, an A5 exercise book, pen, foldable toothbrush and two-inch tube of toothpaste, travel shampoo, a quick-drying blue towel, lip balm, tissues, face wipes, mobile phone, collapsible phone charger, a two-litre Volvic plastic bottle of water that I buckled under the little straps on the very top of the rucksack. And a purse with £115, which was all we had left, and a bank card. I would carry the food too: we'd buy most of that along the way, but to start out with we had a three-inch tin full of concentrated Half Spoon sugar that took up half the space of ordinary, fifty teabags, two packs of rice and two packs of noodles, some strangely orange long-life meatballs in a bag, a tin of mackerel, some breakfast cereal bars and two Mars bars. That was our store cupboard, which we thought we would keep as our emergency rations, and top up throughout the trip.

I forced the top of the rucksack closed and pulled it tight with the compression straps. It was as full and tight as a football. I sat on it and it didn't squash at all.

Moth's rucksack was very similar, although instead of the flowery dress he had a pair of combat trousers which would roll up to his knees to make shorts. He had the first-aid kit, a penknife and a four-inch monocular for spying on the trail ahead. Tucked in the inside pocket was a thin copy of Seamus Heaney's translation of *Beowulf*, which he'd carried with him on every trip for years. Instead of food and cooking equipment, he would carry the tent strapped to the outside of his pack. He put Paddy Dillon in the leg pocket of his combat trousers and we were ready.

Weighing the packs on the bathroom scales, somehow they both weighed in at almost the same weight: only eight kilograms. I still felt it was too much for Moth, but he picked it up and put one arm through anyway.

When he tried to pass his painful shoulder through the strap, it was too difficult, so I took the weight at the bottom of the pack and eased it over his shoulder. I had to do it before I put my pack on, as when it was on my shoulders my arms couldn't reach high enough to move his straps. If I then rested my pack on my knee, I could swing my rucksack round to get my arm through, then Moth took the weight while I threaded my second arm in. Easy.

We stood together like a pair of stranded turtles.

"This is crazy."

Crazy but we had to do it. If we didn't, we'd have to face the fact that the future would stretch beyond this summer and everything that future would hold. Neither of us was ready for that.

"It's a fact; we're not as ninja as we used to be."

Putting the rucksacks in the van, we turned south, driving away, leaving it all behind. It was a dream. Nothing was real. Driving away from twenty years of family life, work life, everything we'd owned, hopes, dreams, the future, the past. Not heading for a new beginning, not a fresh start with life opening up before us. The earth had cracked; we left ourselves on the other side of a void that we could never cross. Running from the rupture in someone else's shell. Just driving away. And ahead of us? The walk, only the walk.

38

CHAPTER
FOUR

Rogues and Vagabonds

A brief note on homelessness

If you ask someone to describe a homeless person, the majority will give you a description of a rough sleeper, unrolling a mat and bedding down in a street, perhaps with a dog, invariably begging for money for drugs or alcohol. A stereotype that evokes a range of emotions from the feet that pass them as they sleep in doorways, from mildly uncomfortable to aggressively violent. But it's this image that informs the view of most people.

Research undertaken by Crisis, the homelessness charity, together with the Joseph Rowntree Foundation, found that in 2013 at least 280,000 households claimed to be homeless, or about to become homeless, in the UK. These were only those who had applied for listing as homeless. However, of these, officials accepted only 52,000 as being statutorily homeless, having neither family or friends who could house them. Of the remaining 228,000 many were helped by local authorities via the relief route. That's 280,000 households requesting help for homelessness. These are households, not an actual head count.

Unfortunately, figures are remarkably inconsistent. Government figures suggest that 2,414 people slept rough in the whole of England during 2013, but these figures are only a snapshot of one night. However, research undertaken by the combined Homelessness and Information Network (Chain), funded by the Greater London Authority (GLA), gives a figure of 6,508 people sleeping rough on the streets of London during 2013. Yet government statistics for this period, using the snapshot method of counting, put the number at only 543, a far more comforting way of counting for those who prefer not to look too closely. So, what happens to the other statutorily homeless as well as the squatters, "sofa-surfers", invisible rough sleepers, and the hidden ones who aren't even a number on a list? Those on the list were just the ones they could find, or who had left a recorded trace. In 2013, rough sleepers in London accounted for 6,508, or 543 if you wear dark glasses. What about the rest of them?

The police have a number of pieces of legislation that can be used to defend the population against the homeless — predominantly the Vagrancy Act of 1824. This came into force after hundreds of years of legal measures against people in public places who the authorities felt were suspicious. Alan Murdie, a barrister writing for *The Pavement* magazine, in his outline of the effects of years of discriminatory legislation, describes the suspicious as anyone from gypsies, actors, prostitutes, suspected witches, artists and beggars, to the homeless.

The Peasants' Revolt resulted in the first Act against begging in 1381, not followed until the anti-vagrancy measures of 1547 after the dissolution of the monasteries. As homelessness increased with the Enclosure Acts and the Industrial Revolution, so did legislation. Then in 1744 the Vagrancy Act laid the template for all legislation that has followed. It categorized homeless people as "beggars, idle, vagabonds and rogues", and designated repeat offenders in the previous categories as "incorrigible rogues". This gave the authorities the right to arrest anyone whom they believed to be suspicious, or without means to sustain themselves. Unfortunately, since 1713, local authorities had been bound to pay five shillings to anyone who apprehended an "idle or disreputable person". This led to a huge abuse of the Act with over five hundred people being arrested in one year alone.

As the homeless numbers grew again after the end of the Napoleonic Wars, calls came for more stringent legislation against vagrancy. This resulted in the Vagrancy Act of 1824, which, although amended over the years, still remains partly in force today. Section One is still used alongside the Criminal Justice Act of 1982 to combat beggars and classifies the "idle and disorderly" as "every person wandering abroad, or placing himself or herself in a public place, street or highway, court or passage to beg or gather alms". Section Four allows "rogues and vagabonds" to include "every person wandering abroad and lodging in any barn or outhouse, or in any deserted or unoccupied building, or in the open air, or under a tent, or in any cart or waggon, not having any visible means of subsistence and not giving a good account of himself or herself".

In 2014, the year after we set foot on the South West Coast Path, the Anti-social Behaviour, Crime and Policing Act took effect. It contains provision for Public Space Protection Orders. Which means that anyone deemed to be causing a nuisance to others can be arrested and ordered by the authorities "to leave and not return to the locality". These PSPOs have been used for reasons as varied as the Forest of Dean's strangely phrased ban on nuisance sheep, to carrying golf clubs in a public place. Put simply, if the local authority thinks you look suspicious you can be moved on, or arrested. This has allowed many councils to introduce orders that directly outlaw actions linked to homelessness: rough sleeping, begging, loitering, and on and on. They can impose a hundred-pound fine for breaking the order and a thousand-pound fine and a criminal record for non-payment. And don't even dream of asking anyone for money, or being seen with a badly behaved sheep in the wrong part of town.

Fear of the homeless is as commonplace now as it has ever been, with a widespread belief that anyone who is homeless must be an alcoholic, drug abuser or suffering mental health issues. Although these are problems rife amongst the homeless community, they are as likely to be problems that result from homelessness as they are to be the cause of it. It's this fear, and the fear of the problem of the homeless affecting tourism, that provoked attempts by central

London authorities to ban rough sleeping and make soup kitchens illegal. Is starving this embarrassment off the streets really the answer? Rogues, vagabonds and vagrants: however you classify the homeless, in the summer of 2013 we became two of their number.

PART TWO

The South West Coast Path

*While some might be daunted at the prospect
of walking for weeks on end, staying somewhere
different every night, while keeping themselves
fed and watered, it is simply a matter
of careful planning.*

*The South West Coast Path: From Minehead to
South Haven Point, Paddy Dillon*

CHAPTER
FIVE

Homeless

We could have been in Taunton two days later. If we'd made it, we might have dodged the worst of the heat. We would have made it, if it hadn't been for the angels.

We'd driven up and down the M5 many times, always with a destination to be reached or a timetable to adhere to. But when the only timetable is when you will eat again, it's easy to be distracted.

"How many times have we driven past the sign to Glastonbury and said, 'Next time'? Let's just go for an hour; we'll still get to Jan's house in Yeovil tonight, leave the van and be away in two days."

Moth's friend Jan had been happy to help us in what small way she could. There was no rush to get there; we could just climb up the conical hill of Glastonbury Tor and see the view from the other side. Then away.

"Yeah, why not?"

A huge mass of Celtic mythology surrounds the tor, where human evidence has been found to date back to the Iron Age. Like every third village in western Britain, it claims connections to the stories of King Arthur. We'd recently passed the side of a lake in Wales where he was alleged to have thrown his sword, so it seemed like a viable diversion. I still don't grasp why a King of the Britons would throw "the" sword into a dingy grey lake on the side of the A5, or hang out in Glastonbury for long enough to be empowered by ley lines and inspire a chain of crystal shops. Maybe we'd be more enlightened by this visit, or by Tintagel, which we would walk through in Cornwall — if we made it that far.

It felt so good to get out of the van and stretch after a long, depressing journey. We took photos of the Somerset Levels on the mobile phone, and photos of Americans and Chinese admiring us, photographing them, admiring the Somerset Levels, and then walked back down to the town. A swell of alternative, New Age, crystal-polishing wonder. And a surprisingly large number of apparently homeless people. Sitting in doorways and alcoves, in blankets and sleeping bags, many of them with bowls requesting money. A boy in his early twenties was tucked in between the bin and the drainpipe outside the white witch crystal shop. Underneath the rough exterior, and despite the grubby clothes, ragged hair and ripped hat, he had the look of a smooth-skinned, perfect-toothed, clear-eyed public schoolboy. We sat on the opposite side of the road, eating a crystal-blessed pie, as he aced the begging market. The well-heeled passers-by were obviously encouraged by the clean, perfect smile and the rounded vowels of his response, to the detriment of his less fortunate peers.

"Look at this." I'd spotted this poster all over town. "Healing with angels at Heavenly End. Three pounds each. Shall we go, just for the Glastonbury experience? It starts in twenty minutes, then we'll be gone. Just a bit of a lark before we go." And what if it wasn't just hokum, what if it could help him?

"No."

"Oh, go on, it's just a laugh."

While we wandered around the car park, trying to find the gateway to Heavenly End, the Etonian beggar went into the public toilet. When he came out, he'd swapped his ragtag coat for the skateboard in his rucksack and for all the world looked like a surfer as he skated to the bank. We sat on a bench as he came out of the bank, returned to the toilets, then left in his ripped coat to resume his position by the bin. Begging in Glastonbury is obviously a career choice.

A woman dressed in white answered the door.

"Hello, I'm Michelle, welcome to Heavenly End. I won't explain anything that will happen, just let the angels be your guides." She took us through the house to her lounge.

"Here's a blanket and a cushion, find a space and relax. Everyone's here already." The room was full of people lying like sardines on the floor, on the sofa, draped over the chairs, all dutifully under their blankets with their eyes closed. I picked my way across the bodies to a space, looking back at Moth as he raised a cynical eyebrow.

"I'll start the music that helps us to summon the angels." Michelle set her stage to the tune of South American pipes and whale calls, lighting a burner that

49

filled the room with "breath of heaven" smoke. Then she summoned her angels.

"Gabriel from the south is here; he's bringing a blue light. Take that blue light in through your toes." Then all her other angels brought lots of other colours and we lay with their angelic power in a hot, smelly, sardine-shaped rainbow. If this is what angels smell like, then heaven's the place for me. I know what we called it in college, and it wasn't "breath of heaven".

"Breathe deeply, take the angels' power to the point of your pain, to your arms and legs, to your heart and brain, to your liver, to your, to your, errr, kidneys. And relax."

The music stopped and the room breathed quietly. The silence was filled by a familiar snore, low at first, as it always is, then louder and louder. I leant up on my elbow; the other fish were lying meekly, inhaling and exhaling. Except Moth, who was fast asleep, snoring with abandon.

"Say goodbye to the angels and rise back into your body, and back to the world."

They all sat up, quietly comparing their angelic trips: swimming with whales, flying with the birds, walking on water. I was just pleased with a three-pound shot of "breath of heaven". But Moth carried on snoring.

I prodded him awake.

"Moth, get up."

"I can't."

"I know you're comfy, but just get up now."

"No, I can't, I can't move. Fuck, do you think this is it? Am I paralysed? I can't move."

Michelle kept her distance, offering a glass of water and then backing away. Did she think she'd brought the wrong angels, or that we might sue her?

"I can't feel my legs. Is this how it will be? What if I suddenly won't be able to walk, really suddenly?"

Eventually he got to his knees, then to the chair.

"It's because you were lying flat out for an hour. You know you can't move when you've been lying on your back."

"I told you I didn't want to come."

"You'll be fine; it's all that snoring, you've breathed in too much 'breath of heaven'." Oh shit, what if this happens on the path? If we even get that far.

As we drove out of town, the Etonian was sitting on a bench looking very clean and well fed, chatting on his mobile phone.

Instead of two days it took nearly two weeks of sleeping on Jan's floor before Moth's back pain and stiffness from the Glastonbury angels had worn off. It was time to move on: we needed to leave before we outstayed our welcome; no one wants to share their bathroom indefinitely. We left the little van on Jan's drive, desperately wishing it was just a bit bigger so we could have slept in it, and she drove us to Taunton, relieved to see the back of her squatters. We said our goodbyes, vowing not to lie still for too long and to stay away from passing angels.

In early August, standing on the side of the road in Taunton, our rucksacks by our feet, we were finally, truly, homeless. I'd never been homeless before. I'd travelled, lived in a van for weeks on end, but this was different. Travelling in the knowledge that you have a point of return gives you the will to keep moving away. There's always a door you can return to and drop your bag, even if that door is the thing you're escaping from. But the feeling that day was entirely different. There was no door. The space I inhabited in that moment was the safest, securest place I had and I didn't want to move.

"Shall we find the bus to Minehead then?"

There was nothing else to do. That was why we were there, to give ourselves a reason to keep moving, to find a way to shape our future. But I didn't expect to pay ten pounds each in bus fares to get to Minehead. Added to the diesel for the drive to Somerset, food in a motorway service station and a couple of bottles of wine to say thanks for keeping the van, and my little red purse was looking thinner. Much thinner. We had fifty pounds left. But that was going to be enough; we'd have forty-eight pounds deposited in the bank every week. Enough.

Sitting on the back seat of the bus, I started to feel calmer. Maybe it was being contained by the bus, but I even felt a small pulse of excitement. We were heading north through Somerset. We could fool ourselves that we were on a day trip to the seaside and got out the chocolate and bananas.

"Where y'all heading there? South West Coast Path, I bet? Us too. Where y'all staying? This your first night? Us too." An incredibly loud American voice filled the bus, from a tiny prim woman with curly brown hair and a very serious jacket, with lots of really useful pockets.

"That's right, we're starting out today."

She scuttled towards the back of the bus, with her equally small partner. He was clearly heading out on safari, in identical jacket and trousers that had even more pockets, bulging with important-looking things.

"No, you can't set off at this time of day. You have to leave early morning. It's a day's walk to the next accommodation after Minehead. Where y'all staying tonight? Come and have a drink with us."

"We're backpacking." I glanced at the rucksacks, stuffed full and sitting like huge turtle shells on the seat next to us, sort of obvious really. "We're camping, so we'll just set off and put the tent up later."

"What? You've got a tent in that? What and cooking stuff too? Ours are as big as that and we're staying B & B and doing luggage transfer."

"What's luggage transfer?"

"Yeah, we're just gonna walk and some nice young man's gonna take our bags to the next B & B. We're going right through to Westward Ho! Where y'all heading?"

"If we make it to Land's End, then we'll probably carry on to Poole, but we're in no rush, we'll just see how it goes." Moth looked at me with an eyebrow raised as he silently created our back story. There were plenty of things we didn't need to tell them.

"Land's End! You can't camp all that way, you're like, well, too old."

"Well, we'll see how it goes. You'll probably pass us in the next day or two anyway, we're quite slow." I'm only fifty; how old did they think we were?

We hadn't even looked at a map of Minehead so had no idea where to find the start of the coastal path, other than knowing we were facing the north coast and needed to be going west, somewhere on the left. We wandered downhill, through curtains of buckets, spades and flip-flops, past crowds of OAPs eating cream teas, until we finally arrived at the seafront. We dropped the rucksacks with relief and sat on the promenade with tea and chocolate bars. A huge hill to the left seemed to rise near vertically from the prom. Surely that couldn't be the hill at the start of the path . . . Paddy Dillon says the path "drifts"; he doesn't say climb a mountain. This didn't bode well.

"No, definitely says down the prom to the monument." Moth's finger traced the orange line of the path, skilfully drawn along the copy of the Ordnance Survey map in *The South West Coast Path*. "It's okay. It probably skirts along the bottom and then rises around the corner somewhere. Right then." He put the map and his reading glasses back in his pocket. "You up for this?" He looked tired, but didn't seem to be in too much pain.

"Nothing better to do."

The crowds started to thin as we walked towards the monument of giant metal hands holding a map that marks the start of the path. Staying at the monument for far too long: taking photos, fiddling with our packs, trying to will ourselves to take that first step. Excited, afraid, homeless, fat, dying, but at least if we made that first step we had somewhere to go, we had a purpose. And we really didn't have anything better to do at half past three on a Thursday afternoon than to start a 630-mile walk.

Halfway up an excruciatingly steep zigzag path through the woods above Minehead, it became clear that Paddy Dillon was going to be the master of underestimation. We sat on a bench with a glimpse through the branches towards the sea, trying to breathe and reread his guidebook.

"No, he definitely says, 'drifts a little inland and uphill'."

"Well if this is drifting, we're in serious shit if he says 'quite steep'."

We'd walked half a mile, drunk half a litre of water and my head felt as if it was going to explode. A large family passed us heading downhill.

"Those packs look really well stuffed; where you heading for?"

"Land's End, hopefully."

"Oh, yeah, right — well, good luck with that!"

The tribe scampered downhill laughing. My hips were screaming and the sole of my foot was sore. They were right to laugh; I'd have laughed if it hadn't been me.

"Do you think they're right? That we're a bit of a joke really?"

"Course they're right, and that's only with what they can see. Imagine if they knew the truth of it? I daren't tell people we're going to Poole."

"Poole? We'll be lucky if we see Porlock."

What felt like hours later we made it out of the woods on to the moorland above, where the ground levelled, ponies grazed and the views opened towards South Wales.

"It's like we can't escape."

The day quickly turned to evening and with it the realization that we were on the open edge of Exmoor, above the Bristol Channel, and night would be coming. We had to find somewhere to put the tent. The open areas of low grazed grass were behind us, and now the only small areas of flat grass were on the path itself, with heather and gorse all around. It seemed obvious to me that the tent would have to go on the path.

"We can't put it on the path. What happens in the morning? There's bound to be someone along to tell us to move."

We walked on, my hips burning.

"Perhaps it's arthritis."

"Perhaps you've spent too long in front of the computer. There's a flat patch over there."

The rucksack was off my shoulders at the mere thought of stopping, but within seconds my feet were covered in ants, thousands of them crawling and flying over the grazed patch of heath.

"We'll keep looking."

56

But looking closer, every patch of short grass was a mass of ants: crawling ants, flying ants. They were in the air; we were walking through clouds of flying black bodies, ants in our clothes and our hair. Running from a black mass before I breathed them in, I stopped in the heather to scratch and they'd gone, I'd left them behind. They were only hovering over the short grass.

Pitching a tent on heather isn't easy. A patch of young, short-stemmed growth was the only option, but a huge risk for the thin groundsheet of the lightweight tent; it could be ripped on the first night. We did it all the same. After half an hour of fighting with unfamiliar poles and ropes, we had the tent up. The base mounded like a feather mattress but we felt as though we were lying in the fork drawer.

"Did we pack some duct tape?"

"Nope."

As the light disappeared, shrinking away, withdrawing into the west, the lighthouses of South Wales began to spike the darkness. So far away and yet the light was still in reach, touchable, while the land they stood on was already slipping away. I screwed my eyes tight and walked up the track to the farm, ran my hands over the stone walls, felt the heat of the fire. I couldn't lose that feeling, had to carry it with me always, the feeling of safety and home.

"I think I can feel homelessness now, like a balloon cut free in the wind. I'm scared."

"I'd hug you, Ray, but I can't sit up."

"Shall we eat the meatballs? I'm sure they weigh the most."

57

★ ★ ★

Cold above, cold to the side, cold beneath. What makes a sleeping bag lightweight? It was obvious at four in the morning, in the grey-green light of the tent as the cold ate through. Less insulation, a lot less insulation. If I lay on my back, the worst of the cold was warmed by the insulation mat. But I couldn't lie on my back; it hurt too much. On my side and my back felt like iced water, exposed to the bone-aching cold. Pressing my back against Moth to suck up some heat, he stirred and turned on to his back and snored. And snored. I piled everything that came to hand over me, put a smelly vest on my head and my feet on the rucksack. Almost bearable. Why didn't I bring a hat?

Dozing fitfully, I dreamt of empty houses and Moth choking. I woke, sweating, heart pounding, head ringing. I'd made it through a horrid night, warm at last as the sun came up, but I couldn't doze off again, I had to get out of the bag. Desperate for a pee, I scrambled through the tent flaps, falling over the gas stove and pan in a rushed attempt to get out and put my boots on at the same time. I squatted in the heather, where the gorse ran into the sea and became Wales beneath a gentle yellow light, the air clear and clean as if it didn't exist.

"Good morning. Beautiful one, isn't it?"

I crouched in the undergrowth with my leggings round my ankles and my arse hanging out in the breeze.

"This morning, yes, lovely."

Dog walkers, how do they get out so early?

58

Moth finally woke at eight thirty, subdued, struggling with stiffness. He hated mornings, knowing that when he woke the pain would come. It had become a habit to hold on to that last moment of drowsiness for as long as he could before he had to get up and acknowledge the day. Painkillers, then a cup of tea, then a second. Ten thirty and he made it out of the tent. Cast-iron bladder. CBD was supposed to cause incontinence, but certainly didn't seem to have affected him so far.

"How is it? Can you carry on?"

"It's like hell, but what else are we going to do?"

By eleven thirty we'd packed everything away, put the rucksacks on sore shoulders and climbed out of the heather. Anyone who writes about wild camping stresses not only the fact that it's technically illegal in England and Wales, but that if you do it it's important to camp away from public places, set up camp late and get away early, and always leave no trace. I looked back; the heather was crushed. So, a fail on every point then. Maybe we'd get better at it.

Descending into Bossington, I was struggling to decide if going downhill with a weight on my back was actually worse than going up. Already making mental lists of everything that hurt — sole of my foot, hips, shoulders, and on and on — by the time we reached the bottom I'd concluded that they were inseparable in pain levels and I was probably insane for thinking we could walk this path.

When we arrived in the idyllic village, the sign for a tea room was irresistible. We knew we couldn't do tea rooms, or cafés, or much of anything else for that matter, but we went into the garden all the same. We ordered our first and last cream tea of the whole summer while I took my boots off. Only eight miles in and a pair of boots that I'd had for over ten years had turned the ball of my foot into one huge blister two inches across. Was it caused by the weight of the rucksack? I added to the weight I had to carry and hungrily shovelled the scone and clotted cream into my mouth. If I'd known then it would be the last I might have taken more time. I created a patchwork of blister plasters across my foot and put my socks back on.

"Walking the path then, are you?" A large man and his tiny wife and child were sitting on a table next to us, obscured by the exuberant shrubbery.

"Yes, that's right."

"You're in for a great time. This is the best bit of the whole path. Got to have a head for heights though when you go over Exmoor."

"Is it steep then?"

"Is it steep?" He started laughing. Were we so funny? Moth looked really unimpressed; he hadn't been good with heights since he fell off the barn roof.

"So how come you've got so much time? I wish I had that much."

"We're homeless. We lost our home and we've nowhere to go, so just walking seemed a good idea."

It came out of my mouth without a thought. The truth. But as the man reached out and pulled his child towards him and the wife winced and looked away, I knew I wouldn't be saying it again. He called for the bill and was gone in moments.

60

* * *

We crossed the marshlands, where the sea had broken through the shingle ridge and turned the farmland into salt marsh. The skeletons of white, salt-burnt trees stark against the grey sky. Dead but still inhabiting life.

As we passed through the cluster of buildings that form Porlock Weir, a voice shouted from a hole in a wall.

"Doing the path? You need some chips before you go into the woods." Two men were looking out of what appeared to be a three-foot square hole in a wall, which was actually the serving hatch for a tiny chip shop.

"Best chips you've ever had."

We caved instantly.

"Go on then."

The round-faced man explained the process of triple-cooking chips, which actually did turn out to be the best chips we'd ever had. And the most expensive. Two miles had cost us sixteen pounds. We couldn't do this. But we were so raw, so lost in spirit, we were saying "yes please" to any scrap of comfort that came to us. It had to stop, or very quickly we'd have no money at all.

We climbed away from Porlock Weir and up into the woods. Moth was tiring and finding every step a struggle. I was leaden and achy. It could have been our lack of fitness, the emotional exhaustion, the CBD, or maybe it was just the chips. Paddy said we would be here at the end of our first day, but in the late afternoon of our second day we were just about done.

The track broadened ahead and in the clearing a man stood on the path who appeared to be practising yoga. We stopped, not wanting to interrupt him, thinking he'd look up and allow us to pass. Utterly oblivious to us, he faced towards a wooded valley. A tall, gaunt, string-thin figure. He looked ill, or something else, suffering some self-inflicted, emotional torment. Bending at the knees he reached out towards the valley and then drew in something invisible, some essence, of what I don't know. Pulling the unseen thing into his body, pressing it through his core and down through his legs. Over and over, repeatedly, cloaking himself in the unknown.

Eventually we gave up and passed him. He continued, utterly absorbed in his movements and unaware of our passing. The path led into the valley and down to Culbone Church, the smallest church in England, ancient, and once the site of a leper colony. Did the man believe there was some power here? I sat in the graveyard and let the utterly peaceful place wash over me. It was profoundly spiritual, nothing to do with God or religion, but a deeply human spirituality. Something of the knot I'd been carrying started to loosen. Maybe there *was* some power here. I cupped my hands and threw some air at Moth just in case.

As we sat and let the green light seep into our aching joints, the yoga man walked slowly and precisely down the hill. He didn't look at us, but stopped. Shouldn't we be here? Was he going to tell us to move on?

"Hi. We've just visited the church. It's very peaceful."

"I know. You passed me on the path."

"Oh, we thought you didn't see us. We didn't want to disturb you."

"I didn't see you; I don't see anything. I heard you." He was blind. Why hadn't we noticed?

"We're just walking the path."

"You are, and you'll travel many miles."

"Well, two hundred and fifty to Land's —"

"You'll see many things, amazing things, and suffer many setbacks, problems you'll think you can't overcome." He reached forward and put his hand on Moth. "But you will overcome them, you'll survive, and it will make you strong."

We looked at each other wide-eyed, mouthing a silent "what?"

"And you'll walk with a tortoise."

We carried on up the hill and camped in a field above the road, hidden from a farmhouse by high hedges.

"You don't see many tortoises running wild in the south-west, do you?"

"Not generally, no."

The morning came, eventually, after a night of cold and lumpy ground. The packs made it on to our backs by eleven and we crept out from behind the hedge, checking each way for onlookers before creeping through the gate to the road like escaping convicts. The path climbed and fell, in and out of fields and along narrow green lanes bounded by high hedges where the wind could barely penetrate. In normal life, we'd rarely pass a day without a bath or a shower, but it had been three days of travelling, walking, and sleeping in the tent. Without a breeze, the smell in the lanes was rich, and not from cows. I'd thought it wouldn't matter that we couldn't afford a campsite so would never be able to wash: we could swim every day. I hadn't accounted for rarely being at sea level. The only time we'd spent near the sea had been in Minehead and the really stony shore at Porlock. We were humming. It was a relief to get on to the wooded cliffs, where hanging forests of oak stood hunched towards the cliff and the sea wind cut through the leaves.

The oaks turned into rhododendrons and we stopped, exhausted. We'd passed into north Devon without even realizing, our first milestone achieved. Two days in and we were still moving. Rhododendrons closed around us, above and below, spreading across the cliffside. Resilient and persecuted plants that, contrary to belief, lived in the UK millennia ago. Fossils have been found that prove they grew here before the last ice age, but native plant status is reserved for plants that flourished after the ice had receded. Reintroduced to the UK in the mid-eighteenth century, they rapidly colonized the countryside: a wave of migrants with rich, glossy evergreen leaves, bringing texture and colour to drab, grey, leafless British winters, followed by a stunning spring display of lush purple and mauve flowers cloaking the hills and forest undergrowth. In a much-loved valley in Wales, May had been a blaze of beauty through a dark ravine until the National Trust decided the non-indigenous invaders had to go. What followed was months of hack and slash plant slaughter,

64

leaving behind hillsides that resembled a battlefield. Years later and debris of the massacre remains, tiny scant attempts at indigenous growth have taken their place, an occasional wisp of birch and heather. But the rhododendron stumps are regenerating, fighting back with tough green speed. Eventually one side will win the battle, but neither will be the better for it.

The cliff rose above and fell below, with barely more than three feet of level ground to support the path in between. We got the stove out and made cups of tea regardless, sitting on the flat of the path. We could hear the Americans coming: the tone of voice in the distance was unmistakable. She was talking about problems at work, unable to leave them behind. I stirred the tea with the odd realization that I had no work to concern myself about, no domestic problems to resolve; I had no problems at all really. Other than that we were homeless and Moth was dying. They stopped for a moment, looking a little put out. I thought maybe they were downwind, but then realized they couldn't get past us.

"We're late already today, should be in Lynmouth by four, we're behind schedule."

They pushed by apologetically. He was sweating magnificently, sweat dripping from his chin and elbows.

"Sure you wouldn't like to stop and have a cup of tea, bit of a rest for a minute?"

She looked at me as if I'd committed a heinous crime.

"No, there's no time; we have to keep to the plan. Y'all don't have a plan, do ya?"

65

They were gone, but for the next few minutes, as her voice trailed into the distance, we heard just how glad he should be that she'd come away at all, with such a full diary and "y'all should just be grateful".

"Do we have a plan?"

"Course we do. We walk, until we stop walking, and maybe on the way we find some kind of future."

"That's a good plan."

Trudging on through the woods it began to rain gently, but the dense canopy of the rhododendrons protected us. As soon as we left the shelter of the trees the weather ripped in off the Bristol Channel, gentle rain developing into a howling gale. Struggling along, waterproofs flapping, I could barely see through the water pouring down my face. Moth was wobbling from the height, the wind and exhaustion as we turned on to the cliff path. Exposed and high, the weight of our packs caught the wind, unbalancing and unnerving us. Around Foreland Point a perfect rainbow formed ahead of us, picking up the colours of the hill and adding a muddy green, brown and purple to its display. Moth clung to the grass at hand height, steadying himself against the growing swirl of black and grey mist where the sea had been. A two-foot wide path, then a void of cloud. Were we on a grassy slope, or a cliff edge? There was no way of knowing. Then suddenly, out of the fog, we could see a church tower.

"You know that plan? It's time to stop walking now." Moth fell into a pew in the church. His shoulder was in agony from bracing himself against the wind and his leg had started to buckle randomly, causing him to stumble. We contemplated spending the night in the aisle of St John the Baptist, until the bright lights of the Blue Ball pub caught our eye. We staggered the short distance from the church to the pub, sloshing through the door, pouring water across the floor and over a dog sitting by the entrance.

A bald man behind the bar looked at us without expression. Then at our steaming packs, and the puddles on the floor. Moth picked his pack up, always the first to make things easy for others.

"I'm really sorry about the mess, mate, we're doing the Coast Path and we got caught out. Shall I leave the pack outside?"

"The Coast Path? No bloody way, put your stuff down there." The barman broke into a torrent of welcome in an Australian accent and we collapsed on a squashy sofa in front of a log fire. As I hung my socks from a chair to drip, I realized we'd come into a pub but couldn't rationally afford to buy anything. A huge dog the size of a small donkey came out of the dining room, sniffed at the socks and, taking one in his big slobbery mouth, went to the bar. I followed him, pulling at the sock, trying to get him to drop it while ordering a pot of tea, which seemed like the cheapest possible option.

"Bob, drop the sock. Okay, tea, very English. Thought you looked like you were up for a night on the single malt."

"If only." I took the sock, now with a big hole in it, and headed back to the fire. Single malt, log fire, hot bath, comfy bed. I hate whisky, but if we had some money it would be a different trip. Instead we spun out the tea and dozed in front of the fire while the socks dried and the rain stopped.

It was pitch black at eleven o'clock when we finally felt ready to leave the warmth of the pub, erect the tent in a niche in the cliff slightly protected from the gale and fall asleep as the wind ripped overhead.

I knew the moment would come. The one thing I'd avoided thinking about when I'd come up with the ridiculous notion of living wild on the South West Coast Path. The moment when I'd have to face the big unanswered question: do bears shit in the woods? Now I had the answer: I wasn't a bear, there were no woods, but without a doubt the answer was yes. Six thirty and I could hear the gulls coming and going over the cliff and the now familiar early-morning battle with boots and tent flaps took far too long. As I stood up I was overwhelmed. Not only by the desire to sit on a white, shiny, flushing toilet, but mainly by a wave of vertigo. Somehow in the dark and fog of the night before we had pitched the tent two metres from the edge of the cliff. Tent, path, scrap of grass, hundred-metre drop. I regained my balance and looked around for somewhere slightly disguised. All I could see was an open hillside with a small clump of gorse bushes. There was no waiting; it would have to do. I frantically tried to dig a hole with the heel of my boot — we hadn't carried a trowel for this, far too much weight and anyway we'd always find a public toilet. My thumb ripped through the waist of my leggings in the rush as I squatted behind the spikey sharp gorse with as much relief as Renton in the toilet scene of *Trainspotting*.

Dog walkers. What is it about dog walkers?

"Morning. You found somewhere to camp then?"

The Australian from the pub walked up the path towards the tent. I couldn't stand up, the gorse wasn't that high, so I stayed squatting and whispered in a small voice: "Morning."

"Well, I'll leave you to it then. Have a good walk."

"Thanks."

The dog dragged him back the way he'd come as I created an artistic wigwam of dead gorse and the crimson embarrassment drained from my cheeks. I watched him disappear through voluminous transparent clouds lifting out of Lynmouth Bay and pouring over the headland, now racing to catch up with the storm that was already miles away. A large area of flat grass appeared through the clouds; we'd walked straight past it in the gale the night before. It didn't really matter; we hadn't fallen off the cliff so our niche was fine. I got back into the tent as Moth woke.

"You're up early."

"Not before the dog walkers though. Thought it was you who was going to be losing bowel control, not me?"

The Coast Path is said to have been established by the coastguards who needed a view into each and every one of the endless coves and bays as they patrolled for smugglers. But the many sites of ancient history described in every guidebook or tourist pamphlet suggest that the path has been trodden by man for as long as he has walked over the land. Natural England primarily funded the creation of the path as a whole route, joining the dots to create our longest National Trail. They finished the last section in north Devon in 1978, the year before I left school. Big hair and kipper ties, running free into a future of outcomes we couldn't see. The trail and us, thrown out into the world together: were we always destined to meet?

The South West Coast Path is said to generate in the region of three million pounds a year. We had forty-eight pounds a week, which certainly wasn't going to add much to the local economy. I was becoming very reluctant to open my purse, but after diverting up a steep, winding road into Lynton I had no choice; we needed more food supplies.

We stood outside a grocery shop on the corner of the street as I counted the coins in my hand, trying to decide what to spend. At the same moment, a woman in a bright yellow and blue sailing coat walked around the corner with a large, white, angry-looking dog. I shouldn't have stood there, between the shop door and a rail where a black Labrador was tied, waiting for its owner. The huge white dog clearly hated other dogs. He lunged for the Labrador, who had been quietly dozing, contemplating the can of dog food that was on its way out of the shop. As he leapt forwards he grazed past the rucksack on my back, sending me spinning into the wall. The coins leapt out of my hand and disappeared down the hill. I threw myself to the ground as a pound coin spun off the pavement, almost catching it as it slipped from my fingers into the drainage grill. Moth followed a two-pound coin as it rolled away, weaving between holidaymakers walking up the hill. From my viewpoint on the tarmac I could see him trying to stoop to catch it, just as a small boy snatched it up with glee.

"I've caught money, I've caught money." No, no, we need that.

"Well done, mate, ice cream van's at the top of the hill." Oh Moth, I'd have liked an ice cream.

The woman with the white dog prodded me with her foot. I was still lying on the pavement with my hand in the gutter.

"What's the matter with you, are you drunk?"

I was momentarily stunned by her assumption.

"I'm fine, it's your dog that's the problem."

"There's nothing wrong with my dog. You tramps should learn how to control yourselves. Rolling around in the street — it's disgusting."

I took my hand out of the gutter and stood up as the black Labrador uncurled itself from the end of a lead stretched to its limit. A tramp. A homeless tramp. A few weeks earlier I'd owned my own home, my own business, a flock of sheep, a garden, land, an Aga, washing machines, a lawn mower; I had responsibilities, respect, pride. The illusions of life had rolled away as quickly as the pound coins.

Moth made it back up the hill, gathering a few stray coppers along the way.

"So how much have we got left then?"

"Nine pounds and twenty-three pence."

"And when do we get some more money?"

"Day after tomorrow, I think. Two packs of rice and something to go on it, do you think? Or supernoodles?"

"No, anything but noodles."

We came out of the shop with a slightly heavier rucksack and two pounds seventy in the purse. But we did have a Mars bar each.

The first time I saw Moth across the sixth-form college canteen I was eighteen. He was wearing a white collarless shirt as he dipped a Mars bar in a cup of tea. I was mesmerized. Afterwards, hanging out of the third-floor window with my friends, we watched him walk through the grounds: old army trench coat flapping in the wind, riding boots up to his knees. I couldn't think of anything else. Weeks passed before he spoke to me, weeks of hiding, watching from a distance, behind bookshelves, in shop doorways, in the bushes. All I could think about was him. And sex. Then he spoke to me, and it seemed that was all he thought of too.

A teenage crush grew into a friendship that had us running in the grasp of its passion through adult life. A life I hadn't known existed, down roads I would never have taken, through days on wind-scoured moors, weeks of screaming resistance at CND rallies, music festivals and pizzas in the park, as he swept me into his eco-warrior life, and talking, talking, talking, in a conversation without end. Years passed with our legs entwined, in endless chatter and laughter. While our friends changed their relationships with their clothes, we needed nothing else. Through our thirties and forties, we watched as couples around us fell into a grey state of companionship, defining themselves by their Saturdays spent shopping or watching the match, and fizzling inevitably into break-ups. And all the time we lived with a passion that didn't die.

Hobbling homelessly through Lynton, there was still something about the way he ate a Mars bar that could lift my spirit in an instant. But months ago, a doctor had given him a drug called Pregabalin to stop the nerve pain in his shoulder, and it had changed everything. Just another loss. Still the closest a friend could be, but an unapproachable physical gap was emerging.

"Can't beat a Mars bar."

"That's a fact." The chocolate-tinged memories made me forget all about the dog.

Out of Lynton the path narrowed to the edge of the hillside, until it became a right-angle bend on a cliff edge. This was our most exposed point so far and we nervously rounded the corner to come face to face with another Australian striding fearlessly along.

"Hi, guys, you're loaded up, where you going?"

"Land's End, if we make it." We still didn't feel confident enough to say all the way.

"Wow, well, good on ya. You're only as old as you feel. Good luck."

I always thought I'd aged quite well. I'd made it to fifty without going grey, or too wrinkly.

"How old did he think we were?"

"Doesn't matter, apparently we're as old as we feel."

"Yeah, right."

"I feel like I'm fucking eighty some days, I'm so fucking tired. I hurt, everywhere." Moth threw his pack down and squatted on the rocks. "Can't tell if I feel half asleep, or wide awake. It's like my head's in fog and I'm walking through treacle. This is the most bollockingly stupid thing we've ever done. I want to lie down."

Stunned, I sat on the narrow path next to him. He'd grown to know this illness over time as it crept up so slowly, namelessly. It hadn't given him the anguish of a suddenly inflicted disease. There'd been a few moments of complete negativity since the hospital, but not many and I wasn't ready for it. Over the years, we'd coped with the practicality of each ailment as it came, but the reality of this diagnosis and the mental wear of living with chronic pain had been deliberately brushed under the carpet. And here we were, rucksacks on our backs at the Valley of Rocks, with no carpet. The sea broke against the base of the cliffs leading up to Castle Rock. We watched in silence. Rhythmically, repeatedly, white against black, white against black, white against black. A group of wild goats, disguised by the scrub and rock, leapt across the path close by, their long hair blown by the wind as they disappeared below, rugged, shifting, the landscape made mobile in the flow of their movement.

I was transfixed.

"Wow, did you see those goats? Huge horns."

"Not still thinking about that Mars bar, are you? What you sitting here for anyway? Let's go. We'll stop soon though, I'm knackered."

I hauled him off the ground and we carried on.

74

The busy Valley of Rocks behind us, a tarmac road led through wide-open parkland to a large country house. Green flat grass everywhere.

"I know it's early, but we'll have to put the tent up soon, I'm so tired."

A placard near the house proclaimed it a Christian estate. Anyone could stay here and be "renewed and refreshed" by God, for a starting price of £120, and absolutely no camping or fires or loitering, or dogs off leads, and definitely no tramps.

Passing out of the parkland into a valley we could hear shouts and laughter. Down in the hollow below us a Christian youth camp prepared for an evening of entertainment. A DJ in an open marquee tried to interest a group of teenagers in a quiz. Christian or not, they were still teenagers and were more interested in sneaking into the bracken. The smoke from the barbecue brought sausages up to the path, and the first real snatch of hunger took hold.

"What are we eating tonight?"

"Rice and a tin of mackerel."

"Do you think they'd notice if we just walked in and ate a burger?"

On and on through the bracken until we stopped looking for a clear patch and threw the rucksacks over a fence, putting the tent up in a grazed field. From Crock Point we could see the last of the light stroking Duty Point in pink and blue. The sea was breaking on the rocks beneath as we finish the mackerel and rice.

"Needed some bread with that. Sssh, what's that?"

"Fuck, I bet it's the farmer coming to throw us off."

The scrambling rustling noise got closer as we prepared ourselves to pack the tent away and move on. The bracken broke apart and two teenagers squeezed through the hedge, twigs in their hair.

"Er, well, hi, we've just been to the . . . beach, but we're going back to camp now."

"Good, better hurry up, or the burgers'll be gone."

CHAPTER
SIX

Walk

We'd expected extremes of weather while we were on the Coast Path, British weather. Wind, rain, fog, occasional hail even, but not the heat, the burning suffocating heat. By lunchtime we'd crawled out of the shade of Woody Bay into an intensely hot afternoon. We shared a cereal bar and banana looking west across some of the highest cliffs in England. Near vertical faces rising as high as eight hundred feet and stretching away to the Great Hangman, at 1,043 feet, the highest point on the whole of the South West Coast Path. But between us and the Hangman was a series of savage rises and falls, which even Paddy admits are steep. From the cliff top to near sea level, from sea level to the cliff top. And repeat. This was why I'd wanted to start in Poole. Then it got hotter.

"We brought sunscreen?" My nose was throbbing in the heat.

"Nope."

"Should we wait for it to get cooler?"

"If we do we'll be stuck on the cliffs when it gets dark. I think we'll be lucky if we find a flat spot here."

"Oh dear. We'd have loved this when we were thirty."

"Old as you feel?"

"Okay."

Legs, hips, shoulders screaming, we reached the top on the other side of the valley and turned towards the sea cliff. The rock path reflected the heat back at our burning faces in waves. A blue wind lifted beneath my rucksack and with my arms outstretched I could fly; the freedom of the height took my breath away. My eyes were watering, my skin burning and in the distance the coast of Wales seemed further away. Every corner was a wash of vertigo and exhilaration. Moth walked with a lean away from the sea and towards the cliff, but I had heather and salt air in my veins and flew with the gulls.

On a smooth stone ledge before another gorge rollercoaster, we met our first backpackers. They looked very young, fresh and efficient, in their matching blue hiking shorts and neat crisp backpacks. But they were backpackers: I felt connected, had to know everything about them.

"Where are you camping? Are you doing campsites or wild?"

"We're wild camping, but it's mad. We get to about six o'clock and all we can think about is flat ground. We couldn't find anywhere last night and ended up on that piece of grass in front of the pub in Lynmouth."

"Where are you heading?"

"Combe Martin, so we're finished today. We've only got the weekend and I've never wild camped before, I'm ready for a shower." The girl had bouncy brown hair and looked squeaky clean to me. I suddenly felt

78

very self-conscious and moved downwind. "What about you, where are you going?"

I looked at Moth; where were we going? After yesterday I wasn't sure, but he replied as if he still knew.

"Land's End. Who knows, depends on the weather, maybe further."

"That's amazing, you're so lucky to have time."

We watched them stride out along the cliff and waved as they passed the headland. *So lucky to have time*. I put my hand on the back of Moth's arm as his hand rested on his hip belt. His skin was hot to the touch and pink below the line of his T-shirt sleeve; same skin it had always been, but wrinkled above his elbow in a way I hadn't noticed before. Did we still have time?

Moth had a hat: a green canvas hat that sat on the top of his head like a cake tin, but a hat all the same. How could I have come without one? I could feel my scalp burning and watched my nose pulsate out of the corner of my eye. We thought we might make the Great Hangman by evening, but it was still a way off. The coastline's deceptive. A viewpoint in the distance seems to be just around the corner, but inevitably the headland in the foreground will be hiding combes and bays and even entire stretches of moorland in between.

"My head's on fire. Have you got a bandana or something?" We headed out on to Holdstone Down; it was late afternoon but the sun was still hot.

"You should have said — with all that hair I never think about you needing a hat. I've got the old hemp one in my pack."

I shoved on the beaten-up hat with its skinny one-inch brim, bought long ago from a hippy market in Ibiza. It held the heat from my boiled head and soon I felt ten times hotter.

Sitting on a bent hawthorn branch, I watched the sun set behind the Hangman and away into the west. The tent was pitched low amongst the gorse and heather where Moth scribbled in a notebook. We'd eaten rice and a tin of peas, but hunger wasn't far away. I swung my feet over the dry bare soil beneath the branch, and then it hit me. A shard of stone made a perfect tool and I dug and dug. Perfect.

"Moth, Moth, come and look what I've made."

He rolled on to his knees then stood up slowly.

"What? I can't see anything."

"Idiot, look, it's a long drop toilet."

"Oh God yeah, ha, me first."

I heated up the last bag of orange meatballs. We'd have more money tomorrow and could buy rations in Combe Martin.

"Second dinner, we're turning into hobbits."

It was almost dark when the sound of marching came from the east. Four twenty-something boys with immense full backpacks romped by at a march.

"There are more of us out there then. Did you see all that kit? Bet they're doing the whole thing." Moth watched them pass. I knew what he was thinking: that he used to be like that.

"Bet they're heading for Combe Martin, catch the pub before it closes."

"No, don't make me even think of a beer, there's only enough water left for tea in the morning."

Down, down, down into Combe Martin, a pretty little Devon village on the beach, with supposedly the longest village street in the country, winding two miles inland up the narrow valley. We wandered around the beach area with one focus: a cash machine. Finding nothing but trinket shops and a café, we tried the tourist information office hoping they'd point us in the right direction. Inside three old ladies were lined up behind the counter; they looked up at us, whispering, smiling and nodding.

"Moth, you speak to them, you always have a way with old ladies."

"That sounds really dodgy."

We dropped our packs by the door.

"Ladies, I wonder if you can help us. We've been looking for a cash machine, but it seems we're out of luck. Could you possibly direct us?"

The ladies shuffled, nudging each other, giggling.

"Of course, it's a pleasure to help. Just go to the grocery store up to the left. They'll do cashback for you, Mr Armitage, but they weren't expecting you yet."

"Sorry, I'm not Mr Armitage."

The ladies looked at each other conspiratorially.

"No of course not, that's okay, our secret, we won't say a word."

Moth looked back in bemusement as the three ladies waved to him. We put our packs on and left.

Supplies in the rucksack, twenty-five pounds still in the purse, chips in our hands, sitting on the beach leaning against the rocks in the heat of the day, nose burnt to a frazzle: it could be any ordinary day on the beach. Living in Wales within a drive of the sea, we'd had many of those. Long days of sand-covered kids, blow-up dinghies, tuna sandwiches, digging holes, rock pools. They'd grown up free to roam the woods, the mountains, the beach. Even now, after they'd been gone for a few years, whenever I felt sand beneath my feet it was with a slight twinge of loss. I had to get over that or it would be a totally dismal summer.

A little boy ran up the beach with a bucket of water for his sandcastle moat; his sister grabbed at the handle, wanting to be the one to pour the water. From nowhere their father leapt up, grabbed the boy and hit him.

"I've told you, don't fight with your sister."

The boy wriggled away and hid behind a rock. The mother stood up.

"Did you have to do that?"

"He's got to be shown." An angry dad, teaching his child to be an angry boy. Strange how the beach seems to bring out the best and the worst in people.

"I was going to say let's have a swim, but I think it's time we moved on." Moth was on his feet, dusting sand off his pack.

"Yeah, time to go, Mr Armitage."

The day got hotter and hotter as we trudged through the sharp rises and falls beyond the village. The pack was much heavier with its new supplies and I dragged along through the dust, following Moth's heels along the path, his feet barely seeming to lift from the ground either. The heat was unbearable. Unexpectedly, a campsite appeared, oasis-like, from the haze ahead of us. The Coast Path passed right through it.

"What do you think, should we see how much it costs? We could just rest, not have to look for a spot to pitch tonight, have a shower." The look on Moth's face said, I'm not asking, I'm begging.

"We can ask."

The site was busy with families, children, bikes, old couples and dogs, lots of dogs.

"That's fifteen pounds for a tent."

"Fifteen pounds? It's a small tent, we could squeeze in a corner."

"Fifteen pounds, any size."

"But we haven't even got a car, we're just walking the Coast Path."

"Well, you should have said." The site attendant pointed at a cardboard notice by the door. "Five pounds each for backpackers."

Ten pounds. We'd got enough dried food to nearly last the week. Moth sat on the plastic chair, wiping his face with a blue spotty bandana.

"Okay, just one night."

The showers were hot and free-running with no time limit. I relaxed into the heat and maybe it was something to do with tiredness, or a second of just letting go, but I couldn't stop crying. I gasped into the running water as I shed a layer of skin and sweat, bitterness, sadness, loss, fear. But only a layer. Whining self-pity: I couldn't afford to let it in.

I dried myself as well as possible on the super-thin, quick-dry towel and rummaged in the tiny toilet bag for a toothbrush. The toothpaste, a hair bobble and a tampon fell on to the floor. A tampon? I picked it up in shock. I'd packed a few, expecting to need them anytime soon, but as I held it in my hand it suddenly struck me that in the melee of our lives over recent times I hadn't realized that it had been over three months since I'd actually used one. Really? What to do in the menopause: become homeless and walk 630 miles with a rucksack on your back. Ideal. Plenty of weight-bearing exercise: at least I wouldn't have to worry about osteoporosis.

We left the campsite clean and rested, but the path to Ilfracombe wound on in a relentless mess of up and down, in and out and heat, and we were quickly as tired and dirty as we had been the previous day. The town was heaving with a mid-season swell of pushchairs, polyester and walking aids. The smell of food was torture, every corner had a new edible choice, but the campsite indulgence meant we could only look.

An old couple with a King Charles spaniel passed by in a bluster of straw hats.

"In all the years we've been coming here, I've never seen anything so shocking. It's not right."

At the end of the harbour, people were standing around taking photos. The great thing about not preparing for a journey, not reading about every place before you visit, is that things can still take you by surprise.

"Jeez, that's big." A huge bronze and steel statue rose twenty metres into the air, towering over the harbour. More polyester rushed away, tutting and shaking their heads. Moth picked up a leaflet discarded by someone who'd left in a hurry.

"Says her name's Verity, and it's by Damien Hirst. How did he get away with that? Mind you, he's supposed to already own a studio and a house here, isn't he?"

"What's it representing anyway?"

"Apparently truth and justice."

"Justice? Could tell him a thing or two about justice." The statue is a cross-section of a pregnant woman. One side whole, the other side showing the baby in the womb. She's holding a sword aloft and the scales of justice behind her back. "No wonder she's hiding the scales. Hide the truth behind a front that distracts the eye. It's a true representation of British justice. Anyone can have it, if they can afford to tip the scales."

"That's so true." An old man was sitting on a bench next to us, smartly dressed in polished shoes. We paused for a moment to chat. He was a retired Gurkha, who had stayed in Britain because he had served Britain and the Queen throughout his career. "But now I am not so sure. We live near here and our daughter wanted to build a bungalow for us in the garden, so that we could live in it now we're old, and she could live in our house so she could care for us. The council, however, do not think that's appropriate to the character of the town. A friend of mine tells me that Hirst is planning to build a housing estate for hundreds of houses on a farm he owns on the edge of town. If this statue is an example of his design, we can be sure they will not be Victorian villas. But if it is true, I do not expect him to have a problem with planning permission either."

"I don't suppose he will."

We shared a bag of chips and left Ilfracombe as quickly as we could, camping on the hill with the lights of the town still shining below. The next day was an exhausting drag. Had we not been so tired it would have been a day of endless photos and admiration of amazing views, but we could only focus on moving our feet.

"What's that blob out there?" I could see something in the sea that hadn't emerged from the haze before.

"What blob?"

"West, down the coast, where the land runs out."

"Looks like an island."

"Could it be Lundy already? Bet it is, Wales is getting further away so where the coast runs out must be where it turns south."

"Such a long way off."

Walking along cliff tops, ankle deep in the seed heads of wild flowers, should have been a delight, but as we passed Bull Point Moth became slower and began dragging his leg oddly. The miles crawled by. I picked some wild thyme and dandelion leaves and stirred them into rice, as the sun set. Woolacombe arrived the next morning: our ninth day walking. According to Paddy Dillon we should have been here four days ago. His timescale seemed to bear no relation to our days. After being driven by the tide on to the leg-draining soft sand of the upper beach, it was a relief to reach solid ground on the cliffs that led to Baggy Point. Even in our foggy, exhausted state, the view took our breath away. A long way out, but Lundy was now in full view and beyond it the coast of Wales curled to the north, then slipped out of sight. Was I relieved to let it fall off the horizon, or did I need it, still tangible, still real? I couldn't answer. And away, away to the west, at least forty miles away, Hartland Point, where the coast would take its second dramatic turn south. As the sun started to dip we put the tent up in the wild flowers and ate more dandelions.

"Mum wouldn't let me eat these when I was little; she said they'd make me wet the bed."

"The amount of times you get in and out of the tent every night, I don't think it can make any difference."

"Shall we get the bus around the estuary, skip Barnstaple and Bideford?"

"We could, but it'll be days before we get more money, and the Braunton Burrows looks really interesting: massive sand dunes made of windblown shells."

"Okay, but if you're in too much pain or your leg's hurting, or you're too tired, we'll cut in for the bus, okay?"

"Okay." Under the sunburn, black rings were spreading beneath his eyes.

The white, granular dunes rolled away down towards the Taw estuary, a fine shifting gravel like ground coral, not really like sand at all. The Burrows seemed to stretch on forever, one of the largest sand dune ecosystems in the country, covered in vegetation and humming with insect life. As we walked on I didn't see much of the view, most of my attention being taken by large pieces of skin peeling from my nose, and I passed more than a mile cross-eyed, trying to pull bits off. Moth was shuffling through the shell sand, watching his feet, when suddenly as if out of a desert haze we were confronted by a fully kitted-out commando, a real-life camouflage-clad, gun-hugging soldier. I've never been so close to that much camo paint, and didn't know how to react: whether to fall on the floor with hands behind my head, stand to attention, run away. What?

"I'm afraid you can't go any further today, you'll have to turn around and go back."

"We can't go back, we're going forwards." What a stupid thing to say. But Moth seemed unfazed.

"Hi, mate, what are you up to here? Manoeuvres or something?"

"That's right, sir, and you can't go through."

A big group of twenty soldiers streamed over the dune and collapsed on the sand as a canvas-backed truck pulled up.

"We can't go back, Moth's not well, we're going to Braunton to catch the bus. We won't be able to make it if we go back." Did I look desperate enough?

"Stay there, I'll see what can be done." Seconds later the soldier returned with a canteen of water.

"Don't move from that spot and we'll take you out with us when we go. Didn't you see the sign that says the dune's closed?"

"No."

"Don't move." The soldiers threw their kit into the truck, lifting their immense packs and waist belts as if they were nothing; they took mine and added it to the heap. Close-up, the soldier looked like a boy.

"What's this? Call this a pack? Feels like a handbag." They were all laughing. Then they picked up Moth's.

"Piece of cake. We pack more weight than that in the shower." Raucous laughter as we were bundled into the back of the truck, the canvas rolled down and we bumped away. They might have been more disciplined and in better physical shape than many, but it was soon obvious they were just a truck full of young men having a great time. In the heat of the back of the vehicle I realized that any day now these boys could be in a war zone, within a few weeks any one of them could be injured or dead. Young lives over before they'd barely begun, and for what?

"Where are we going?"

"Can't say, sir. In fact, best not to mention this to anyone." The truck bounced along, hit tarmac, then shortly after ground to a halt. "Okay, out you go."

The truck disappeared around a bend in the road, but I kept my fingers crossed for the generous men inside, hoping they stayed as full of life as they were at that moment.

The bus took us to Barnstaple, and then we changed on to another for Westward Ho! I felt as though I was cheating, and didn't understand why.

We arrived in Westward Ho! disorientated by the unexpectedness of it and surprised by its greyness. The exclamation mark had made me expect something spectacular, but nothing I was seeing quite matched the ostentatious name. Paddy says the town is named after a novel by Charles Kingsley, including the exclamation mark. Maybe the book's more interesting.

The break in the trail had left us feeling disconnected and slightly lost. Moth was irritable and, regardless of the dwindling pound coins, he needed a beer. We found ourselves sitting in a dismal bar overlooking a concrete walkway where children dodged waves as they broke over the sea wall. Moth drank his beer in silence and I held a glass of iced water to my head.

"Pub quiz, guys, take part, it's fun, there's prizes." A round little man in a waistcoat forced a pen and paper on us. "Only fifty pence to enter and you could win ten pounds first prize. Can't go wrong."

"Okay."

"Moth, that's fifty pence."

"What can you buy with fifty pence, and what if we win?"

The little man managed to rustle up three teams, so was about to make a serious loss.

"So, let's start with TV."

"I told you this was a waste of money."

"And on to sport; in Formula One racing . . ."

Why are we here?

"Who was the captain of the *Black Pig*?"

Moth jumped in his seat and scribbled on the paper: Captain Pugwash.

"And last of all, what went up in 1961 and came down in 1990?"

I've got this one, I've got this one: Berlin Wall. Maybe I shouldn't have been grumpy over fifty pence.

"The winners with the ten-pound prize are . . . the family at the bar!"

They took their ten pounds and immediately handed it back for another round of drinks.

"And in second place, taking five pounds: the backpackers."

We rushed to get our rucksacks on and collect our winnings.

"Another drink for the winners?"

I kicked Moth below the bar, and he glanced at me with narrowed eyes.

"No, sorry, we've got to make a move."

Diddley-dee, diddley-dee, we skipped our way back to the path. The waves broke over the wall behind and in front, but somehow missed us. Buoyed by our win, and the unfounded thought that maybe things were going in our favour, we escaped from Westward Ho!, singing the Captain Pugwash theme tune. Diddley-dee, diddley-dee. It was always going to be a shortlived high and we couldn't find anywhere to camp, so resorted to trampling a patch of bracken and thistles on a slope, in the dark. Gravity took control of the synthetic sleeping bags and we woke in the night curled in a pile at the door of the tent. The sea was very close, booming into the ground, more of a sensation than a sound. We piled the rucksacks by the tent door and propped our feet on them, knees locked, virtually standing.

Hobbling around the thistle patch in the grey morning light, knees refusing to unlock, we realized that we'd camped on an overhang of stone and clay, where the sea scratched away at the earth in the hollow below. A patch of land nearing its end, about to relax into oblivion.

Heat climbed up over the cliff and bound us in a cloak of airless, flat suffocation as we headed out on to Greencliff. Black rock sliding away into the sea, in layers of dark molten exposure. This seam of blackest black runs from Bideford to the cliff edge and fades into fingers running out to sea. It used to be mined as fuel to fire the lime kilns that scattered this patch of coast, turning Welsh limestone into fertilizer and building materials. Now Bideford Black is used as an artist's pigment, fuelling the cash tills of trendy art galleries.

And it got hotter. My nose was glowing red, the new skin burnt before the old skin had shed. Moth was stumbling more often and for the first time tripped and fell, grazing his arm and leaving him shaken.

"I've got to stop. Can you get the water?" He drank, trying to satisfy an unquenchable thirst, until there were only two inches of water left. We'd filled the bottles in the bar in Westward Ho! and used most of it overnight, but now were quite some distance from a tap, unless we diverted inland in the hope of knocking on someone's door.

"Shall we carry on? It looks like we'll cross a stream near Babbacombe Cliff."

"I'll try."

We shuffled on, as Moth got slower and I became increasingly anxious. By the time we crossed the dry stream bed, the afternoon had become a burning shimmer. No shade, no trees, just cliff top, sea and sky. At three o'clock Moth dropped his pack and lay on the ground.

"I'm done, I'm just done. I can't do this. I feel shivery."

"Do you think you've got sunstroke, or are you just exhausted?"

"I want to go home, get in my own bed and never wake up."

I lay on the grass next to him and stared up at the sky. Don't even think it. Don't let the thought in. I sat up, found my glasses and read Paddy's map.

"We're nearly at a little ravine, think it's called Peppercombe. There's a stream there and trees, so we can get out of the heat. You'll feel better if you cool down." The heat had built until I could feel all the moisture evaporating from my body, turning me to parchment. We couldn't stay there.

"I can't."

"Well, I'll leave my pack here then and just go and have a look." I walked away from him; without the weight of the rucksack I had springs in my boots and balloons on my shoulders, but anxiety didn't let me appreciate it. Don't let this be real. Don't let him be getting worse, please don't. Let it just be the sun.

A stripe of green trees and undergrowth followed the narrow valley towards the sea and the sound of water. Crouched by the side of the clear-running salvation, I splashed the icy coldness against my burning skin, feeling sure I could hear it hiss. I drank over and over from my cupped hands, before filling the two-litre bottle to the brim and heading back up the hill.

"You have to come down. It's so cool under the trees, you'll feel a lot better. Only half an hour and you can drink this, when the water-purifying pill has done its thing." I didn't tell him I'd drunk a pint before even considering bacteria.

We dozed the afternoon away under the green shade until a black ball of hair leapt into the stream, followed by five others.

"That's the way, jump in and cool down, boys." The owners of the pack of spaniels stood on the bridge, efficiently dressed in pockets, hats and walking poles. So glad I'd already filled the water bottles.

"Well, hello there. What a pleasant afternoon. Come far, have you?"

"Not far today, it's been very hot."

"Yes, rather warm. Where are you off to then?"

"Land's End." Poole still isn't coming out of my mouth. Just the thought of it seems ridiculous.

"Land's End? Oh, Land's End." The tall brisk man looked at the woman with a nod. "I heard you might be coming this way. We're from south Devon; heading home tomorrow, so unfortunately we won't be able to see you. Unfortunate, that. Well, must go, hope it's a profitable journey. Let's go, boys." A tidal wave of black left the stream and bounded up the road, heading inland.

"Profitable journey? We're meeting some odd ones."

"Too right. Let's go down to the beach — it's getting cold under these trees." I instantly regretted leaving the path as the track to the beach headed sharply downhill, which meant we would eventually need to climb all the way back up.

A beach of smooth, sea-worn stones sat above black rock that slid down into the low tide. The sun-warmed cobbles soothed our aching muscles as we sat in the shade of some scrubby vegetation, sheltered from the early-evening sun that still burnt our red skin. The sea swayed, syrup flat, in a moment of indecision before its inevitable return. Moth was shivering, but burning hot, his joints aching and feeling nauseous.

"What if this is it, what if I'm dying?"

"You're not dying; it's probably sunstroke. Anyway, this thing isn't going to hit you in the afternoon and you're dead by tea."

Knowing the blackness was coming, waiting in the background, had put him on constant alert; every rustle in the grass was his nemesis creeping up. We knew it wouldn't be sudden, that we were on a downward slope with a long way to run before we reached its end. We were both nervous all the same. I had thought, in the days after leaving the farm, when we were packing rucksacks and preparing, that walking together over a vast distance would give us the space to think things through. Time to talk about the huge loss we were feeling, and calmness to try to face a future not with CBD in it, but carved out by it. But I hadn't thought much at all, and we'd mainly talked about food and the heat, or the rain. I'd plodded along as if my head was in a paper bag, thinking of nothing, just taking it out occasionally to shake it around and see if there was anything inside. Putting one foot in front of another in a metronome of blankness was strangely satisfying and I didn't want to think. But as Moth struggled on, one thought had crept in; how stupid it was to be doing this, the irresponsibility of dragging him here. Clearly he was getting worse. If we weren't walking, he wouldn't be going through this daily muscle-grinding torture. I hardly dared to look in the guidebook; from the tiny glimpses I'd taken, I could see it would soon get harder. What if by suggesting this insane trip I'd accelerated the CBD? It would be my fault. After all, the consultant had said, "Don't tire yourself, or walk too far, and be careful on the stairs." All I'd thought about in those days of planning was leaving Wales, running away, forgetting that we'd lost our home, that our family was spread all over the country, that Moth was ill. I once heard a lecture by Stephen Hawking, when he said, "It's the past that tells us who we are. Without it we lose our identity." Maybe I was trying to lose my identity, so I could invent a new one.

"Have you taken the Pregabalin today?" Moth had been prescribed this drug, not for its use as an antidepressant, but for relief from nerve pain. It seemed to work, but I didn't know how it could relieve pain and not have the antidepressant effect. He certainly seemed slower since he'd taken it. Less pain, but less Moth.

"No, I took the last one at Baggy Point. I forgot to say: have you got another box?"

"No, you've got them."

"I haven't."

"Oh shit. Why didn't you say? We'll have to get some more. We can walk back to Westward Ho! and get the bus to Barnstaple, see if your GP can send a prescription."

How could we have forgotten them? As I thought about it, I could see them sitting on a bag in the back of the van ready to be put into the rucksack. Completely forgotten after the encounter with angels. There could be a town inland, a chemist within a short walking distance, but we would never know. Paddy Dillon's great little guidebook contains copies of Ordnance Survey maps covering the entire South West Coast Path, fantastically comprehensive and detailed; you couldn't want for anything better. The drawback is, they only cover roughly half a mile inland. Our world had become this narrow passage, with half a mile of land to our left and a wet infinity to our right. The path covers vast tracts of English coastline and only a few places can be considered remote, but on that beach it was as clear as the salt water running over the Bideford

Black that civilization exists only for those that can afford to inhabit it, and remote isolation can be felt anywhere, if you have no roof and an empty pocket.

"They're in the van. We could get them posted somewhere. To Clovelly maybe."

"No, Jan's on holiday until late August. Like you say, it's just sunstroke. Let's make some tea and eat something. I'll be fine."

"You're not supposed to just stop taking them. This could be withdrawal; it could make you worse." What had the doctor said? "Whatever you do, don't just stop taking the Pregabalin." The immense list of withdrawal symptoms could begin with headaches, nausea, diarrhoea and sweating, and lead to insomnia, anxiety, depression and suicide. That's if you're lucky.

He couldn't eat, but after heaving up a few spoons of rice, he drank and drank. The shakes became more pronounced as we erected the tent on a flat patch behind the hedge. He put on the clean T-shirt he'd kept at the bottom of his pack while I washed sick into a rock pool.

In the pitch black of the night I could see nothing in the tent; there was no moon to give even a faint outline to anything. Every moan and whimper made me switch the torch on, checking on what I'm not sure; it wasn't as if I could do anything anyway.

"Water, need some water."

There was no phone reception and by four o'clock the battery had died in the cold. To get help I'd have to leave him there and try to find a house. I didn't want to

98

leave him. I switched the torch on, recklessly wasting the batteries.

"Smell, that smell, sickly shit smell, what is it?"

"I can't smell anything."

"It smells."

All I could smell was washing powder on the only clean T-shirt.

"Lotus flower and melon. Try to sleep."

"Stinks."

I ran the torch around the tent, checking everything was in its place, familiarity soothing the panic. Over the days on the path, the green dome of the tent had become our home. Every evening we began a ritual of filling our home with our possessions. The self-inflating mattresses first, then a small fleece blanket over them, then the sleeping bags, then us, then the rucksacks by our feet at the entrance. Then we unpacked the rucksacks, putting cooking equipment in the porch, then clothes spread across the remaining uncovered groundsheet to block the cold, before attaching the torch to a karabiner hanging from a loop above the entrance zip. Finally, I made tea while Moth read from the tiny slim volume of *Beowulf*, the only book we carried. Is it human nature to crave ritual? Is it instinctive to construct a safe environment before we allow ourselves to sleep? Can we ever truly rest without that security? It was all I could cling to in that tent, somewhere on the coast, with a dying man falling into withdrawal from a central nervous system depressant, a Class 5 controlled substance in America but still uncategorized in the UK.

I lay close to Moth to stop him shivering and passed the night flicking the torch on and off, imagining myself two hundred years ago attracting smugglers to the shore. I gave up on sleep when a faint light crept into the green. He was finally peaceful and breathing deeply. I quietly got out of the sleeping bag and unzipped the door but managed to fall out of the tent, breaking the leg off the stove support as I went. My torch-flashing had done no good: never a crate of rum when you really need one.

Moth eventually woke at nine, as I was sticking the stove leg together with a roll of micropore plaster. He'd stopped shaking but had a crushing headache, his joints ached and the shoulder pain was worse. I made tea, twice, and then went to the stream to get more water. Mugs of hot tea had become a lifeline. Initially the soothing effect of the hot liquid on jangling nerves had been priceless, but now it filled a hole where food should be. I couldn't be bothered to take the tent down and Moth wasn't strong enough; if someone came to throw us off then I'd pack it away. The rock pools made a perfect washing bowl and I scrubbed the clothes with water and shampoo; they smelt better but dried crusty with salt and slightly sticky. I cut the ripped leggings off at the knees with a tiny pair of nail scissors to make a pair of shorts, and left everything to dry on the rocks.

The Bideford Black stretched and split into the sea like a muscle of land reaching to its furthest point. In the narrow gaps between the shiny, smooth blackness, dark pools formed in hidden depths of salt water. The sunlight reflected from the surface, but when I put my hand in to feel the empty, smooth, cold rock at the base of the pool, it wasn't there; the hole went down and down, opening wider as it went. No ammonites or crabs, but a deep, mysterious hole that might hold unknown caverns and mysterious creatures. Slightly spooked by what could be beneath my feet, I scoured the beach for driftwood, building a small fire as the evening began to cool, slowly feeding it as Moth huddled in his sleeping bag next to me and shivered. Then another night of wasted batteries.

Wandering along the beach in the early light, I collected more bits of driftwood for a fire. On the sharp grass at the top of the rocks, amongst the pink thrift, was a rough shelter made from bits of wood and washed up plastic. Someone had put benches inside and hung seaweed around. I was playing house, arranging some shells with the seaweed, when Moth hesitantly walked over the rocks towards me with two mugs held precariously in front of him. I took the mugs of tea and we sat inside.

"Welcome home, Ray. What do you think to our new place?"

"It's great. I always wanted somewhere with lots of light and a sea view."

"Should we go back to Wales, camp somewhere and beg the council for a roof? Or shall we just stay here, make the shack better, live on the beach? I mean, what exactly are we going to do when this is over?" The great unspoken question. What would we do?

"I don't know."

We sat around in the shelter and in the shade of the hedge watching a group of turnstones. Compact and beautiful little wading birds with white chests and mottled chestnut backs, hopping deftly between the black rock and the seaweed on spindly orange legs. Their strong pointed beaks quickly flipping stones to find the edible treats beneath. They must have been on their way north or south, or perhaps non-breeding birds just hanging out for the summer. We hung out with them: Moth, cold and aching in his sleeping bag, dozed fitfully in the sun, while I collected more driftwood and dried seaweed for the fire. As the sun set we realized that we actually couldn't see Wales any more. It had slipped away without us noticing. The only land mass was Lundy, getting much closer. The fire crackled to embers and Wales had gone; we were alone on a beach in Devon, no home, no hope of getting one, just the path and our feet.

Moth groaned through the night, the aches in his joints getting worse until finally he fell into a sound sleep. Was the Pregabalin hell over? I lay and watched him, but he didn't wake and finally my own eyes closed. He woke around midday, more alert, a little stronger, ate a cereal bar and was ready to move on.

"We can't stay, we've only got food for one more day. Let's go to Clovelly. We can get some more supplies there, I'm sure, and it can't be more than five miles."

We climbed up from the beach and back on to the path that rose and fell in relentless jerks. Very quickly Moth was exhausted. The little shop in Bucks Mills had closed ten minutes before we reached it, so we headed up into the woods. Not even halfway to Clovelly and we had to stop. A glimpse of green through the trees made us scramble through the undergrowth, throw our packs over and paratrooper roll under an electric fence into a lush green corner of a field, surrounded on three sides by trees and in a slight dip, completely hidden from view. We pitched the tent and, desperately hungry, ate the last of the rations, leaving four digestive biscuits for breakfast. It didn't matter; we'd be in Clovelly the next day.

CHAPTER
SEVEN

Hungry

I sat outside in the soft, dewy light of another dry morning and made a cup of tea to dunk the last of the biscuits. My legs itched in my newly cut shorts, probably because of the salt-water laundry.

"Moth, come out, I've made the tea." Actually, my legs were really itchy.

"Wow, look at your legs, amazing." Was he still ill? My legs aren't bad, but they're definitely not that remarkable either. "Look at that: ladybirds."

Rather than layers of sweaty salt, my legs were crawling in ladybirds. I stood up and found they were all over me. In fact they were everywhere. Over the tent, the stove and, as he stood up, Moth too. Their tiny feet all heading towards the sky as they lifted into flight, migrating towards their first breakfast from our outstretched arms. A lifetime spent in the natural world had taught me how the ladybird parent lays hundreds of eggs in an area where there's a high population of aphids, so that when they hatch they're in the right place for a ready meal. But they were too special and the shiny red wonders too numerous: there had to be more to it than that; they had to have a meaning for us.

We stood in the early morning, watching hundreds of tiny creatures stretch their wings for the first time and lift into flight from our fingertips. No, I couldn't be scientific about it, and clung to the myth of the ladybird bringing good luck, carrying it with me in a rosy, spotted glow. I watched the pink aura lift from Moth and tried to believe in miracles.

"You know, I'm feeling good today."

"Was it the ladybirds?"

"No. I think it's because I've stopped taking those tablets; I feel as if I've just walked out of a fog. It's really quite painful, but I'm going to see how it goes without them. I'll take a few ibuprofen, but I feel different, clearer. Let's go to Clovelly and get something to eat. I'm starving."

"Still think it's the ladybirds."

The weather changed rapidly and rain began to fall relentlessly through the trees. The gravel track of the Hobby Drive wound on around endless corners that never opened on to Clovelly. Reminders of our hunger were everywhere, even in flocks of juvenile pheasants eating from grain containers at the edge of the wood. We'd been hungry for a week, but my stomach had started to squeeze and I was feeling lightheaded. Could we boil the pheasant grain?

Clovelly is run as an estate, all the houses being owned and rented by the estate company, controlled by descendants of the family who've owned it for nearly three hundred years. It's known mainly for its very steep cobbled street running down to the harbour through picture-perfect cottages. But it didn't appear and the road, the woods and the pheasants went on and on.

"The actor from that film lives here. His wife died of motor neurone disease, you know."

"That's really sad. What actor?"

"You remember, that film about walking from Land's End to John o' Groats. But they lived with carers and a house, not actually on the path. I don't want to die in a tent."

"You're not going to die in the tent. Do you think he actually walked much at all or was it just for the film?"

I realized that I envied the actor a little. Not for losing the woman he loved, but for still having their home, full of their memories and their life together; he could close his eyes and picture her reading in her chair, or looking out of the window. What would I have?

"Do you think this is just a masochistic way of pretending we're not homeless? That we've still got a purpose?" The pheasants drifted away from our feet and re-clustered behind us. The hunger was intense now, and I had a headache.

"Of course it is." Moth had stopped, amazed by what he was seeing. "What the hell is that? Tell me I'm not still hallucinating."

"No, that's a really big turkey."

"Why is there a huge grey turkey in the woods with the pheasants?"

"I have no idea."

"I can smell cars; we must be here."

We dodged the sign that said six pounds fifty each to enter and headed down the cobbled street of Clovelly, the weight of our packs adding to the momentum. The shop wasn't really a shop, more a glorified tuck shop with sweets and ice cream for the visitors.

"You'll have to go to the pub if you want food, or the visitor centre."

We carried on down to the harbour, and sat in the clearing drizzle.

"Maybe they'll do cashback at the pub if we share a bowl of chips."

A spotty youth walked across the stone arc of the harbour, dressed in black as if he was about to start work in the bar. Eating an enormous Cornish pasty. I was so hungry I contemplated putting my hand out to catch the flakes of pastry as they fell to the ground. He was just a youth, he wouldn't mind.

"Mate, where did you get that pasty? There was nothing in the shop."

He looked slightly shocked to be spoken to by a middle-aged, smelly tramp and contemplated us while he finished chewing.

"They sell them in the visitor centre."

"We thought about going to the pub. Are the meals reasonable in there?"

"No. I work in this one; they charge a fortune. They even charge me. That's why I always go to the visitor centre to buy a pasty before I start work. I mean, that and the girl with pink hair that sells them." He smiled.

"Sorry to hear that, mate. Oh well, thanks for the tip. It's tough to find a cheap pub around here."

The boy seemed to sense we were kindred spirits and perched on the bench nearby.

"Tell me about it. I won't pay a penny into the pockets of the upper class around here. They've got plenty of their own. That's the way it is here. It's all owned by Him up on the hill."

"You're not keen on it here then? I thought it would be a nice place to live."

"Well, bad boy in the posh village. I'm joining the army soon. Time to get away from here."

"There must be a lot of positive things about living here though? I mean, it's idyllic, and there's the girl with the pink hair."

"No, she ignores me anyway. I do go beating with the shoot though; the estate boys are a good laugh."

"You know about the shoot? Tell me: what's with the turkeys?"

"What, the turkeys in the woods? Not many people spot those. They keep them because they encourage the pheasants to come to eat, then at the Christmas shoot there's a bonus paid if you bag the turkey. They get to shoot their own dinner and win a bottle of whisky for doing it. We just get a fiver for a whole day trudging around the woods. Anyway, I've got to go. Enjoy your walk."

"Good luck in the army." I feared he may be just swapping one hierarchy for another, but he seemed as if life had equipped him with the resilience to deal with it.

We were nearly on our hands and knees by the time we reached the top of the hill and the visitor centre.

Having only eaten one biscuit all day, my head was spinning.

The big restaurant looked really promising and we had cash in the bank. We laid our waterproofs over the chairs to dry, plugged the phone in to charge and decided on the cheapest thing on the menu. The girl with pink hair looked at us apologetically and explained that they had closed five minutes ago and she wasn't allowed to sell anything else.

"Well, could we just have a pot of hot water maybe?"

"Oh, I don't know." She looked over her shoulder. "Go on then, if you just put some money in the tip jar."

"Couldn't I just buy two of those pasties? We're walking the coastal path and we've run out of food. We thought we'd be able to buy some at the shop . . ."

"Oh no, you can't get food there. I can't sell them now we're closed. Go and sit down, I'll bring your water."

The clothes steamed as we sat and waited.

"What are we going to do? We have to get food." The table next to us had been vacated by a family, leaving behind plates of untouched salad. I was just trying to gather my courage to move two plates to our table, when the girl with pink hair came over.

"Just got to wait until the boss goes, then you can have some pasties to take away. I'm supposed to throw them away if they're not sold, but that's such a waste, you might as well have them. I can't let you go without taking some food. It'd be like letting my gran go to starve under a hedge. It wouldn't be right." Her gran? Wow, I must be looking rough.

"Thank you so much, that's really kind." Maybe I could do something in return. "We've met some really nice people here, like the boy who buys pasties and works at the pub — he was really nice, very chatty."

"I know, but he's joining the army. I really don't want him to go."

"Maybe you should tell him? You never know, I think he might feel the same."

"Do you think?"

"Definitely."

We left with a bag of pasties and bought four packs of fudge and a bottle of locally brewed pear cider from the trinket shop on the way out — paying with the bank card so we could get some cash back.

The boy on the harbour had got under my skin. I understood his sense of them and us in the village. Growing up as the daughter of a tenant farmer on a large country estate, I didn't have to ask him to explain who "He" was. As a child watching people in the village "doff their caps" to the landlord, treating him and everyone connected to him with a reverential respect, I empathized with the boy's disdain. It was that upbringing which drove me to join socialist rallies, protest against the poll tax, protest against the American nuclear warheads at Greenham Common, protest against anything really. When my parents tried to make a match between me and a farm owner's son, it was the anti-establishment, anti-control sense of rebellion that drove me to run as hard as I could towards Moth and his belief that freedom is the most important right we have. Mum never really forgave me for giving up the security of a life married to a man with acres, and until the day she died never accepted Moth as being worthwhile. Walking through the woods in the falling light, the damp smell of the undergrowth acidic in the air, I could almost hear her laughing at me.

"Bet you regret it now, my girl." No, Mum. No, I don't.

The path followed the edge of the woods as they ran up to an open area of grassland, the wire-netting cones around the sapling trees marking it as a deer park. The lights of the big house were coming on in the distance.

"Do you think He's dressing for dinner?" I was imagining a warm fire and dry clothes.

"You're only jealous."

"No, I'm really not. Let's camp here — it's perfect."

"It's not worth it. There's bound to be an estate man round in a Land-Rover in the morning, telling us to clear off."

"Then we'll have to get up early."

The owls in the woods hooted theatrically all night, flat soft grass and I still couldn't sleep. I tried to count them, there could have been four or five, or maybe it was the same one flying around in circles. However cosy "He" was in the big house he didn't have this, he couldn't hear the beat of an owl's wing through the oak branches, or the scratch of his talons against the bark of a beech tree. He wasn't breathing the sweet smell of nettles or the sharp tang of gorse as he put his head on a pillow. But then again, he did have a pillow.

When I finally woke Moth was already up, writing a note on a piece of paper.

"What are you doing?"

"Writing a thank-you letter. What do you think?"

I found my glasses in my boot and read the crumpled piece of notepaper: "Dear Sir, thank you for a very nice night camped in your deer park. I'll be sure to tell all my friends of your hospitality."

"I'm just going to leave it in the top of the cider bottle and tuck it in the wire cone. They're bound to find it."

"What about 'leave no trace'?"

"It's not rubbish, it's a thank-you letter."

Eight thirty, the earliest morning so far. We shooed ladybirds from the tent and walked.

CHAPTER EIGHT

The Corner

Lying in the sun on baking-hot grass, having walked four miles before lunch and eaten a handful of elderberries straight from the tree, there's a lot to be said for being a vagrant. Lundy was directly ahead; we'd been walking towards it for days and very soon would be walking away. On the other side of the combe we'd just crossed, the woodland faded out through steep bracken, down to yet another stream before rising up again to where we sat. Two small figures scrambled through the gorse, bracken and nettles on the other side, and we indulged in our favourite entertainment: watching other people get it as wrong as us. The figures disappeared from view and we ate some fudge. Fudge for breakfast, fudge for lunch, and it was looking like fudge for dinner. Our smelly, sweat-soaked clothes were dry and it was nearly time to move on. Then a rare sight. Two backpackers appeared over the brow of the hill. Backpackers with full packs who looked like they were doing a long distance. The young men stopped for a moment with the cursory questions about how far we were going.

"Land's End? Great, more backpackers." They took their packs off and dropped down beside them on the grass. "Hey, we've seen you before. You were camped near the Great Hangman. How the hell did you get in front of us?"

How the hell *did* we get in front of them? They rummaged in their rucksacks, packed with the complete abandon of youth, everything shoved in supermarket bags and bulging from every pocket. Their rucksack straps were bound with bubble wrap and their sleep mats tied on with string.

"Where did you camp last night? We couldn't find anywhere and ended up on the grass square in front of the visitor centre."

"The deer park; it was great, except for the owls. I thought there were four of you at the Great Hangman?"

"There were. One dropped out at Woolacombe, so we spent a couple of days there. Then the other's just given in on Greencliff; it was so fucking hot, he couldn't take it. We walked back to Westward Ho! with him and got the bus to Barnstaple, saw him off, stocked up with supplies at the supermarket, then bus back to Westward Ho! and had to do Greencliff all over again."

"Greencliff was a nightmare. We nearly gave up there. Such a good idea to go to the supermarket. There was no food in Clovelly except a bag of pasties and fudge."

"We missed the path at the top over there and got stuck in the brambles." He peeled off his socks to examine his blisters and pick thorns out of his ankles.

114

"Yeah, we watched you." It was so warm to be in the company of these two young people, so random, scattered and carelessly enjoying life. I felt a stab of longing for my children, the same age, with the same lightness of being. I swallowed the tears and dressed his wounds with antiseptic wipes and blister plasters.

We talked for an hour in the hot sun, stories from the path uniting us in mutual comfort. Josh and Adam had set off from Minehead a few days after us and somehow their diversions and our slow motion had landed us here at this moment. They would be in Bude and on their journey home the next day; we would be somewhere a few paces or a few miles south of here, and we would never see them again. But that didn't matter.

"Are you really going to Land's End? I wish we had the time. I've got to be back — we're supposed to be moving house in three days."

"Yeah, Adam's girlfriend thought he was only away for a week. You're going to be in such shit, man."

"What the hell, she'll get over it."

"I'm sure she will. We might carry on to Poole if we can." It seemed an impossibly long way off, but just saying it made it sound a little closer.

"You lucky bastards."

We swapped some sachets of coffee for a bag of couscous and waved them off. When they'd gone from view, we followed slowly behind. Hand in hand in the hot mid-afternoon sun. Homeless, dying, but strangely, in that sweaty, dehydrated moment, shyly, reluctantly happy. *Lucky bastards.*

$\star$　$\star$　$\star$

Hartland Point is a geologist's delight. The rock on this coast changes and changes and changes again, but at Hartland Point it's unlike anything else. Created in shallow seas 320 million years ago, the sedimentary strata are formed from layers of sand, shale and mudstone. Around 290 million years ago, when the Gondwana tectonic plate moved up from the south and collided with the Laurasia plate in the north, they met in a huge upswell of rock known as the Variscan orogeny. It formed mountains through Portugal, western Spain, Cornwall, Devon and on through the south and west of Wales and Ireland. The Hartland Point cliffs are carved out in sandstone ribs that rise up into chevron-shaped rock folds. A movement millennia old, still visible, still alive beneath our feet.

But all I could see was a football on a stick. An absolutely giant football in the sky ahead of us. On a stick.

"Get a grip, Ray, it's a radar station; it says so in the guidebook. It's used for air traffic control."

"I've got to sit down."

"Have you eaten too much fudge? I think you're having a sugar rush. You just need some real food, but there's nothing 'til a hotel at Hartland Quay. That's going to be ten miles in one day; I don't know if we can do that."

"I'll be fine. We've got half a bag of fudge and some couscous."

I've always liked bunting. Happy, cosy, childhood garden parties and canvas camping trips. But the bunting hanging from the tiny café in a shed at Hartland Point was the most perfect bunting I've ever seen. A bunting oasis. Bunting with heart. Bunting with food. Unexpected food supplies are like waking up one morning and realizing, unexpectedly, that it's your birthday.

"Can we pay four pounds each for a panini, or shall we share one?" Please say one each, Moth, please.

"No, you need to eat, and who knows when we'll get to somewhere to stock up on rations. One each."

Mozzarella, basil and tomatoes combined into some kind of wind-whipped, gull-swirling heaven. I sat with my back to the football and the wind in my face, looking out over the end of the Bristol Channel and the start of the wide, endless Atlantic Ocean. It's wild here, a corner where tides, winds and tectonic plates collide in a roar of elemental confusion. A place of endings, beginnings, shipwrecks and rockslides. The viewpoint by the railings caught the air and rushed it up in a jet of cold, oxygenated, sea-spray fizz. I flew with the power of the uplift; alive, we were alive.

"Shall we carry on?" Something's changing. Something's forming. I can't see it yet, but I can feel it coming. We turned left and headed south. I kept my eyes fixed on the sea, and away from the football.

The ground climbed and fell. The vegetation became shorter, treeless, tough and stubbornly rooted in shallow soil, resilient to the full pelt of the Atlantic forces. Rocky headlands fell repeatedly to streamed valleys. An outcrop of rock ahead called the Cow and Calf, like no cow and calf I've ever seen, became a

117

well-known friend shrinking in the distance behind while the rocky headlands kept coming. The sun set through scudding clouds to the west and the light dimmed as we reached a flat area of short grass on an exposed cliff top. The view through the doorway of a ruined tower caught the fading light as it framed the tower of Stoke Church. We considered camping close to the tower, hoping it might afford some protection from the wind, but in the dark it was hard to tell how stable it was, so instead faced the tent head on to the Atlantic air as it rushed over the open cliff, too tired to care.

I woke to the sound of torrential rain. Water thundering on to the taut flysheet. My eyes were gritty, still in the fog of sleep, but the water was only coming from the south. It should be coming from the north, or west, straight off the sea, but the rain wasn't beating on the opening. Then it stopped. Torrential rain covering the back of the tent, then stopping. Weird. I stuck my head out of the door to view the strange clouds that must be passing very quickly. There were none. The sun was just lifting on to the sea, blurring the water into the sky with the white blue of early morning. Not a cloud. But the source of the rain was trotting away east with a smug look on his wiry muzzle; the dog on the end of the lead seemed equally satisfied. I could make a cup of tea or wash pee off the tent: there wasn't enough water for both. I went for the tea and hoped the pee dried quickly.

A slow, slow, leg-pumping morning confirmed that Paddy Dillon is probably superhuman. In fact I'm convinced he's ex-SAS, eats raw seaweed for breakfast, runs marathons when there's nothing on TV, and wears camouflage pyjamas. He seems to think this is day nine when it's really day seventeen, that it's quite feasible to cover fifteen and a half miles "of the most scenic" but also "one of the toughest" stretches, and still have strength to admire the waterfalls. He also thinks it can be "quite tiring" in wet and windy weather. Does that mean it's a walk in the park on a hot sunny day? At least there were plenty of streams from which we could refill the water bottles. He's right about it being the most scenic. Treeless open headlands, ragged water-torn rock formations and a coastline that runs from Hartland Point to a fading grey smudge on the far horizon: a smuggler's paradise. The heat kept rising. On cliff tops with no shade, my cheeks were beginning to feel like leather and my third nose was emerging from the peel.

Dropping into a shady combe and over a wooden footbridge, a sign unexpectedly welcomed us to Kernow, the local name for Cornwall. The north coast of Devon had passed under our feet, leaving a new county stretching away to the west, disappearing into the horizon. It was evening when we dipped into another valley. The climb up the other side rose above us so steeply that without discussion we pitched the tent on a small patch of grass near running water and fell asleep for half an hour. Five miles, six pieces of fudge and the day was over. I left Moth fiddling with his rucksack and followed the stream to where it disappeared over a two-metre drop, then down a rocky slope towards the sea. Peeling off my sweaty, dusty clothes, I climbed down on to the slope and stood under the ice-cold water as it fell in a waterfall from the edge above. I'd been in the sea at Peppercombe, but hadn't been in clean water since Combe Martin, eleven days ago. Sand, salt and a profoundly disgusting stench washed into the sea. My skin was red, brown and peeling, turning into cured leather on my arms and cheeks, red and swollen on my legs. My hair felt similar to the coarse grass on the headlands and my big toe was now half its depth but twice its width, flattened by the reinforcement of my boot. The cliff reached out to sea in a jagged fin of rock, shielding the water behind from the harshness of the currents, creating a calm pool of stillness. Behind a notch in the black line of rock, the sun seemed to be held up, prevented from finally sinking. Foam broke against the fin and ran exhausted and calm into the bay behind. I climbed back up to my clothes, checking that there was no one walking past. As I put the stiff rags back on, I thought I heard cricket commentary. At the tent Moth had his feet up on a rock with another cup of tea, listening to the little radio that I thought was in storage.

"How have you carried that so far? It weighs as much as a bag of sugar! No . . . *why* have you carried it?"

"So I could listen to the cricket."

"Right." I was uncomfortable. The radio seemed out of place, an intruder in the wild space that had become our new reality. "So what's happening?"

"Five overs left. They're talking about the light. There's a chance it could be a draw; it's a shame — we could win this."

We lay in the grass by the tent and watched seagulls flying over in flocks as England won the Ashes, but the match was a draw and Jonathan Agnew got in a flap about it being a "disgrace".

The light had almost gone and the seagulls kept coming, calling quietly, not with loud and raucous chattering as they do in the day, but longer, quieter calls.

"Where do you think they're going?"

We watched as the gulls dipped over our heads to the cliff edge, then dropped towards the bay to join hundreds of others floating on the calm water, protected by the rock fin.

"They're sleeping on the water; it's their safe place."

"It is safe here, isn't it? Protected. I'd live here if I could." Moth paused for a moment. "When it's over, you could bring me back here if you like."

"What do you mean? When the walk's over?"

"No. When it's all over."

His body moved the air next to me, my skin sensing the shape of him in the falling light.

"Shall we swim?"

The deep water was cool, but pockets still held the warmth of the day. Floating in the darkness, Moth pushed out into the gently moving bodies of grey, bobbing in near silence around him. The moon caught their white heads, occasionally turning towards him in untroubled curiosity. We hung weightless in the salt as

121

everything drifted from us and was lost. All that remained was the water, the moon and the murmuring forms that shared the sea.

The gulls settled into a dark blue rhythm, as the cool dampness of night finally drove us into the tent. It'll never be over; we'll never be over.

PART THREE

The Long Fetch

Often, for undaunted courage,
fate spares the man it has not already marked.

Beowulf, Seamus Heaney

CHAPTER
NINE

Why?

Robert Stephen Hawker built himself a hut from driftwood, precariously positioned on the cliffs below Morwenstow. It's now the smallest property owned by the National Trust. Hawker was a devout Cornishman, with a passion for the county and the people who lived in it. According to one of his many poems, "twenty thousand Cornish men will know the reason why!" I didn't know why the men in his poem wanted to rescue Trelawny, but I was beginning to understand why they loved this piece of land so much, and why Hawker was driven to build his shack in this exposed spot. Because sheltering in his wooden hut surrounded by the gorse-filled air, amongst the rocks, sea and sky, his thoughts were set free.

So free in fact, that he passed his days as the vicar of Morwenstow, walking the lanes and cliff tops in a purple coat, pink hat and yellow cape. We would at least have had bad dress sense in common. I wish I'd known him, spending his years rescuing shipwrecked sailors from the sea and giving the dead a Christian burial in his graveyard. It seemed fitting that we were finding shelter from the burning heat in his hut, shipwrecked from life, lifewrecked in the driftwood.

He might have given us some food too. We were well into our second day of the fudge diet and it wasn't going well. Headaches, dizziness and hunger were now constant. We could have diverted inland to a café in Morwenstow, but that would have used unknown amounts of money that we barely had, and when you start a diet it's best to stick to it. We'd be in Bude later anyway.

A mile further on and we knew we'd been stupid. We should have gone back and refilled the water bottles, but we couldn't bear to retrace our steps and so kept moving forwards. The heat was intense on the open cliff top, bouncing back from the scorched earth and reflecting from the blue sea. Not a breath of wind, just heat wrapping around in a hot, dusty, sweaty, suffocating fog. Then we drank the last drop of water. The heat pressed us down; it took every ounce of willpower to stay on our feet and keep moving. Where there should have been streams, there were only dried-up cracks in the earth. The thirst overtook the hunger in a primal craving for water: we needed it and we needed it now.

Stupid, stupid, stupid.

Stupid to think we could walk this path, to not have enough money, to pretend we weren't homeless, to get the court procedure wrong, to lose the children's home, to not have enough water, to pretend we weren't dying, to not have enough water.

Stupid, stupid, stupid.

126

Shouting, crying, throwing the water bottle in anger. Angry with ourselves for making the wrong decision; angry for all the wrong decisions. Die — just do it and die now. Don't drag me through death with you. If you're leaving, just go, don't condemn me to years of letting go, sitting by, waiting for the iced blade to cut my heart out, rip me bone from bone, leave me macerated, spewed out, screwed up. If you're going, just go, get it over with. I can't say goodbye, can't live without you. Don't leave, ever. Leave. I'm already dead. I died when you let that demon take our home and throw our children into the street. Yes, death come and save me, save me from you, save me from ever having to say it's okay again. It's okay, we're okay, it was no one's fault. We spat out words of pain, self-pity, hate — for judges, doctors, false friends, each other. The scratching, desperate need for water took over from every other need, hid the pain in our joints, the battered and blistered feet, the sunburnt, cut and bruised skin. Nothing else mattered; we needed water and we needed it now.

Moth threw his pack down.

"We have to go to Duckpool."

"Why, why, why do we *have* to go to Duckpool?"

"Because on the map it's got a bigger blue line, so it might not have dried up. And if it has, half a mile inland there are some houses. They'll give us water."

I hated him, for reading maps better than me, and always being so bloody right.

"And Paddy says there are toilets."

Steeple Point came out of the heat haze and then disappeared. The path followed the sheer edge of the point and then it too disappeared. We sat on the hot grass, our legs weak, mild nausea building, not just from heat exhaustion, but also from the view. The path followed the sharp edge to the point and then just disappeared. It had to lead somewhere, but wherever that was, it was going to be down a steep, near vertical hillside.

Inching along the tightrope of air, wind and gulls, the path reached the nose of the point; then it turned abruptly left down a bank that appeared to fall on to a thin track far below. Every step a deliberate and careful act, clutching handfuls of grass as the loose stones rolled underfoot. It took a thigh-trembling, knee-crunching, toe-crushing eternity to reach the bottom.

The toilet block was locked, and the stream had dried up.

Stupid, stupid, stupid.

We dropped our packs and melted into the dusty ground.

"Bet you'd like an ice cream."

The gravelly voice drifted over us like a wave of tormenting flies. We ignored it.

"They don't have any water left, but you can get an ice cream."

Moth mustered the strength to respond.

"Yeah right, mate, course we can. And where are the ice creams? I can't see any."

We stayed flat out, with our eyes closed, unable to move.

"In the ice cream van up the road."

Slowly, we got to our feet. Just along the track was an ice cream van; it had no signs or jingling music, just a man selling ice cream from a van.

"All I've got left are rhubarb-flavoured lollies."

We bought four and turned back to the man to thank him.

"So what are you up to, carrying full packs in this heat? It's been thirty-eight degrees here; cooler now, it's dropped to thirty-four."

"Started in Minehead. We're heading for Land's End, maybe a little further." Thirty-eight degrees?

"Really. Really." He hesitated, squinting into the sun and looking Moth up and down. "Have you arranged somewhere to stay tonight?"

"No, we're camping. We won't make Bude, so somewhere between here and there."

"Really? I'm renting a farmhouse, about twenty minutes away. Come and camp in the orchard."

We sat in the back of Grant's sleek 4 × 4 as he drove inland through the shade of high hedges. In his mid-forties, a tall, gaunt man with a bald head that glowed pink from the sun, white socks in his sandals at the end of thin pink legs. He explained that he rented the farmhouse with his wife and household staff. He seemed very interested in the people we'd met on the path, and the hospitality we'd received.

"We've got a huge lasagne, so plenty of food; we'll have a few beers and you might feel like telling me a bit

129

more about what you're really doing." All we heard was lasagne and beer. Suddenly our legs weren't so tired.

The picture-perfect stone house stood in an orchard, next to a stream, an oasis of cool greenness. We pitched the tent beneath the apple trees on perfectly flat mown grass.

"Come in, have a shower. I'll pour a beer."

The sense of age in the cool house made my chest tighten. Wide walls, low dark beams, open fires: it was as if I'd walked back through my own front door. Think of something else, think of something else. It was a near physical struggle to put the sense of loss back in its box.

"The shower's through there in the back porch. Then come and meet the girls."

I drank pints of water straight from the tap; then I stood in the shower with my mouth open. The water ran like mud from my hair as I washed it over and over with expensive shampoo and drenched it in conditioner for the first time in weeks. It made little difference; the large mirror above the sink still shone a battered reflection back at me.

In the kitchen three beautiful young women greeted us and I was suddenly very aware that it wasn't just my home I'd lost. I shook hands with a stunningly tall, curly-haired woman: the wife; then an immaculately bobbed, ivory-skinned nanny; and a floating, ethereal, white-blond PA. Standing on the cold slate tiles, I felt every inch a scruffy fifty-year-old, with ragged hair and a face like a lobster. Grant was opening beer bottles at the table, still wearing his white socks. Why were these gorgeous young women here? He caught my look, raised his eyebrows and carried on pouring the beer.

The PA took Moth's arm and guided him to the table, ladling a huge portion of lasagne on to his plate. I drank the beer. I hate beer, but it was the best thing I'd ever drunk. I followed it with a jug of iced water, while Moth was on the third beer. I hungrily shovelled in the lasagne, a pile of salad and half the garlic bread while the others were talking, then said yes please to seconds.

The blond hair swished around Moth as she slid her hands over his shoulders and started to massage his back.

"I used to be a sports therapist before Grant enticed me away. Would you like a massage? I can see you have a lot of tension in your shoulders."

Without a blink, he was on the sofa in the other room, while I ate more lasagne.

"Tell me about yourself then, Grant." He had to have something special, and it was soon evident what it was. He told a long tale of leaving home as a teenager to walk across Europe with a knapsack. Living on his wits with only a piece of bread and cheese in his pocket until he reached Italy; finding himself in a vineyard, where he lived for years, sleeping in the barn or under the stars, learning everything he needed to know about wine. He eventually came home and started importing the wines he had encountered on his travels, trading from a disused warehouse, until he eventually became a multimillionaire and attracted all the beautiful girls that made up his household. So they were there because of the quality of his wine cellar, of course.

The wife got up to leave the room.

"Take no notice of him. He studied wine at night classes and his father got him a job with a merchant he knew."

Grant rolled his eyes at her as she left the room.

"When I retire, I want to write. I believe I could be a great writer. But it's a good story, isn't it? I think that Moth, if that's what he's calling himself for this trip, could use it. It would be marvellous material for him, don't you think?"

I thought about Grant's tale and why he felt driven to tell it. When you tell a story, the first person you must convince is yourself; if you can make yourself believe it's true, then everyone else will follow. Grant wanted to be the person he had created: hard done by, struggling through life's adversities, but making good on his own wits, rather than the son of a wealthy father with connections. Our story was born out of self-protection. The public's perception of the homeless immediately assumes drink, drugs and mental health issues, and prompts fear. The first few times we'd been asked how it was that we had time to walk so far and for so long, we had answered truthfully: "Because we're homeless, we lost our home, but it wasn't our fault. We're just going where the path takes us." People recoiled and the wind was silenced by their sharp intake of breath. In every case the conversation ended abruptly and the other party walked away very quickly. So we had invented a lie that was more palatable. For them and for us. We had sold our home, looking for a midlife adventure, going where the wind took us — at the moment it was blowing us west. At the end of the path where would we go? "We don't know, just see which way the wind's blowing." That met with gasps of "wow, brilliant, inspirational". What was the difference between the two stories? Only one word, but one word that in the public perception meant everything: "sold". We could be homeless, having sold our home and put money in the bank, and be inspirational. Or we could be homeless, having lost our home and become penniless, and be social pariahs. We chose the former. Easier to have a brief passing conversation; easier for them, easier for us.

The more times we repeated the lie, the less we felt the grief. If we told ourselves the lie for long enough, would the loss fade away, until eventually we could face it without pain? Maybe I was doing that with Moth's illness too, or did I genuinely believe the doctor had made a mistake? It was hard to tell. Rather than the walk being a time to get our thoughts straight and make a plan, it had become a meditation, a mental void filled only with salt wind, dust and light. Each step had its own resonance, its moment of power or failure. That step, and the next and the next and the next, was the reason and the future. Each combe climbed out of was a victory, each day survived a reason to live through the next. Each lungful of salt scouring our memories, smoothing their edges, wearing them down.

"Moth is his name, but he's not a writer."

"Okay, mum's the word, have some more lasagne."

I ate while Grant poured a glass of red wine; the rich aubergine purple swirled through the glass, my head spinning from the aroma alone.

It was only when the glass of wine had mostly gone that I noticed the wife and nanny had gone too. Grant and I went through to the other room; Moth lay topless on the sofa as the PA massaged his back and the nanny rubbed oil into his feet. The wife sat on a chair, flicking through photos on her digital camera and then taking more shots of the scene.

"Girls, you're keeping my guest from me! I need to hear his stories, or maybe a poem before bed?"

I may have had two glasses of wine, but it would take more than a massage to get a poem out of Moth. He sat up and put his T-shirt back on.

"A poem? What, you mean from me?"

"Don't be coy, we all know. And now I've got some great photos to go with the story."

"I don't quite get it."

"Never mind, come and have a glass and tell us about you. For a start, your name's not Moth, is it?"

"Of course it is."

"Brilliant, brilliant, but we'll just call you Simon."

"Call me what you like, mate, we're just grateful for the hospitality."

"And you don't mind if I use the photos? Nice little publicity thing?"

"Nice? Don't quite get how a scruffy old bloke sitting on a sofa is publicity for a wine company, but go for it."

"So where's your next gig?"

The third glass of wine was making everything blurred. Sleep was about to put my head on the table. Moth drank a second glass, and I could see he had no more idea what Grant was talking about than I had.

"Bude. We'll be in Bude tomorrow, then heading for Boscastle . . . Can't remember what comes after that."

"And will you be at the Minack?"

"The Minack? Where's that?"

They all exchanged looks, laughing and patting Moth on the back.

"Oh Simon, you're so funny. Go on, give us a poem before we go to bed."

"Well, I do know one my dad used to recite in the works cabin on the building site." Moth took a deep breath and sat back in his chair.

"The boy stood on the burning deck.
All but the goat had fled . . ."

I'd heard it so many times; I really needed to sleep.

"You are a corker. This is going to make such a good story."

I fell asleep within seconds on the flat, soft ground beneath the apple trees in the orchard. We were woken only by apples falling on the tent and Grant saying that bacon sandwiches were waiting in the kitchen.

After they had all taken selfies with Moth and we were stuffed full of bacon sandwiches, our packs full of apples and water, we left, Grant dropping us back on the path.

"So, Simon, what happened in the other room?"

135

"No, I'm sorry, what happens in the orchard, stays in the orchard. More importantly, who is Simon? That wine went straight to my head, but still, that was weird."

" 'What happens in the orchard'? You can't get away with it that eas —"

"And a poet. Do you think it's the hat? I look a bit like my Irish grandad; maybe I look like a wandering Irish poet. The girls thought I had very artistic hands."

"The girls what . . .?"

"And they wanted me to go and read to their friends when they're back in London."

"Why, are they illiterate?"

"No, read poetry."

"You've never read poetry, unless you count *Beowulf*, or your dad's poem about the goat."

"I've always had a feeling for poetry."

"No you have not. Ha, is that what they called it, feeling for poetry?"

"That's all you think about; what happened between the girls and me was on a much higher level."

"Get lost, Byron, or shall I call you Simon now?"

"I can take abuse; we poets are used to being misunderstood."

"Bollocks."

Paddy Dillon walks from Hartland Quay to Bude — one of the most remote and difficult sections of the whole path — in a day. It had taken us three. But we survived, as we were surviving all the boulders of pain that had brought us to the path. Things we thought we would never be able to bear were becoming less jagged, turned into round river stones by the movement of the path. It was still a heavy burden to carry, but just a little less painful to hold.

The mornings weren't getting any easier though. I was still crawling from the tent in a scrunch of agony. My ankles cracked with a hot, grinding sensation that felt as if the bones were rubbing together, wearing themselves away. My hip hurt until my pack was on and I'd walked a couple of miles and I tried not to think about my big toe. Maybe it had been the lasagne, or the red wine, or the massage, or the thought of bacon, but Moth had got out of the tent that morning without any help. He was losing weight fast, his lean frame becoming really lean. Was he moving just a little more easily or was that me hoping for a miracle?

The path dropped into Bude, and us with it. There would be money in the bank, and a supermarket for affordable food to last the week; we'd walked for an hour without noticing as we imagined fresh bread and fruit. Bude is a quiet little town without the bustle of Ilfracombe; we followed the path as it skirted the outer edge, diverting in for the cash machine. I inserted the card, expecting the usual sum of money to be available, but instead my gut twisted in a strange spasm. Eleven pounds. How could there only be eleven pounds?

"What are we going to do, where's it gone?"

"Fuck, fuck, fuck."

I took the ten pounds offered by the machine, holding my hand by the tray, desperate that there would

137

be no mechanical change of heart between the instruction and the action.

We stood in the bank and listened to the clerk explain that the usual sum of money had gone in, but a direct debit payment had gone out. How could we have forgotten to cancel it?

"But it's a standing order for insurance on a property we no longer own. Please, can't you refund it?" we pleaded. We knew it was hopeless but we had to try.

"I'm sorry, but that's between you and the insurance company." Stupid, stupid, stupid. How could we have forgotten to do that? "Do you know any of the insurance details? Maybe they'll refund it?"

We didn't, and even if they did it would be weeks before we got it back. Fuck. "Can I withdraw the other pound, please?"

We should have sold the last of the furniture, instead of storing it in a friend's barn. We might have got a few pounds for the pine cupboard we bought in an auction when we moved into our first house. Or the kitchen table that had held everything of family life, from Rowan sleeping on it as a baby because she wouldn't sleep anywhere else, to the last meals before they left home; it was where we'd planned our future and agonized when we lost it. We could have sold it. Or Dad's chair, or Moth's family pictures. But we couldn't let go.

"What the fuck are we doing?" I sat on the wall outside the bank, unable to hold back the tears of self-pity any longer. "We're lost. No money, no food, no home. You need to eat; you're ill, for fuck's sake. Why

138

didn't I get the procedure right? Bloody juvenile mistake. Now I've dragged you out here when you should be somewhere safe, resting, not hauling a bag round the edgeland of life. And to where? What then? What fucking then?" I couldn't stop myself, couldn't hold it in any longer. I shook with sobs and snot. "And those girls, so young and beautiful. I used to look like that; you used to want me. I don't blame you, I don't, I'm fat, ugly and old. Don't blame you, it was there on a plate, but why don't you want me any more?" I rocked with gasping self-pity.

Moth's arms wrapped me up, as they always have.

"You know what happened in that room? I had the best massage I've ever had, and they talked about how they have a great life with Grant — wine-buying trips and parties and they never want for anything. They wanted to take photos because they thought they might use them on the company's social media. Don't know where they were going with that, makes no difference to us. I was just teasing you earlier; it was fun to see you pretending not to mind."

"You arse."

"And I still want you; I just don't feel like me any more. Maybe when things change, I'll feel different."

"You won't. I'll still be fat and ugly."

"You've lost a bit of weight actually, and you were never ugly."

"We'll have to eat noodles all week."

"I know, but we'll survive. If we can survive Duckpool, we can survive anything. But we can't run out of water again."

We left Bude with enough twenty-pence packs of noodles to last a week and a lot of water. Walking out of the genteel holiday spot, past the retired ladies' tennis club, past the strangely folded rocks and the tower on the headland. The path felt remote now. Without money, we had moved into a world apart. It was nearly dark when we found the corner in a field of thistles, ate noodles and slept.

CHAPTER
TEN

Green/Blue

Dawdling along the gentle path from Bude towards Widemouth Sand, a table appeared unexpectedly between the gorse and thistles, offering a selection of books for ten pence each. We only had *Beowulf* to read and it was too much of a temptation. Amongst some trashy paperbacks, Moth picked out *Robinson Crusoe* in hardback. We left pennies and a beach pebble in the honesty box to offset the weight and dipped down on to the beach, crowded with surfers and sandcastles.

We'd found that cafés don't charge for hot water, so we stood for a moment in the gleamingly clean, air-conditioned café and ordered two mugs of hot water, taking them outside before we dipped a teabag in. We watched families on the beach while cancelling the direct debit for the insurance, using all of the phone credit to do so.

A group approached from along the shoreline. Some walkers stroll, some limp forlornly, and some stride with purpose, but these were yompers. They yomped. Dressed in the walking uniform as issued by all outdoor suppliers: quick-dry trousers with important pockets, even quicker drying T-shirts, and wide-brimmed bush hats. Their packs were lightweight, but big enough to make them backpackers, not daypackers. The serious group of four sat on the table next to us, rapidly taking out wads of money and queuing for drinks.

"Hurry it up, John, you're taking too long."

It seemed only polite to talk to fellow long-distance walkers, although they obviously had a tight schedule. Moth queedled back in his chair.

"All right, boys, are you doing the path?"

"Yes."

"Great. Are you doing the whole thing? Looks like you've come from the Poole direction."

"No and yes." They fixed their eyes on the table.

"Hurry up, John, we need to go."

Moth, never one to acknowledge a brush-off, carried on.

"So, doing it lightweight then. Bet you're covering some miles in a day?"

"Yes." They cracked. "Three days: Padstow to Hartland Quay."

"Wow. So where are you heading today?"

"Hartland Quay." He stole a glance at our packs, and my grubby, ripped frock. "Daypacking, are you?"

Moth was visibly suppressing a self-satisfied smirk.

"No, we've come from Minehead."

"On the bus?"

"No, walked the path, wild camped. Heading down to Land's End."

The older member of the group turned briskly round, annoyed by our presence.

"All very well in this weather, but blindly irresponsible. What will you do if the weather turns?"

"Put a coat on."

"John, it's taking too long, let's go."

We watched them march over the headland, heads down, metronome. When we stood to leave, Moth had grown; his shoulders were a little straighter as he lifted my pack for me to put on.

"We're not running away, or hiding, you know. We should actually be proud of ourselves for doing this. Let's carry on."

"Okay."

Two miles further on we realized I'd left my fleece behind and had to retrace our steps in the hope that it hadn't been taken. The man behind the counter handed it over.

"The waitress picked it up, said it belonged to the old backpackers. We think it's great what you're doing. Good luck."

We walked away, glowing. This wasn't just about being homeless; we were achieving something. Even if we were old.

Beyond Widemouth, pronounced Widmuth by the locals, the path put us into a trance, but then became just painful. Looking ahead it rolled into an endless succession of headlands disappearing into an infinity of blue and green. Blue — green — blue — green. Or for variation green — blue — green — blue — blue — blue — green — green — blue. It came and went in waves of up and down, up, up, down, down, down, steeply up, really steeply up, really very steeply up. Down, down, green, blue, green, up. Tent up, noodles, sleep, noodles, tent down, squat in the bracken, walk. Green, blue, up, green, down.

Crackington Haven was picturesque, and we dawdled for a while watching two women eat a cream tea at ten thirty in the morning. When they'd devoured the last crumb and sucked in the last of the sloppy strawberry jam, we moved on. I worked on a business plan for turning virtual eating into a weight-loss tool. Up, up, down, green, blue, blue, green.

We got into Boscastle at five minutes to five, and nearly made it into an outdoor shop to buy a new bootlace, but the door shut before Moth's foot could stop it. He knotted the broken lace together and walked up the street. This village is famous, or infamous, for the floods of 2004, which washed away shops, cars and people, leaving the village devastated. I had thought it would be a friendly, welcoming place, happy to be rebuilt and back in business. But instead it was shut, everyone rushing away to put sandbags out just in case. The chip shop was open, but even a bag of chips was out of our price range, so we carried on and camped on an old hill fort just above the village. Tent up, noodles, sleep, noodles, tent down, squat in the bracken, walk. Green, blue, up, down, down, green.

Paddy Dillon eats spinach for breakfast, wears a hair shirt and sleeps on a bed of nails, obviously, because he walks from Bude to Boscastle in one day.

Green, blue. This coast is rugged, rock stacks standing defiantly against the power of the Atlantic.

The Ladies' Window coming and going as the waves rushed in and out of the rock arch. Hot and sweaty, cold and shivery. The wind picked up and dark clouds poured in from the west. Sweating. Up, down, green, blue. I stopped to pee in the undergrowth and it burnt like acid. Head pounding, body aching. Next stop and I'm peeing blood. Blue, blue, green, rocks.

A queue formed through the Rocky Valley as a family in flip-flops struggled to negotiate the boulders. The phone rang as rain began to drop, heavy and determined. We sheltered under a rock overhang. It was Rowan, on her way to a late-summer job in Croatia but stuck in Venice. She thinks she's missed the connecting bus. Before, when I was a parent, we'd have sent money to put her on a flight, make her safe. But now, just a helpless friend, I sheltered in a rock crevice, useless, hopeless, pointless, and talked to my daughter, stranded in a foreign country, alone. She talked and talked, panicking; the warning for a failed battery sounded . . .

"It's okay. The bus is here. I hadn't missed it; it's just late. Love you, Mum, be safe . . ."

I curled up on the rock ledge and sobbed. Moth held me, stroking my hair until I could breathe again.

Paddy says "ignore the Camelot Castle Hotel" and just look straight ahead, but it looked like an oasis to me as I shuffled into Tintagel. Moth put our packs in a corner of the lobby and ordered a jug of water.

"You need a doctor. Stay here, I'll see if I can find a campsite, put the tent up, then I'll come back for you."

145

"Don't need a doctor, just need to drink loads, and sleep. I'll come with you, I'm supposed to look after you."

"Stop, just stop. I'm not Rowan; I'm not Tom. Don't be my mother. Just let it be, Ray. And stay here."

I curled into the armchair and slept. I half opened my eyes and thought I saw a knight on a horse. Then slept again. When I woke, Moth was back.

"I saw a knight; am I hallucinating?"

"Probably, or dreaming. Think all this King Arthur nonsense has got to you. There's a campsite at the end of the road, tent's up, let's go. It's got showers that don't need tokens."

"We can't pay."

"I know."

Wind ripped in from the west, roaring through the grey broil of cloud, hurling the cumuli east into Devon long before their water burden hit the ground. I stood outside the tent in the darkness and let the wildness in. Swirled up, bound up in the storm's ecstasy, part of a cycle of molecules without end. Contained, boundless, imprisoned, set free.

I'm a farmer and a farmer's daughter; the land's in my bones. The end of August: September was coming when I should have the sheep penned in the corner of the field. Catching and upturning each one, trimming the hooves, dosing for worms, preparing the ewes for the ram. Turning the earth, ready for sowing the winter corn, autumn preparing for spring, in defiance of the winter to come. I'm cut free from that connection, from

146

the meter of my existence, floating lost and unrooted. But I can still feel it.

As a child I was sent to the field to collect a ewe and her newborn lamb, to carry the lamb for the ewe to follow, to bring them both safely to the shelter; I picked the lamb up but realized the ewe was about to give birth to a second. So I waited, lying on my back in the wet spring grass, clouds rushing overhead, the ewe only feet away, giving birth, as the first lamb found its feet. I knew then that I was one with everything, the worms in the soil, clouds in the sky; I was part of it all, within everything, and everything was within my child's head. The wild was never something to fear or hide from. It was my safe place, the thing I ran to.

Our land gave that to our children. Growing like saplings in the storm, bent by it, but strengthened at the core, rooted but flexible and strong, running free in the wind, but guided by it. Now our land was gone, would they keep what it had given them? I'd feared I would lose it, that tie to reality, when our land was lost. Sitting in the grass, wet air rushing past, roaring overhead, the dangerous, self-willed, uncontrolled, wild strength of the wind filled me up. Caught by the storm. Held up. Bonds rebound, chelated. Released. Regained. I could never lose it; I was as much the storm as I was the dry dust and the high-pitched call of the oystercatchers. All material things were slipping away, but in their wake a core of strength was beginning to re-form.

* ★ *

We left the far corner of the campsite after two nights. Feeling slightly weak, but well enough. Walking confidently past the reception and not looking back.

Tintagel and its Arthurian legends behind us, we paused by St Materiana's church to drink more water. The phone rang again. Rowan. She'd been offered a job with a PR company in London and they needed her to start straight away. How would she get back? She was already on the train; she'd worked it out for herself.

CHAPTER
ELEVEN

Surviving

Slate quarrying marked the way in patches. It was the forerunner of things to come, the inescapable evidence of man's need to take everything he can. Even the spoils of the destruction were taken to create the Cornish banked walls. In Wales a drystone wall like this, cambered in on both sides with soil in the middle and a hedge grown on top, is called a *clawdd*. But here, with zigzag patterning in the laying of thin stones end on end, the spoil created the "curzy way" walls. They gave a sense of moving to another zone, another way of living, another way of generations fighting to hold the wild at bay. We walked on, between the wall and the sea, in the strip of wilderness that was ours.

The path dropped quickly down into the narrow inlet of Trebarwith Strand. The patchy white clouds were inviting, but the storms had left the sea raging, forcing itself violently on to the rocky shore. A tiny café offered a cone of chips for a pound. We had five pounds seventy-five left, so rashly ordered two, plus two mugs of hot water, and sat down amongst the surfers, just out of reach of the waves. Poseidon reared up, and then fell away, a Rottweiler on a retractable lead.

The path had a steepness that kept my nose close to the ground, passing gardens filled with fishing nets and buoys, until eventually at the top we passed a couple eating huge pasties, with a scruffy whippet/lurcher/greyhound patiently waiting for crumbs. One whole, large pasty each. Next to them two enormous backpacks.

"Hey, backpackers." He nearly choked on the pastry in his rush to greet us; probably, like us, he'd found there were few of us around.

"You too." We stopped for a moment to exchange the usual wayfarer details. They'd started in Tintagel and were heading as far as a week would take them. When they asked where we were heading, Moth told them with confidence that it would be Land's End, and maybe further. Buoyed by their astonishment that we were tackling the entire north coast, we walked on with a spring in our step.

We carried on through open grassland, where plump white mushrooms were starting to show, gathering a few, with handfuls of tart, unripe blackberries through wooded valleys.

A collie dog stood facing the bracken, barking. We passed it and stroked the friendly face, before it returned to barking. There was no one with it. We looked around the cliff top in fear that its owner might have fallen off, but saw nothing so carried on. Looking back into a steep-sided cove, there were people on the sand, but apparently no way in. Had they come by boat? Suddenly a boy jumped out from the undergrowth on to the sand below, followed by the dog.

150

There must be a secret tunnel. We didn't have the energy to explore, so carried on, in and out of deep combes until the sun began to dip and the sky lit into peach, lemon and mauve. We pitched the tent on Bounds Cliff and ate noodles with mushrooms as the colour faded into starlight, and the gulls called their long night calls.

We were packing the tent away when a group of old people in smart multi-pocketed shorts marched up to us.

"Brace yourself; we're going to get our first bollocking for camping where we shouldn't." Moth put his best "granny's favourite" face on, while I tried to look away.

"Where's the coastal path?" a red-faced man gasped demandingly between breaths.

"You're on it."

"No, this isn't it. Coastal path, on the coast. We're going to walk to Tintagel."

"This is it. It's not on the beach, it's here on the cliff."

"Well, are there any more hills like that one?"

"Six or seven? Don't know, I lost count."

"Well, forget that then. We're going back." They turned around and stomped away grumbling. "It should be called a cliff path, not a coast path."

Port Isaac used to be a fishing village. The owners of the few boats on the beach would tell you it still is. But the thousands of visitors who come by car and bus trip know it's the village where Doc Martin lives. We threaded our way through the narrow, heaving streets, crowds of people trying to take selfies with Doc's house in the background. A whippet/lurcher/greyhound bounded through the crowd, knocking telephones and ice creams flying.

"Simon, oi, Simon, catch the dog, will you?"

Moth caught the dog's collar and hung on to him until the pasty couple made it through.

"Knew it was you. We knew it."

"Who?"

"Knew it was you. Answered to your name, didn't you?"

"Only because people have called me it before."

"Yeah, course, ha, your mum."

"Look, stop now. Who is Simon?"

"Simon Armitage."

"Who the fuck is Simon Armitage? We've been hearing the name since Combe Martin and we still don't know."

"God, you're good, aren't you? Keeping it hidden. We'll catch you out, though. Don't forget we're on your trail."

Moth handed back the dog and we struggled through the hordes and up the hill out of the village, where a group of smart elderly ladies were gathered.

"Simon, Simon, can we have a photo near the Doc's house? Two birds with one stone, so lucky!"

"No."

"Ooh, Simon, what a great Doc impression. Good luck with your walk."

152

I followed Moth as he pounded on ahead, marching up a steep gorse path without looking back until I gasped up behind him and had to call a halt.

"Why's it annoyed you so much?"

"I don't know, I just want to know who this person is; he could be anyone."

Rising and falling between gorse and stone, with the sea booming always. A rhythm of pain and hunger, mellowed into ache and thirst, softening eventually to just a booming rhythm. Needs slipped away as the winds chided the water and the gulls guided us forward. Fishermen used to live in Port Quin, but now it seems a lost collection of weekend homes. Rumour has it the fishermen went to Canada, chasing a better haul, leaving their lobster pots to rot as garden ornaments. The views behind marked the miles passed, but the views forward were shortening, heading inexorably towards another corner, another drop south.

The sun lowered, painting the tiny islands of the Mouls in a low September light as we dropped off Com Head. A kestrel that had hung in the sky for an endless time quietly landed on the fence ahead, the early-evening sun lighting his back in a russet glow. We hesitated before passing, not wanting to disturb him. As if sensing our indecision, he lifted off, circling and then landing on a rock just behind us. We carried on. The edge of an arable field was a possible campsite, but, fearing for the groundsheet on the stubble, we kept walking and found ourselves at dusk on Rumps Point.

There used to be an ancient fort here, looking back towards Tintagel headland and away into the Atlantic. If there had been a King Arthur he would have put his castle here, not amongst the trinkets and pasties further east. Here, where he could see his enemies coming from every side. A secret place of forgotten stories. We hid the tent behind the grassy mounds of the old earthworks, on an active rabbit warren, and climbed to Rumps Point as the sun slipped away, leaving only deep unnamed colours.

In the darkness we ate the last pack of noodles. We had water, but no more food. I contemplated hunting rabbits. It would be nothing new: Dad and I had shot rabbits, hundreds of them, as they ate the corn in swathes, destroying a whole year's crop in a week. We filled the freezer, sold them to butchers, made stews, pies, skewers, pates, soups, sandwiches, until no one could face rabbit again. I lay in the darkness thinking about making a snare, but had neither the energy or enough gas to cook a rabbit if I caught one. I woke in the night to the sound of them tearing and chewing grass. From the volume of the snuffling, it could have been a big stew.

In the pink half-light of dawn, the holes were everywhere. Fresh droppings piled up under the flysheet of the tent and as I undid the zip tens of fat rabbits hopped only feet away. I could have just reached out and taken one to put straight in the pot. Instead we made tea. Moth found a hairy wine gum in his pocket, so we cut that in half.

Looking back at the Rumps as we headed away, the patch of earth we had camped on hovered above a great gaping cave. Landfalls had exposed the runs of the rabbit warren, coming out of the earth and ending in mid-air. How many rabbits had landed in the sea, and how many more would be washed away? Or would the pounding sea beneath their warren eventually be a loud enough warning for them to move on?

We rounded the headland past a memorial to "The Fallen". Too tired to get my glasses out and read the whole plaque, I didn't check if it was for the fallen in war, fallen from the cliff, or to us, fallen from society, fallen from hope, fallen from life.

Of course the memorial must have been to the men who died in the wars. Dead, gone without chance for self-pity. I tightened the hip belt on my pack, shut the door on the whining voice and kept walking. Life is now, this minute, it's all we have. It's all we need.

The path dropped into the Polzeaths, New and Old. A building site from end to end. New builds, extensions, renewals, building, building, building. A long beach stretched ahead of us, from Daymer Bay to the small ferry at Rock. The tide was way out, thinning the wide River Camel to a two-lane highway for boats and jet-skis. We had no idea how much it would cost to use the ferry. I was certain the few coins in the palm of my hand wouldn't be enough, but prayed they would be, unable to face the long detour inland to the bridge at Wadebridge. Moth dropped his rucksack and sat on the sand.

"Feel really lightheaded. When do we get some more money?"

"Tomorrow, maybe, I'm not sure. We can make it if we keep drinking."

"Don't know, I'm feeling a bit weird." Thin or not, his six-foot-two frame couldn't keep moving on nothing. I looked again at the coins in my purse and headed through the dunes to the snack hut.

The hut was full to bursting with buckets, nets, parents and children. I scoured the shelves for the most economical way to buy some food. Only confectionery, but it looked like a five-star menu and needed as much consideration. I settled on six fudge bars, at twenty-five pence each, which could be spread through the day. The cold fridge air wafted over me while I held a bottle of Coke to the side of my head, wet with condensation and beautifully cold. I put it back and stood in the queue. The long queue. I was near the door. The girl behind the counter was focused on the till. Children ran around, noisily distracting. The queue didn't go down. I was near the door. The coins burnt in my palm. And I walked away.

I crossed the sand to Moth, briskly, calmly, inconspicuous, but with a neon sign on my head flashing thief, thief, thief.

"Come on, let's get to the ferry, see what it costs." Helping Moth to his feet, anxious that we should move on quickly.

"Don't you want to just eat something now?"

"No, there might be some shade down there and we can probably get water while we wait." Moth, just move quickly. Thief, thief, thief. This was it, the barrier crossed. A homeless stereotype. Dirty, hungry, and now thief. A social pariah.

"Eat one as we go, it might help us walk faster."

There was no water, but the ferry cost less than two pounds each. I had just enough to go back and pay for the fudge, but held on tightly to the coins and put them back in my purse.

On the other side of the estuary, Padstow was heaving. Another quaint village that had been a fishing hub in a previous life, but was now more famous for Rick Stein's fish restaurants than for its fish. Busloads of tourists listened to buskers in the harbour, while devouring half the north Atlantic's cod stocks. Rick seemed to have taken over the village, with his name on the restaurant, the chip shop, a pub, bistro, patisserie, in fact most places claimed a connection to him. We sat on the harbour, dangling our feet over the stone edge, listening to the young buskers rattle out cover versions of rock ballads, while their guitar case filled with coins and notes.

"Wish I'd brought my guitar."

"Wish you'd learnt how to play it."

"Don't think they are playing, I think it's a recording."

The salty smell was inescapable torture. Eating noodles for a week had reduced our appetites and when we did eat we needed far less to feel full. But the onslaught of food was unbearable and virtual eating just wasn't curing the hunger.

"Shall we go? I can't watch this any more."

"Let's check the bank before we leave, in case."

"In case?"

"The balance of your account is thirty-two pounds and seventy-five pence, and the amount you can withdraw today is thirty pounds". Not the forty-eight pounds we thought might be there, but we didn't care where the other sixteen pounds had gone, or if the thirty-two pounds should have been there at all, or that it was Tuesday when we thought it was Thursday, and held the notes like precious gems.

Moth bought more packs of ibuprofen and we went back to the harbour to share a bag of Rick's chips.

"What do you think?"

"They're okay, just taste like chips."

Fighting our way off the harbour, through the crowds with people tutting and complaining about our packs, we stopped for an ice cream, a ridiculously expensive indulgence, but we'd forgotten to fill the water bottles and they were empty.

"Thanks, and would you be able to fill our water bottles?"

"No. You can buy a bottle. We can't just fill water bottles for free when we have it for sale."

It was the first time anyone had refused us water and we were stunned. Passing a pub at the edge of the harbour we filled the bottles in the toilets and then left the village, finding the path again with relief.

The tent sat low among the sand dunes at Harbour Cove, hopefully out of reach of the dog walkers and the tide. The river had refilled and oystercatchers ran in chattering lines up and down the strip of sand left to them. Further down the beach a group of terns huddled quietly, and further still herring gulls were slowly gathering. All keeping to their own patch, segregated by choice.

September now, and getting dark by nine o'clock, the nights in the tent were becoming longer, and chillier. We hadn't slept on sand before and it was shockingly cold. Inescapably cold. I put on the short leggings over the long ones, two vests, the long-sleeved T-shirt, the fleece jacket, the Ibizan hemp sunhat, and shivered inside the one-season super lightweight sleeping bag.

Morning didn't come soon enough, and I was out moving as quickly as I could. But not as quickly as a hairy Labrador/spaniel/terrier that dived through the sand, knocked the water off the stove and jumped into the tent, rummaging through the bags. Moth sat up as the hairball leapt all over him.

"There's no food in here, mate."

He bounded out again chasing his master's whistle, skidding sand behind him.

"It's not a campsite, you know. You can't camp here. It's disgusting, sleeping in public."

"Yes, good morning, lovely day again."

The dog owner stomped on, as the hairball bounded after him.

Trying to shake the heavy beach condensation from the tent we succeeded only in spreading sand over the now wet inner walls, so gave up, rolled it into a ball and walked on in the early light. The sea birds were out at sea and the dog walkers were heading home for breakfast as we rounded Stepper Point, the wind welcoming us back to the edge.

CHAPTER
TWELVE

Sea Dancers

Stepper Point could easily have been missed by cutting across to Gunver Head. But our feet instinctively followed the path, drawn west on the dusty umbilical cord that was allowing us to grow, unseen, in our strip of wilderness. Trevose Head appeared in focus, with endless headlands disappearing south into the mist, yet to be trodden.

Tamarisk flourished in greater numbers, forming banking walls of hedgerow, their feathery branches stroking the air. Softer, gentler, more welcoming than the gorse and bracken further east but tough and resilient at its core, flexing in the breeze and gale alike. On a bench, tucked into the stems, was a pile of rags, surrounded by supermarket carriers full of possessions and hovered over by flies.

An old man with his life in plastic bags.

He was motionless. Like a rabbit in the hedgerow, picked over by crows, swarmed by flies, eggs lain, maggots growing, sucked up and absorbed into the cycle. We stood by the body on the bench, feeling our place beside him, our place in the cycle, one foot in the hedgerow of decay.

"Fuck off." Not dead then.

"Do you need anything, mate? I've got some bread."

"Fuck off."

"Or a chocolate bar."

"Leave it on the bench, then fuck off."

Moth put half our rations next to the rags and we walked away, willing ourselves to turn our back on the flies. Not our place, not yet. But if we stopped, stood still for a moment too long?

We begged some water from the lifeguards at Harlyn Bay. They'd come from South Africa and Australia to watch over the hapless holidaymakers on their foam body boards, before returning south like geese in the winter. If only we could head somewhere warm before the dark coldness of winter crept in. We left them, envious of the ease of their life, crossing the broad stretch of clear sand to a rocky outcrop on the other side of the bay. Pouring our stinking, dirty clothes into a rock pool we left them to soak while we leapt into the foaming waves, washed clean, salt scoured, shrieking. An oasis of clarity: clear water, tide-rippled sand, free from time.

Lying on the rocks, our clothes stretched around us, air dried, preserved, we slept into mid-afternoon. When we woke we found ourselves with a large family, cut off by the incoming tide. As we scrambled up twenty metres of rocky cliff, the grandad explained that they always came to Harlyn Bay, and had done since his children were as small as his grandchildren, staying in the caravan park on the hill. At Mother Ivey's Bay they

162

disappeared through vast metal gates into a city of caravans, laced with concrete and stadium lighting. They might have been sleeping in a concentration camp, but at least their days were spent free on the beach. We turned right, the headland luring us forward, returning to our line of wild.

Trevose lighthouse dazzled in the late-afternoon sun, shocking against the blue, too bright to focus on. Lying on the dry grass, peeling burnt skin from my nose, most needs had slipped away. Less hungry, less thirsty, less everything. We slept soundly until early evening, when a cool wind woke us and we left the headland, dropping down towards a perfect beach backed by marram-covered sand dunes. We pitched the tent on the grass hoping the hard-green shards would insulate us from the cold, opening the tent to the wind to dry the sodden fabric.

The tide turned, bringing pristine barrelling waves on to the beach. And then they came. Neoprene figures, surfboards under their arms, running from the road, the path, out of the sand dunes, every direction, sleek black bodies waddling, ungainly, their boards blown by the gusts. They paddled out beyond the breakers, huddling together as a black shoal until the waves came and as individuals they broke away, standing, becoming one with the rise and fall, elegantly curling their way to the shallows. Humans transformed into sea dancers.

We sat in the door of the tent in our sleeping bags, until the light had gone and with it the last of the surfers. The tide headed away and, as it hesitated before

163

returning, the birds came to claim the empty beach for their own. To run and call through the night, between the sand and the water.

The next morning brought the heavy beach condensation, but we waited for it to dry, drinking tea and watching dog walkers and early-morning surfers, before Moth smoothly left the tent without help and we finally packed it away. The hunger was still there, but like the aching joints and hardening blisters, was becoming something to observe rather than feel.

The wind continued to rush in from the west, cool and gusting. Whipping the sea into foam against the tiny rocky islands just off the shore. The rocks grew bigger until they became the Bedruthan Steps, the legendary stepping stones of the giant Bedruthan. No one seems to know where the legend came from: ancient Cornish inhabitants or the National Trust who sell the rocky stacks to the vast number of visitors that fill the path and the tea room. We'd heard mutterings amongst the locals of a dislike for the National Trust who own over a third of the coastline of Devon and Cornwall, bought by Project Neptune to save the coastline from development. There were complaints that the Trust are too restrictive and don't understand the need of local people to make a living. I've lived on the land, and making a living is hard. I've also been to Mother Ivey's Bay, and without a doubt the coast should be saved from that. But walking past the heaving car park, stone paths and cash tills, I had a strong whiff of hypocrisy.

164

"Just go inland up the valley; there's a little campsite. Bit quirky, but it's dead cheap." The rain had started as we sheltered under the awning of a beach shack. The girl was trying to be helpful.

"Shall we go up, see how much it costs? We could always pitch in that wood if not; they'd be more sheltered than the cliffs in this." The wind had increased with the rain and shelter was tempting.

The lane to the campsite was lined by a horsebox, a cattle truck and a grain silo, grown through with tall grass; they didn't appear to have moved all summer. The trees opened up to a handful of chalets, a field of pigs, two donkeys and a marquee. A man in a ripped jumper with a wild curly beard came from behind a chalet carrying a mop and bucket. Five pounds a night for the tent, and cold showers. The rain kept coming, so we took it.

Beyond the marquee, we trudged through a zinc barn lined with old sofas and a washing machine, past wooden sheds, stone sheds and another horsebox, to a field in the trees.

"Come down to the barn later, the boys'll be there, they've usually got a few beers." The boys? There didn't seem to be a soul around.

I started to undress in the shower shed, a garden shed with two showers and a chair, but grabbed for a towel when I realized I wasn't alone. A woman on the other side of the room looked up at me: hair like a bird's nest, burnt brown face with a shredded red nose, red

165

calloused feet, lean athletic legs and ribs poking through saggy flesh. I ran my hand down the ribcage in the mirror: it looked alien to me; it hadn't been visible for years. I attempted to untangle my hair in the cold water. It didn't work, so I dried quickly and shoved the hemp hat back on. Cold showers on a cold day are like virtual eating. You can put a scrappy thin fleece on afterwards and it feels like a down jacket, but the feeling doesn't last long; quickly the cold comes back, like the hunger, sharper than before. Rather than shiver in the tent, we headed for the barn.

The side door of the horsebox opened and a tanned, blond youth jumped out. The wooden sheds along the way similarly released more young, tanned twenty-somethings, and as we reached the barn a young couple with dreadlocks came out of the stone shed. We attempted to drop ourselves on the sofas with the same cool, languid fluidity, without success.

"What are you all doing here? We didn't think there was anyone around. Are you on holiday?" We felt so old and alien, struggling around for something to say.

"No, man, we live here. We work here, Kurt lets us live in his sheds if we do odd jobs and errands, then in the winter it's away with the waves."

"You live in these sheds, not just an odd night then? Where do you work?"

"Lifeguards, most of us, a couple of waitresses, but we're all surfers. None of us could afford to rent around here — the rental prices are crazy. So yeah, the sheds are so cool. This'll be my third year, but next year I'm upgrading to the horsebox."

166

"What about the stone shed?"

"No, you've got to be one of the chosen ones to get the stone shed."

The Rasta hair at the washing machine turned around as he heard this and tipped his chin at the boy on the sofa.

"Wanker, go and get the beers. So, old folks, what are you doing here, washed up in the barn?"

Moth glanced at me and shrugged his shoulders. No need to lie.

"We're homeless, lost our house, business, everything we've ever worked for all our lives, penniless, and I'm dying, so we thought: What the fuck, let's go for a walk. We've come from Minehead, going west, who knows from there."

"Wow. That's a story, right?"

"Nope."

"Fuck."

"Yep, fuck."

"But that's okay, you're like a wave, man."

"A wave?"

"Yeah, how good a wave is depends on what nature's doing. It starts to pick up when the wind blows on the water, way out at sea, then it's all down to how strong that wind is, how long it blows for and how far it travels across the water — we call that the fetch. A big wind, a long fetch, a good stretch of coastline and you've got it, you're barrelling. But you, you're blown up by a fucking gale, man, and your fetch is still running, you're heading for the biggest, cleanest barrelling wave, man.

167

Don't you get it? You're gonna swash in style! Kurt, Kurt, they're cool, open the lock-up."

The bearded man unlocked the back of a Portakabin. It was chock full of every kind of alcoholic bottle you could possibly need. The boys relayed boxes to what appeared to be a stable in the corner of the barn, but when the door swung open Kurt was behind a built-in bar, stocking the shelves.

It was early evening and we really needed to eat, so inevitably hungry bodies that had barely touched alcohol in weeks didn't last long before it was all a blur. Colonel Roots billowed reggae from the speakers on the washing machine and nothing mattered any more. We were with the best friends we'd ever had, in our favourite place in the world.

"So, what's wrong with you, man, why're you dying?"

Moth was dancing, smooth, relaxed, his body moving with a rhythmic flow, a glass of Jack in his hand. I didn't know he drank whiskey, but you can't know everything.

"My legs are going to stop working, then all the other bits that matter, then I'll choke."

"Fuck."

"Yeah, fuck."

"You know, Kurt's a herbalist. He might have something for that."

"Kurt. Is that really his name? What do you really do with him, why do you really hang out here?"

"We feed the pigs, cut the grass — you know, help each other out; works for all of us. Then he comes

168

surfing with us to Costa Rica, we carry his boards, drive the van — like I say, help each other out. We get to stay in the sheds for free. It's all good."

Kurt emerged from behind the bar.

"That's really my name. Take this and breathe deep: all the pain will just disappear."

"But I don't smoke."

"You will, you will."

A beautiful haze of happiness filled the barn and I curled on the sofa in bliss. Moth was still dancing and the world was good.

It was the following morning when I raised an eyelid to wave to two of the lifeguards as they left with their surfboards strapped to their bikes, but it was close to midday when we packed our things and unsteadily headed away.

"Take this with you, my friend, it's medicinal. Anytime you need a place to crash, we're here."

"Thanks, Kurt."

The skies were clearing, the remaining clouds scudding fast across the blue as Watergate Bay stretched endlessly ahead. We followed the beach, too fragile to face the up and down of the cliff top. The wide expanse of sand lay pristine and empty beyond the restaurants and cafés. The only person ahead came into focus as an old man with two spaniels. He stopped to speak as we passed.

"Are you walking the coastal path?"

"Some of it. To Land's End at least."

"I've always wanted to do that . . . just walk for days and days."

"Then do it. Just pack a rucksack and do it now. You never know how long your fetch will be, depends on the wind."

The man and dogs grew small behind us, passing between the land-slipped cliffs and the foam. The waves high and crashing on the incoming tide seemed to stretch the vertical horizon, folding us in between the land and the sea. Confined and set free, on the edge but part of it all. Blown up and still building our strength through the fetch.

Towards Zacry's Island the rocks were blue with thousands of mussels. We filled our pan and boiled them, picking the fat bodies out with the penknife. Occasional people passed, but we were becoming observers, not participants. Crows crawked in the damp air, their calls eerily clear against the cliff face. Our world was changing, the edges fading as our journey drew us on between sea, sky and rock. Becoming one with the wild edge we inhabited, our fetch redefined by the salt path we trod.

Camped on the fort at Trevelgue, the lights of Newquay ahead, the darkness of Watergate behind, we were openly exposed to the Atlantic. The wind picked up, bringing torrential rain. We put on all our clothes, laid our waterproofs over the sleeping bags and slept for twelve hours without waking.

CHAPTER
THIRTEEN

Skins

The sprawl of Newquay was a shock after the wilderness, but strangely welcome at the same time. The urban blanket begins in Porth and stretches all the way to the Gannel: a collection of headlands, intersected by sandy beaches, catching some of the best surfing waves in the country. The town built its reputation on the newly growing surf culture of the sixties, but that heyday has passed, leaving a town becoming down at heel. Home now to the ever-growing tribes of stag and hen parties, shrieking through the streets in fancy dress, filling shop doorways with empty bottles and pools of puke. It's off-putting to the locals, families and surfers alike: all the trade that the shopkeepers would like to attract. But the pubs and restaurants need the party revenue to keep them open during the winter. This contradiction has left the town pivoting on an awkward catch-22. Only a handful of surf shops now remind us of its past, and its best hope for the future.

Being separate from people for large chunks of time had reduced our tolerance levels, but for a moment it was comforting to feel part of humanity. For a moment.

And it was a good place to shelter from the rain ripping in on a horizontal westerly. I zipped the waterproof hood tightly round my face and viewed Newquay through a tunnel.

It was quickly evident that beyond the holidaymakers, still there in numbers in September, there was another side to the town, a side the vacationers ignored. The invisible ones. The homeless street dwellers lining the shopping areas in greater numbers than we had seen since Glastonbury. Wet bodies curled in doorways. But these weren't well-honed professional beggars, these were tough, hardened rough sleepers. A tall, broad ex-soldier asked us for money, and when we told him we had none and were homeless ourselves he didn't question it, but gave us directions to a soup kitchen. Moth gave him some coins and his last chocolate bar. We had very little left, so wandered up to dodge the rain and claim our free bowl of soup.

The soldier's directions had sent us to St Petroc's, a charity aimed at helping the single homeless who fall through the net of social care provision. I didn't ask what happened to couples that fell through the net, but they redirected us to the soup kitchen anyway. Depending on which statistics you read, Cornwall has the second or the fifth highest rate of rough sleepers in the country, outside of London. It was claimed to be just forty or sixty-five people, or thereabouts. If that was true, every homeless person in Cornwall was currently dipping bread in tomato soup in a disused church in Newquay. The anomaly in figures was explained by a volunteer; apparently, only those people

172

on the street in the given area between the set hours of the count could be included in the figures. And that was if the person confirmed that he was homeless and sleeping rough. And if he was asleep, or appeared to be, you couldn't wake him to ask.

"So, does every homeless person sleep on the street in the given area at the right time?"

"Of course not, they're everywhere. There's a group that sleep in the woods, but the council want to get them out so they can create some sort of public access space. What they really need are shelters for overnight stays, not pretty paths in a woodland, taking away what little safety they have. They're opening some new shelters this winter, ten beds here, ten there — it's better than nothing, but it's nowhere near enough."

"Trouble is, people think we're all addicts of some sort; puts them off helping. They think it's a waste of time."

"Of course there's a high proportion of addicts on the streets, but whatever makes you homeless, you still deserve help."

The rain had cleared and the sun flickered through the clouds with a thin, watery light. We sat on a bench on the steaming pavement and watched people go by. Shoppers, holidaymakers, mums with kids fresh out of school in shiny new uniforms, skaters on longboards, dog walkers, a homeless boy with a duvet over his shoulder. We were all of those people, and none of them. The bakery by the post office was selling the last of its pasties for twenty-five pence each. Moth bought

173

as many as he could, handing one to each of the people sitting on rags in doorways, keeping the rest for ourselves.

Fistral Beach was loud with booming waves and neoprene dancers heading out to sea. The street behind was lined with blond, tanned boys in VW vans, anxiously watching the waves for a good set coming through. But we carried on, crossing the Gannel estuary by the wooden footbridge, just ahead of the tide. Then on, out on to open headlands and our room for the night.

The sky held only the faintest haze of light as Moth got out of the tent alone and made tea. I was still in the sleeping bag, under a thermal blanket that we'd traded for *Robinson Crusoe* in a charity shop in Newquay. A flock of sheep were surrounding us when he opened the flaps, but dashed away with the sound of the zip. A rock just off the headland, oddly named the Chick, was swarming with sea birds. The cacophony of noise drowned out the sound of the swelling sea rushing through the gap. Herring gulls, black-backed gulls, oystercatchers, cormorants and terns, all bickering over the same lump of inhospitable, jagged rock. It seemed every living thing in the area wanted to occupy Kelsey Head, and none of us were happy to share the space. We left the birds to it, passed the empty army camp at Penhale, with its abandoned Nissen huts, and headed down on to Perranporth Beach. I could live in one of these corrugated iron huts. With a little imagination, the whole site could provide housing for the people of

174

Newquay who desperately need shelter, but undoubtedly it'll be converted for leisure use.

The beach is flat, straight and as long as a landing strip. Moth's shoulders were stiff, and I was more tired than normal, so we sat in the sand beneath two sculptures made from beach debris. Human rubbish fashioned into human forms. We made some more tea and shared the last of the ibuprofen. An old man carefully laid out a towel close by, then methodically took off every stitch of clothing and lay very precisely on the towel. There was something close to tortoise-like about the naked old man, wrinkling, drooping as if his old skin was sliding away, soon to reveal a pink, exposed, smooth new body. I had to stare. We hide ourselves so well, exposing our skin in youth when it has nothing to say, but the other skin, with the record of time and event, the truth of life, we rarely show.

One naked man was interesting, but two became a little awkward. When a third shouted "good morning" as he strode past in only walking boots and blue socks, I felt I had to put the stove away and carry on. The alternative was to make them tea and discuss anti-wrinkle cream. We left, feeling overdressed and half tempted to go for a full body tan.

The beach didn't end but became a desert, stretching on remorselessly. The scorching sand scalded our bare feet and we put our boots back on. Cutting up into the dunes to find some shade we lost all sense of direction. Rather than showing the way out, every peak just revealed more never-ending dunes reflecting the heat. Dried out, turning to dust, we slid through the sand back down to the beach and fixed our eyes on the cliffs beyond Perranporth, a shimmering distant oasis that we might never reach. Eventually, a swarm of people and windbreaks emerged from the haze near a car park. The end. We begged iced water from a café and slugged it down, listening to our bodies hiss with pleasure.

I peeled more skin to find yet another nose.

The cliffs of St Agnes Head are desolate, scraped and scarred by its mining history. Littered now with open shafts and ruined buildings, left open and weeping with sulphur fumes and dust, the land stained with a rainbow of ore.

The days had fallen into a routine. Between morning and early evening, camping spots abound. After six, they're nowhere to be seen. The nights were getting longer and colder; as soon as the sun sank, the air temperature dropped quickly behind. That morning had been our earliest start and without realizing we'd walked through a day which had become our longest. But now we were exhausted, desperate to find somewhere for the night. The Nancekuke Common RAF airbase rose to our left, with its high steel fence trapping us into a strip of gorse and bramble. The land was dead and still and the fence endless. Dropping down into a shallow valley, a patch of grass seemed promising. But the valley had been barricaded on the landward side with a man-made dam of rubble, grown over with gorse, brambles and thistles. The land around the dam oozed water, running with ore-stained mud.

We carried on, the light falling, darkness coming, until eventually the fence turned inland and the airfield turned to farmland and fields of brassicas. In the final moments of light we pitched the tent in the corner of a grass field. No longer a twenty-minute battle with hooks and pegs, the tent was up in five minutes in semi-darkness. I heated a tin of soup; our legs were throbbing, our strength drained to zero by sand and fences.

The sky lit into colours we hadn't seen since the Rumps, fading to blackness, then a silver light that moved with the sea.

"Am I seeing things, or are those cabbages glowing?" Moth was wandering around the grass field, trying to stretch the aches from his body before sleeping. "Do you think it's a trick of the moonlight?" The field had a light green aura, a supernatural hue.

"No, they really are. Could be just the angle of the moon."

"What on earth do you think goes on inside that fence?"

Now a radar base, the site was originally built during the Second World War as RAF Portreath. By 1950 it was no longer needed and was given back to the government. Using equipment brought back from Nazi Germany, the government turned the airfield into a chemical-weapon production plant as an offshoot to Porton Down and began manufacturing the deadly nerve agent Sarin B. Production continued for two or three years alongside other chemical weapons. An investigation by the *Independent* newspaper reported that forty-one deaths and a high incidence of serious illness occurred amongst the workers involved in the production of Sarin B. In the study "Sickness Experience at Nancekuke" in 1970, it was found that workers at the plant who had been involved in Sarin B production were 33 per cent more likely to suffer serious illness than the average and 50 per cent more likely to suffer respiratory disease, the classic outcome of nerve-gas exposure. The government denied any errors on their behalf, suppressing the report and altering its conclusions, declaring that during this period there had merely been a "higher than expected level of absenteeism". However, in 1971, they admitted negligence, and made "generous" payouts to sufferers, in the region of £120 each. In 2000, the government finally admitted that they had dumped the machinery used to produce Sarin B in the mineshafts on the common and began to clean the site in 2003.

The next morning the cabbages were just plain green and the holidaymakers were already arriving in the valley of Portreath, not far away.

The path skipped around the rims of deep hidden coves and in and out of car parks as it ran parallel with the road, the nearness to the road making it perfect dog-walking country. We had grown to appreciate the challenges dog walkers face every time they encountered a stile. A lot of wooden stiles on the path have an open section at the side, with a piece of wood that slides away to allow the dog through. Which seems to work fine for small dogs, but anything bigger and it needs to be circus trained, or collected up as a huge, hairy, muddy bundle and manhandled over to the other side. Some stiles are made of stone slabs trapped horizontally into the wall, which necessitate the walker going up the stairs on one side, traversing the top of the wall, then down the staircase on the other side. Some are huge, sturdy constructions that would befit a castle: perfect for big dogs, but small ones need to be carried.

We were at a gate. Gates are great for dogs, even if, like this one, it's a kissing gate. These are ingenious constructions: a C shape of fence has a gate inserted into it that's hinged on the opposite side, allowing the walker to enter the C from one side, then open the gate and pass out the other side. Great for everyone: walkers and dogs can get through easily; great for farmers, unless they have really intelligent sheep. But not great for backpackers, or fat people. I'm convinced that the usability of the kissing gate depends on the size of the person constructing it. If they're large they leave plenty of space between the edge of the gate and the back of the C, enough room to pass behind the gate and out the other side. If they're small their concept of space is completely different. After being trapped repeatedly in these gates, the backpacks wedging us in, we had developed a way of getting through that prevented us getting stuck. Enter the C with the gate fully open, climb up the back of the C until the backpack is higher than the gate, kick the gate to fully closed, then climb down and exit the C.

After spending a morning at stiles waiting for dogs, lifting dogs over, catching dogs that had been thrown

179

over, we came to a tiny kissing gate. I climbed the C, just as a chubby man in early retirement, who had been following us, rushed up to the gate, obviously in a desperate hurry to get home to read the newspaper. He completely ignored me hanging precariously from the top of the fence and let his three dogs through one at a time. Then stood angrily getting redder.

"Well, are you going through or what?"

I climbed out of the C, followed by Moth, and let the chubby man go rushing past. There was loud clapping from the other side of the hedge.

"Wow, that was so good, what a perfect way to get through the gate." A smart elderly couple were clapping excitedly. "Could you possibly do it again so I could film it?"

Moth obligingly climbed in and out of the gate while the couple cooed over the camera, shaking him vigorously by the hand when their masterpiece was finished.

"The book club are going to love that; do you mind if I put it on the blog?"

"No, feel free, mate."

"We're coming to see you in St Ives. We can't wait."

"Are you really?" Moth pulled his hat lower and stepped back. "Well, who exactly do you think you're going to see?"

"You, of course! Oh, is that a clue? Is that the theme, our different personalities? Perfect, who are you today?"

"I'm just a homeless bum going for a walk."

"Oh, that's perfect, perfect. Oh, we're so excited now, can't wait to see you perform, Simon. Bye for now." They carried on in the opposite direction. "Split personalities, contradictions, opposites. Thrilling to have a heads-up, let's blog this as soon as we get back."

We watched them go, deep in conversation.

"Why didn't you deny it?"

"It's just funny now. Imagine the stick he's going to get when his book club read his blog. He'll never live it down."

"Cruel."

"But we still don't know who Simon Armitage is."

"No, but we have a clue: he's interesting to book clubs, so he must be a writer."

"And they're going to see him perform in St Ives."

"Writers don't perform, do they?"

"Could be a book signing or something, but you wouldn't call that a performance."

"Corker. Whoever he is we might even get to meet him."

"Don't know if I want to now, quite like the mystery."

We were hanging over the edge of Hell's Mouth to see the seals on the rocky shore beneath, grey forms lying in the sun or dropping into the water, so lucky to have caught a moment of silence between the tourists that walk here in droves from the car park and beach café. An ozone wind rushed over the edge, bringing the creatures' deep, sorrowful calls echoing up through the rocks. Their sadness was surely an illusion, a human interpretation of the animals' noise. The sound held no sense of doom, or longing; they were probably bickering over space, living and dying between the rock and the sea. Not emotion, just an echo of the low tone of life.

We moved away as more tourists came, past Godrevy Lighthouse, glittering in the sun as it reflected from the sea. A bright shining light along the endless headlands all the way back to Trevose Lighthouse and possibly, faintly, in the far, far distance, Hartland Point. It was impossible to think that we were the same people who had stood at Hartland Point, with its bunting café; less still the broken shells that had stepped off the bus in Minehead. And before that? Out of reach, too far away now, our home had drifted out of range. It existed, but the distance made it untouchable. The raw, jagged, visceral pain of loss had gone, but the memory of it was still there, if I closed my eyes and let it come. It wasn't at Godrevy though; it had been left on another headland, the pain was only in the echo.

The wind picked up, whipping the sea into a frenzy. Hayle Beach stretched for miles ahead, basking in the white glow from St Ives, clearly in view now across Carbis Bay. We walked easily across firm sand, not like the grasping, soft horrors of Perranporth, our eyes always on the sea as it closed in quickly, rising and crashing in froth and spume. Herring gulls calling daylight calls, tossed up by the air currents, mocked our slow progress. Kite surfers lifted from the waves, harnessing the air and the water, and, just for a second, hanging between the two, free from both. At low tide and with extreme care it's possible to cross the mouth of the River Hayle, but as soon as the strong currents start to fill the estuary it becomes a deadly trap. The tide pushed us inland and we followed the path along a string of tiny wooden shacks, gilded with shells, buoys, driftwood and collected beach debris. I could have lived in a little wooden hut, a tiny blue shelter for the winter that was coming. The summer visitors were thinning with the shorter days and most of the shacks were empty, soon to be shuttered against the storms to come.

The path disappeared into a concrete sprawl near the old quay and then became a pavement that would follow the side of the road for miles. Paddy says some walkers opt to miss the urban section between here and St Ives and get the bus. It was late afternoon and the walk would have left us stranded in a residential area after dark with nowhere to camp, so we opted for the bus. We had just enough money left for the fare and there would be a headland for the night beyond St Ives, so we queued at the bus stop.

"Where are you guys off to? Getting a bit late in the season for backpackers." A twenty-something in long shorts and a hoody was in the queue ahead of us.

"Land's End, then it's all down to the weather. We might just carry on."

"How long have you got?"

"As long as we want."

"What, nothing to go back for? That's amazing, doing this at your age. Just getting out there and doing what you want."

"It's not quite like that."

"Oh, it is, man, if you haven't got to go back, you're free, living the life. Good on ya, guys." He got on the bus going the other way, but shouted back. "Live the life, old guys."

We sat on the bus; it was a strange sensation to move so quickly, covering a distance that would have taken us hours on foot in just a few minutes. The path had taught us that foot miles were different; we knew the distance, the stretch of space from one stop to the next, from one sip of water to the next, knew it in our bones, knew it like the kestrel in the wind and the mouse in his sight. Road miles weren't about distance; they were just about time.

We got off in St Ives, an hour before dark, on the wrong side of town from an open headland. It didn't matter; nothing mattered. Moth still filled the air next to me and we were free, living the life.

CHAPTER
FOURTEEN

Poets

Even in the falling light St Ives has a luminous quality. Facing north, but surrounded on three sides by the Atlantic, the town bathes in a high level of ultra-violet light reflected from the sea, giving the painted houses a shimmering unreality, even at dusk. Bernard Leach set up a pottery here in 1920, still in production now, followed by Barbara Hepworth and her giant sculptures. The light attracted artists from all over the world and the little fishing village became a colony of bohemian life. Then the tourists came, then the Tate St Ives art gallery, then more tourists, then the pilchards left and the town's fate was sealed. A heaving Cornish tourist mecca, where the fishermen run boat trips instead of trawlers and there are more galleries than artists. But the light is still real, reflecting from the narrow streets and terraces of fishermen's cottages in a white Mediterranean glow.

"It'd be good to stay for a day, have a look around."

"We can't; there's nowhere to camp."

We sat on the harbour wall, watching the lights coming on. An old man in a ripped woollen jumper, short wellingtons and a beanie hat pulled down to his beard was packing away a collection of new lobster pots and a half-woven one. For a moment we could have been 1930s artists absorbing the atmosphere for a painting.

"Do you fish locally, with your pots?"

"I'm not a fisherman, my lovely, you won't catch me on a boat."

"What are you doing with the pots then?"

"Sell them to the tourists. Why, do you want one?"

"No thanks."

"You look like you need a campsite more than a lobster pot. Follow the village out past the Tate, get on to the coastal path and you'll see a campsite up the hill on the left."

We left the path and headed up the hill, through a gate and into the final field in a long string of fields that made up a caravan and camping site above the town.

"We can't pay for this."

"No, but it's dark: they won't come and check now. We can leave early."

The tent fitted perfectly into the furthest corner of the furthest field, behind the gorse bushes. We slept as if we'd walked thirteen miles across hills and rocks, sand and tarmac. When we finally woke, we took a chance and stayed.

I took my boots off in the shower block and peeled away the socks that had been on my feet for three days and nights. The big toe was flat, the nail lifting around the edges. I cut the loose nail away leaving a thin strip still attached to the middle of a pink throbbing toe. But the floor was warm: underfloor heating in a shower block — unheard of. I dried the socks with the hairdryer beneath a huge mirror, blowing sand, dust and skin across the immaculate counter top. The radio was loud with a clotted-cream voice talking about free petrol vouchers if your car displayed a Pirate FM bumper sticker. "Da da da da Pirate FM." The little jingle got stuck in my head, and even Bon Jovi belting out "Dead or Alive" while I was in the shower couldn't shift it.

I dried my bird's-nest hair, the warm dry air a forgotten pleasure. Living wild on the path we were always wet. Wet with sweat, wet with rain or just wet from the moist air. Our clothes were damp, always. Damp or wringing wet with sweat during the day, damp from the moist air during the night, damp and ice cold in the morning. There would be moments of dryness, when we sat in the sun, packs off, socks off, drying, to be put back on and wet again within minutes. It was as familiar as dryness is in normal life, so familiar we didn't really think about it any more. Maybe that was the reason why my socks hadn't left my feet in days. We'd tipped over the edge from modern-day civilization to a state of just existing, surviving. The hot dry floor was spa therapy to the soles of my feet, and I stood for what felt like forever with hot feet, dry hair and Pirate FM. I like civilization. *Da da da da Pirate FM*. Fuck. If the shower block was this good, this site must cost a fortune. We needed to go before someone asked us for money.

St Ives was heaving, a swarm of people squeezing through the narrow streets. Banners hanging overhead

187

announced that St Ives September Festival would begin at the weekend, but the place was already full, people obviously checking in ahead of the crowds. We walked through the streets, springing in our boots without the weight of the packs.

"You know, there should be some money in the bank."

"It's lethal; there's so much food."

We pressed our noses against the window of a seafood restaurant. We had a virtual breakfast of poached eggs and smoked salmon, almost followed by a cappuccino, not quite drunk when a waitress came out and asked us to leave as we were putting people off their food. Delis, doughnuts, ice cream, clotted cream, patisseries and pasties. Pasties. We went to the cash machine.

Balance today: twenty-five pounds and sixty-two pence. Available to withdraw today: twenty pounds. Why so little? There was nothing we could do about it; we had none of our tax credit details and even if we had we couldn't afford the cost of the phone call to find out what was going on. We withdrew the twenty pounds and sat in silence in a tiny green park by the church.

Moth put an arm round me.

"We'll manage. We did before."

"I know, but I really wanted that pasty. Let's just wander round anyway." I was trying hard not to cry.

"More noodles then. We love noodles."

"Yaaay. Love noodles."

The streets swelled and swayed with people and buskers, but the light seemed just a little dimmer. We followed the tiny lanes beyond the church and peered through the windows of an elegant hotel, waxed floorboards and painted through in tones of white with tongue-and-groove panelling in Nantucket blue.

"How do you know that?"

"They're the same colours I used in the kitchen of the barn. Don't you remember?"

A New Age trinket shop caught our attention, the window filled with bits of silver jewellery, crystals and dreamcatchers, A notice on the door said: "Tarot reading today". We stared into the window, not really looking, just resting our eyes on a haze of sparkly things.

"Would you like a reading?" An old lady in jogging bottoms and a twinset held the door open for us.

"No, no thanks, we can't afford it."

"Well, come in anyway. All the business in town seems to be missing me — I'll do a short one for you."

I took a step forward.

"Okay, why not."

"No." Moth stayed on the doorstep shaking his head and wouldn't cross. The lady put her hand out to him and guided him in.

"I'll just read for your wife. You can sit in."

We went into her booth in the back room, surrounded by curtains and knick-knacks, where she shuffled the cards and I picked out nine. She laid the cards down in turn.

"Oh my, you have the sun at the centre of your reading, and the moon at the top. Your final three cards are Mother Earth, the arts and the scales. A prestigious, beautiful reading. Give time for what you know you must do and you will have what you desire the most."

"Really?"

"Really." She reached out to Moth and held his hand. "And you will be well. She has a long lifeline, and you're in it."

We walked back to the sea and along the concrete sea-defence wall. An artist on the shore was balancing rocks end on end, sea sculptures in a gallery for viewing until the tide came in, while his audience dropped coins down a drainpipe into a bucket on the beach.

"So, you're going to live forever."

"And you're going to be there with me."

"And you're going to have whatever you desire."

"Let's do it then."

"What?"

"Buy a pasty."

There are lots of pasty sellers in Cornwall and most of them claim to either be the best, or the oldest, or the original. We bought one large pasty from a shop that claimed to be all three and sat on the harbour to eat it. Crowds of people filled the benches, gorging on bags of chips and ice creams. We dangled our feet over the concrete wall, while Moth ate his half of the pasty. The gulls were loud, cackling in angry, fast voices, perched on rooftops, railings and lamp posts. One particularly savage-looking bird was holding his ground on the boat-trip shed, his sea-glass eye fixed on us. I held the precious crumbly pastry close to me, wrapped round with its grease-stained paper bag. It really was the best pasty I'd ever eaten. Perfectly soft beef, potatoes and swede and just enough gravy not to run down my hand. I took a second bite, trying to eat slowly and make it last, always with one eye on the seagull. My hand left my mouth and I heard a rush of air as something scraped across my head from behind, and the pasty was gone. Dumbfounded, I held the empty paper bag as the boat-shed gull took off, calling raucously. What a fool. I hadn't looked behind me. Do seagulls hunt in packs?

"She said you'd have all you desire — didn't say how long you'd keep it though."

"All right for you, you'd eaten your half."

"Oh, come on, you've got to admit that was funny."

"No."

Moth stood up and threw the paper bag in the bin.

"Well, you can sit here and feel sorry for yourself. I need something from the tent. Don't move or I won't find you."

And he was gone into the crowd. There was a strange thing about the way he'd moved, smooth, straight, not stuttering with pain. Normal. Weird. *Da da da da Pirate FM*. We had barely been apart since we left Wales and I felt oddly dislocated, as if he'd stood up and taken half of me with him. A half-eaten pasty. The gulls massed near the fish and chip shop, not totally abandoning their instincts — they had a clear preference for fish — but would take anything given the chance. Swooping, snatching, they had occasional success. *Da da da da Pirate FM*. I tried to make up a ditty about St Ives. "As I was going to St Ives, I met a man with . . ." No, that one's already been done. What if he didn't come back? Sick of me whingeing, he could just pack his rucksack and go. No, he wouldn't do that; I had the money. Then it lowered on me, the roof beginning to caving in, the roof I'd held off with pit props of denial all summer. What would happen when he didn't come back, when he left me behind for good? I'd always be a half-eaten pasty, never whole again. I hugged my knees and focused on the gulls, anything to keep the thought at bay. *Da da da da Pirate FM.*

"I didn't mean actually sit here."

"Well I have. What was so important?"

"I needed *Beowulf*. C'mon."

"What?"

We pushed through the crowds to a space where the street widened, where the buskers stood. He took up a spot near the deli and opened *Beowulf*, the so-familiar plain dark blue cover with the red writing.

"Ready?"

"No, no, you can't . . ."

Moth leant against the wall, casual, as if it was the most normal thing in his world. But he always could tell a good story. He'd told stories in builders' snap cabins, in queues for the bus, to children on his garden tours, to the visitors in our barn, to anyone who sat still for too long. Captivating people with his tales of everything from history to botany. But this was different. These were streets full of total strangers, not a captive audience. And a lot of them weren't bucket and spade holidaymakers, they were art-savvy visitors here for the festival.

"No, Moth . . ."

" 'So.' "

192

Oh jeez. Cringingly embarrassed, I tried to back away. He's always had such a loud voice, never one to whisper.

"The Spear Danes in days gone by
and the kings who ruled them had courage and
    greatness . . ."

A few people had stopped and turned towards him. Then two old men, arms folded, nodding. He was well into it now, oblivious to the crowd, back in the builders' snap cabin.

"'Then a powerful demon, a prowler through the dark . . .'" He threw me his hat — surely he didn't expect me to — and coins fell into it. Pound coins. I walked through the crowd and the coins came: twenty pence, fifty pence . . .

"Have you got a licence?" A voice pitched up from somewhere to the side of the crowd, which had expanded to nearly block the street. A licence?

"'"Time and again, foul things attacked me . . ."'"
He closed the book.

"So that's it for today, folks, thank you to Seamus Heaney and *Beowulf*, and thanks for listening." And they were clapping, and clapping.

"Well done, a great tribute, he would have been proud." One of the old men was shaking Moth's hand. "Hope he's looking down on the festival this week."

"Sorry, remind me, when did he go? I've been walking, lost track of things."

"Two weeks ago. A perfect, perfect tribute, thank you." The crowd dispersed and I shoved the hat under my fleece.

"I didn't know he'd died. I feel such a disrespectful tit."

"I don't think he'd mind. Probably would have made him laugh."

"We should go. Did you hear that about a licence?"

Back at the quiet end of the harbour we emptied the hat and counted the coins. Shiny, shiny coins. We counted them again. Then again. Twenty-eight pounds and three pence. Twenty-eight whole pounds! We jigged on the spot and jumped around laughing until we cried, re-enacting the scene.

"I loved it when you swung round that post, so dramatic."

"Food, food, food, food."

We tipped our coins on to the Co-op counter, filling our bag with bread, fruit and green things, everything we'd craved that wasn't noodles. A woolly jumper each from the charity shop and two cones of chips and we still had ten pounds to add to the twenty in our pocket. And five pounds still in the bank. Living the life.

On the way back to the campsite, we spotted a poster in a gallery window. Simon Armitage. A poet. Walking from Minehead to Land's End, doing readings along the way. Doing one here in St Ives on Sunday. Free. Fully booked.

"Well, at least we know who he is now."

"Looks nothing like you though."

194

"What can I say, maybe people are just drawn to my poetic nature."

"Bollocks."

We spent the evening hanging out in the shower block, washing our clothes and playing with the hairdryers.

Da da da da Pirate FM. I tried to complete my St Ives ditty without much success.

> "*A Tribute to Simon Armitage*
>
> Seagulls, seagulls everywhere,
> In my hair.
> Pasties, pasties everywhere,
> In the bird."

"Ray, that's complete crap."

"No, it's iambic heptameter."

"Bollocks."

PART FOUR

Lightly Salted Blackberries

Spoilt for choice — which one to throw,
which to pocket and take home.

"The Stone Beach", Simon Armitage

CHAPTER
FIFTEEN

Headlands

It was one of those mornings that are just too perfect. Crystal-bright light from the moment the sun broke the horizon. The headland of Godrevy sharp green, and Trevose visible on the horizon with stark clarity. It couldn't last; these mornings always descend into a mess of cloud at the very least, often far worse. But we'd discovered that the campsite charged twenty-five pounds a night and we knew we couldn't stay another day.

From Clodgy Point the green light stretched east, but in the west towering white-topped cumuli were gathering, breaking to send forerunners rushing by on the rising wind. The path led on, into a wilderness of headlands: Hor Point, Pen Enys Point, Carn Nuan Point and on out of sight. Headlands and the Atlantic, craggy, primeval, and foreboding. Always another headland. We walked on, the west becoming darker, broken rock falling into the sea, white foam beginning to build as the water took on the growing density of the lowering cloud. A hidden land of weather and rock, remote and isolated. Unchanged through millennia yet constantly changed by the sea and the sky, a contradiction at the western edge. Unmoved by time or man, this ancient land was draining our strength and self-will, bending us to acceptance of the shaping elements.

The ground breaks and heaves, pushing up boulders, turning the path into a spew of sharp, impassable rock. We scrambled on, through, around, over, behind. The sky met the land; we met the sky. Water passed through everything, through clothes, swelling out of boots. The sea roared on the rocks somewhere to the right, but we didn't see it; the rain ripped past leaving a grey, hanging wet air, so dense that there was little hope of following the path amongst the rocks. With no way to set a point ahead to make for, we stumbled on through the giant scree, giving in to the possibility that we may be destined to wander the boulder fields forever, in a wet grey Hades.

At some point, without knowing how, bowed by the wind, at one with the rain, I realized my feet were on open ground; they had instinctively refound the path as it climbed to Zennor Head. The rocks gave way to bracken as we squelched on, eyes fixed on the path, afraid to let it go. Eventually it flattened and I looked up, finding myself face to face with two elderly Germans, the first people we'd seen all day.

They were just as grateful to see us.

"Oh thank God. We thought we would die here. We have passed this place three times now. Where are we?"

You thought you would die? I thought I had died. Moth took a sodden Paddy Dillon out of his pocket and delicately peeled the pages apart as we stood in a circle, all trying to dry reading glasses on wet clothes.

"Where are you heading?" asked Moth.

"Zennor. We have a room booked at the Tinner's Arms."

"Down the hill then and follow the road inland."

They turned away and within two metres had disappeared into the fog.

"Tinner's Arms?" The thought of a warm, dry pub was irresistible.

Our legs dragged from exhaustion along the tarmac road, our packs were now twice the weight and draining streams of water, but the flat surface was heaven after the boulders.

The legend of the Mermaid of Zennor tells of a beautiful woman with a magical voice, who occasionally visited the church. One day she came and set eyes on Mathey Trewella, who was duly entranced and left with her, never to be seen on land again, except maybe once out at sea, when the mist was rising in the west . . . or so the girl in the Moomaid of Zennor ice-cream shop in St Ives had told us. Apparently, in memory of the couple, the villagers had carved a mermaid on to the wooden pew where she had sat, and it was absolutely not created by a marketing-savvy, fifteenth-century congregation who had just invented a vanilla dessert.

So when St Senara's church appeared out of the fog we had to go in. And there she was in all her fish-tailed glory. We were just considering sheltering in the church for the night when the door was flung open and two men with backpacks with efficient waterproof covers marched in. The larger of the two beelined straight to the carving, turned and looked down at it.

"Well, there it is."

He then swivelled round and marched out, taking the smaller man with him before he had even reached the carving. Yompers.

We found some stools in a dark corner by the bar of the Tinner's Arms, peeled off the waterproofs and ordered a pot of tea. The Germans waved from the other side of the room, already tucking into huge plates of food. I hung my red socks over the edge of the table and the water from them drained into the pool beneath the rucksacks. We were soon so hot that we began to steam, obscured in a dark corner by our own fog.

The door flew open and the two men from the church marched in, followed by four others. No longer wet, they were showered and wearing clean dry clothes. We waited for them to announce what they were doing; backpackers just can't help themselves, sooner or later they have to tell others what they're doing. It didn't take long.

"We're walking the coastal path. Minehead to Plymouth. We must be in Plymouth in two weeks max. This is our eighteenth day, so on schedule." The big man was the spokesman.

"Why are we doing it? Well, charity of course. No one would do it and not support a charity, that would be just downright indulgent. We have back-up; the support van follows, of course."

This is the point in the conversation where any other walker would come out of the woodwork and the room would convivially discuss walking stories. The Germans had already gone and the other occupants clearly weren't walkers. Well, actually, we're doing the path too. No, not for charity, just thought we'd go for a walk. Do we have back-up? No, just our rucksacks. Camping? Yes, that's right and yes, the tent is absolutely saturated. Where are we staying tonight? Haven't the slightest idea. We decided against it and ordered another jug of hot water from the fog. They marched out at ten o'clock to "get an early night, ready for an early start".

At eleven o'clock it finally stopped raining and the fog lifted slightly. We put our wet clothes back on and headed out into the dark. A field by the side of the road seemed like a good spot, but the compost heap gave it away as the end of a garden. We'd spotted a bare patch on the headland and headed back up to that. A scramble through the bracken and we were into a field, the lights of a farmhouse just far enough away to risk it. The wind picked up while we mopped the tent out with a wet towel, so we sat in the field hoping it would dry enough to unroll the sleeping bags. Wet and shivering, eating rice and tuna at one in the morning on an exposed headland. Rising through the wet air from the cove below the low, moaning calls of seals; then fainter, slightly further away, a reply. Calling to each other through the black, wet night:

"Fucking wet over here."

"Same here."

"Sick of that bloody mermaid. Won't she ever shut up? I can't get any sleep."

Or they could just have been seal calls; it was hard to tell. Either way, as I got into a wet sleeping bag in a wet tent on a windy headland and listened to seals in the night, I was grateful that I wasn't on a piece of cardboard behind the bins in a back alley.

Cows that have been grazing on a rich pasture make a particular gassy noise. And it was right by my head. If a cow was belching right by my head, it meant her hooves were right next to the tent: one missed step and she'd be tangled in a guy rope or, worse, put her foot through the fly sheet. I tried to whisper quietly.

"Moth, Moth, there's a cow right outside."

"So?"

"So, she's right outside."

"Ignore it, she'll go away."

I couldn't ignore it and tried to open the zip slowly, so as not to scare her and cause her to jump into the tent. It's impossible to open a tent zip quietly. Then I tripped over the stove and fell on to the wet grass. The cow had already turned and was walking slowly away, grazing, utterly unconcerned. Steam rose from her back and in the cold, still air I could see her breath as she wandered away into the mist, joining the herd of apparitions at the edge of the fog. I listened to them tearing grass, chewing, belching, breathing in the wet half-light of a moon somewhere out of sight. The seals continued to call, low and repetitive, occasionally silenced by the sharp cry of an oystercatcher. I pulled the sleeping bag out and wrapped it around me as a glow began to shape the eastern horizon, illuminating the headlands one by one, until the moon was dimmed and the fog began to lift. The gull calls changed to daylight volume and lights came on in the farmhouse.

The clouds had lifted far enough to make out the lump of Gurnard's Head and the headlands in between, but the sky still hung low and grey, threatening to stay if the wind didn't resist. The path passed through a ravine cut by a small stream, the banks filled with flowers, as if all the gardens of Zennor had shed their seeds into the water, to be caught up by the damp soil and bloom in profusion in a wild, hidden garden.

And on to another headland. We sat on a bench and ate a wet fudge bar, listening to voices and marching feet.

"I damn well don't care about your blisters. We'll pass Land's End tonight, on schedule." They marched by, oblivious to us, and were gone. Land's End today? We were days away from the question mark of Land's End, the big "what then?"

Two other figures wound their way up a tiny track from Pendour Cove and on to the path next to us. Old men, stooped, of similar size and age. One fully dressed in boots, waterproof and woolly hat, thin with a sunken, grey complexion, carrying a bundle of clothes. The other, slightly younger, in swimming trunks and flip-flops, a towel draped round his neck, carrying a Tupperware box. As they got closer, the movements, the shape of their heads and the bickering made it obvious they were brothers.

"Good morning. Are you off for a swim? We've just been. Well, I have — he won't take his boots off. Don't know what he thinks will happen if his skin sees daylight, maybe something will fall off." The swimmer was also the talker. The other brother just stood quietly with a half-smile.

"Perfect air this morning. Warm and damp, great for the skin. A drop of cold salt water, a warm mist, I keep telling him, keeps illness at bay and keeps you young." He held out the Tupperware box, half full with glistening, ripe purple fruits. "Do you want a blackberry?"

The blackberries we'd picked along the way had been small, tart and sharp, so I took one only out of politeness, but when I put it in my mouth it was like no blackberry I'd ever tasted. Smooth, sweet, a burst of rich claret autumnal flavour, and in the background, faintly, faintly, salt.

"You thought blackberries had passed, didn't you? Or you've eaten them and thought you didn't like them. No, you need to wait until the last moment, that moment between perfect and spoilt. The blackbirds know that moment. And if the mist comes right then, laying the salt air gently on the fruit, you have something that money can't buy and chefs can't create. A perfect, lightly salted blackberry. You can't make them; it has to come with time and nature. They're a gift, when you think summer's over, and the good stuff has all gone. They're a gift."

He put his arm around his brother, now shivering and pale, obviously ill.

"Let me carry my clothes, old boy, and we'll get you home by the fire." The other brother just smiled and they walked away into the ravine.

We ate handfuls of blackberries, winding our way towards Gurnard's Head, our hands stained purple.

The sky came down, sucked up the sea and dropped in on the land, turning us into slithering mud bodies sliding along the broken rocky path. Huge, crashing rollers battered the headlands, as the rain battered us. Water ran through not-waterproofs, through clothes, collected in boots and shot out again in jets of muddy, sweaty soup. By mid-afternoon we gave up, put the tent up in a field, changed our wet clothes for slightly less wet clothes, ate rice, played I spy (a very limited game in a tent), played what to do after Land's End (a very limited game when there are only two options: carry on or don't), enacted *Beowulf* (a very limited game of "who's got the biggest sword?" and not advisable in a tent), then slept for twelve hours.

A bright light crept into the tent, a brighter light than we'd seen for two days, but it didn't matter if it was light or not: my stomach was twisting in blackberry cramps, shocked by the huge volume of fruit after weeks of rice and noodles. I squatted by the side of a curzy wall with purple relief and watched white fluffy cumuli track across a blue sky. Then I spotted her. A woman, sitting on a stool, head resting against the flank of a cow that was eating from a bucket. What was she doing, sitting in a field milking a cow? Was I ill, hallucinating, or caught in a *Tess of the D'Urbervilles* time warp? No one sits on a stool to milk a cow any more, especially in an open field. Then she waved at me. Oh fuck, she'd seen me squatting in her field. I'd reinforced the local belief that visitors are uncivilized, soya-milk-drinking heathens.

"Moth, get up, we need to go."

The path flattened and curved slowly down to Portheras Cove. Our clothes were drying in the wind as we followed a stream towards the beach. A Border collie rushed by, leaping from rock to rock, followed by a small woman with blond-grey hair, so long that even in a plait it was below her waist.

"Hi, are you walking the path? Where are you heading?"

"Land's End, or maybe beyond."

"Not far now then. Where have you come from? Are you camping?"

"Minehead, and yeah, we've wild camped most of the way."

"I can tell; you have the look."

"The look?"

"It's touched you, it's written all over you: you've felt the hand of nature. It won't ever leave you now; you're salted. I came here thirty years ago and never left. I swim here every day, and walk the dog. People fight the elements, the weather, especially here, but when it's touched you, when you let it be, you're never the same again. Good luck, wherever your path takes you." She followed the dog and disappeared effortlessly over the headland.

"Is this coast the land of sages and prophets? They seem to be around every corner."

"Salted. I like that. Flavoured, preserved, like the blackberries."

"Sun's warming up. Let's dry our stuff."

The contents of the packs lay spread around us on the rocks, lightly steaming in the midday sun. Items that had seemed alien but acceptably practical when we bought them weeks ago were now like family. We saw all their quirks and failings, infuriating as they were, but each item was something we couldn't live without, something we'd defend to the last. Even the paper-thin sleeping bags that we were coming to hate were as essential as an annoying sibling. The rough granite absorbed the heat, reflecting it back, warming our damp, wrinkled skin, soothing aching muscles, and we woke from a midday nap in late afternoon. I stood up stiffly, burnt skin creaking, as crisp and dry as the kit on the rocks. I started to repack things. The sleeping bags and charity shop jumpers were warm and dry at last; if only they could hold that heat into the night.

"Shall we just stay here tonight, move on tomorrow?"

"Yeah, why not? I'm going for a swim."

Moth stretched into the deep water as it shelved away beyond the beach. His body was thinner than I'd ever seen, bright white inside his dark T-shirt tan. The muscles moved across his back, not strong as they had been after summers of building *clawdd* walls, making hay and digging ditches, but leaner and more defined than they had been since the shoulder pain and muscle wasting began. He swam, reaching his arms forwards in a front crawl, a full rotational stroke, out into yet deeper water, the sunlight dropping lower, lighting the darkening water with golden streaks. Then, in the dark blue and wine gum hues, a darker grey, a smooth grey, arching, diving and reappearing. And another, and a third: bottlenose dolphins working their way closer to the shore. Moth had spotted them and stopped swimming, bobbing still in the water as they crossed the bay, an occasional nose or tail flipping as they curved silently through the sea, hard to distinguish them from rising waves. They were the water, the falling, running sea, of the same element. They left with the tide and the light, slipping towards the horizon and the deep ocean.

The Cornish population of bottlenose dolphins, unlike those of Wales and Scotland, are offered no specific spatial protection. The numbers in this area have halved in the last ten years, whereas in other areas they have stabilized. To receive local protection, they must be recognized by statutory conservation bodies as resident, but without sufficient study they can't be declared resident. Scientists found, as an absolute proof of residency, that bottlenose dolphins in Cardigan Bay were speaking with a different dialect to those in Ireland. Therefore, without doubt these dolphins were local as they were speaking Welsh. Unquestionably, the pod in Portheras have profound clotted-cream accents; what more evidence is needed?

Even if they are eventually afforded some protection, it can't be guaranteed to save them, not until we can rely on governing bodies to show consistency. The Welsh government now thinks that marine life in the Cardigan Bay and Pen Llyn Special Areas of Conservation have been special for long enough and have put forward a bill to reopen the areas to trawlers dredging the sea floor for scallops. Having left the previously heavily dredged area for a few years, marine life has been slow to return, allowing the Welsh Assembly to conclude that a sandy underwater desert is the natural state of our coastal waters. But along with the scallops, the metal claws have ripped out all the sea life: mussels, anemones, sea fans, sponges, seaweeds, all manner offish, a marine world that cannot recover in a handful of years, but will take decades, centuries even. The exact marine life that dolphin mothers feed on when their calves are young and slow moving.

The cliffs that backed the beach were shale and unstable, so we pitched the tent well away from them, on the other side of a stream of fresh water and far above the tideline of seaweed and shells. Weeks of ebbing and flowing with the tide had given us a feeling for the point where the tide would turn. Darkness fell; the light from Pendeen Lighthouse swung rhythmically over the headland never reaching the beach; the oystercatchers came and with them a biting cold, eating up through the sand, chilling us to the bone. I wore all my clothes and some of Moth's, who wasn't cold at all, and eventually shivered into that state of deep sleep which doesn't last for many hours in a tent.

That's when the sea came, rushing in with urgency and force, rising above the tideline and not stopping. We'd chosen that tent for its ability to stay upright even without tent pegs, but staying erect when being hoisted in the air with airbeds and sleeping bags still inside was beyond any expectation. More amazing than the staying power of the Vango tent was Moth. Running up the beach in his underpants, holding the tent above his head. Even wading knee-deep through the salt water as it ran up the fresh-water stream, he kept moving. He'd changed, there was no question, he'd changed and according to the doctors that wasn't possible. CBD is a one-way ticket.

He knew it too.

"I'm stronger. I feel as if I can put one foot in front of the other and trust where it'll land. I'm not dropping things as often. But it's my shoulder too — it's not as painful. It was really bad when I stopped taking the Pregabalin, but somewhere before Newquay I realized I wasn't feeling it as much. It's been years since it felt this good, and my head's so much clearer; I can think straight. I don't know if it's temporary, if it's even possible, if it will all come back the moment I stop walking. I don't know."

"Before Newquay? Probably Kurt's herbal remedies."

"I think it's extreme physio. Maybe I'll have to keep walking all my life."

"Don't joke — we might have to anyway. But I don't care. If it keeps you well, I'll walk forever."

"What are we going to do, after Land's End?"

"I don't know."

★ ★ ★

The need for food drew us into Pendeen. A tiny shop had a pile of home-baked loaves the size of footballs; we had to have one and devoured the whole thing in one sitting. Gagging for a cup of tea we blagged a pot of hot water from the café and tried to charge the phone, but it hadn't survived the rain and refused to leave a white screen.

"So, where are you heading?" The owner of the café was clearly curious about the smelly scroungers in the corner.

"It was Land's End, but we're not sure now; we may carry on."

"Don't you have to be back?"

"No, homeless now."

"Wow, selling up to go on the road? Brave at our age — there aren't many that would do it."

That's not what Moth had said, but we went along with it anyway.

"I have a dream of cycling and canoeing through France, towing my canoe behind the bike. You could come. I've got a house in northern France; you could rent that for the winter, five hundred pounds a month. We'll cycle there."

"That sounds amazing. We'll be in touch when we finish the path, whenever that is."

We left the café in the heat of late morning. Someone had offered us a place to stay. We couldn't afford it, it was in another country and, stronger or not, it was doubtful that Moth could cycle six hundred miles towing a canoe. But all the same, someone had offered.

213

Even if it was based on the notion that we had a sackful of money from a house sale and they probably wouldn't have offered if they'd known the truth. There were possibilities; there was hope.

Geevor was a working tin mine until it finally closed in 1991; in the same decade that saw the last of the English tin mines close, its pumps were switched off and the shafts flooded to sea level. Some miners dispersed as far as Australia, others went to work on the building of the Channel Tunnel. The end of an era that had lasted centuries — Cornwall's mining history was over. But not for long; as with most things Cornish, it became a tourist attraction and now forms part of the Cornish Mining World Heritage Site. The site no longer turns out tonnes of metal ore; instead it mines the pockets of the visitors, a more sustainable and long-term project. The mining may be over but the heritage remains, and we'd be the poorer without it. After all, without the tin mines we might never have had pasties. Or *Poldark*.

That day it was closed, a silent, deserted tin mine in a perfect state of repair. Beyond Geevor, back on the path, and the ruins of a dead industry are all around. Shattered engine houses and broken chimneys, a land of shale and destruction, a war zone. Man's battle with the rock leaving desolation that can never heal. The earth in submission. We passed the surreal landscape, and the tourists revelling in it, as quickly as we could.

The path stayed just back from the cliffs between gorse, blackthorn and brambles, and always to the right was the mound of Cape Cornwall and the mine chimney that marks its summit. In old Cornish it used to be called Kilgooth Ust, or goose's back of St Just. It didn't resemble any goose I've ever seen, but it had the edge-of-the-world presence of an island in the foaming water. Until two hundred years ago it was believed to be the most westerly point in Britain. And it should be: it feels remote, projecting, a last sentinel heading into the ocean. We sat with our backs to the warm granite of the summit chimney and looked out to the horizon. Even the phone sprang back to life in the heat.

Land's End was only a few miles to our left, but from the chimney we had the impression of being on a huge liner heading out into the ocean, as far west as we could be. A baked-bean-label plaque on the chimney commemorates the purchase of the cape for the nation by the Heinz Company in 1987; it now belongs to the National Trust. Moth's always been a big fan of baked beans and as the sun dropped lower and the sky lit into endless, bright, late-summer whiteness, reflecting from the foaming water in blinding brilliance, he stood on the seat, arms outstretched, shouting into the wind.

"Thank you!" Even if it was a clever tax dodge, it would have been a crime for this place to be lost to development.

"Thank you, Mr Heinz!"

The End was so close we could almost touch it. Longships Lighthouse was clearly in view, standing on the tiny islet of Carn Bras just off the final headland. We could have made it that day, but there was no rush. Why hurry, when beyond there was the great unknown?

If the earth was flat, then Land's End was the edge. We wandered on in the early evening, the path closed in with low, tough, scrubby growth. Resilient to wind and salt and impossible for camping. A few flat patches in Porth Nanven were taken by camper vans, so we climbed away from the rocky beach with a sense that we might not find anywhere for the night and would have to keep walking. Glancing back as the path turned away into more scrub, we saw a flat green patch on the side of a finger of rock pointing out from Carn Leskys into the sea.

"What do you think?"

"Exposed, really exposed."

A narrow path led to the tiny green shelf, just big enough for the tent if we didn't use all the guy ropes. At the edge of the ledge the cliff fell vertically away twenty metres to the rocks below, where the waves crashed, fizzing spray almost within reach.

"Just don't get out in the night."

"We'll be on Pirate FM tomorrow; 'Last seen on Leskys' Ledge'."

The sun finally dipped from sight between the peaks of the Brisons islet, sending shafts of every colour across the sea, swathing the headland in pink and orange. We lay awake with the tent flap open, herring gulls perching on the crags close by, as Long-ships Lighthouse began to flash.

"What is that? That light moving; look, coming out from behind the lighthouse." We were on the corner; it was our first sight of the shipping lanes of the English Channel.

216

"Oh fuck, Moth, we're here, what are we going to do?"

"Sleep. Sleep and see what tomorrow brings."

I slept and the morning brought water sprayed repetitively at the tent. Half opening the flap the water came again with fizzing closeness. The tent roared in a vibrating frenzy, wind-whipped. There was no rain, just a sky full of fast-moving cloud and bursts of water every thirty seconds. We packed everything, put waterproofs on and raced the rucksacks to dry ground between breaking foam. The Atlantic was driving something big our way, but thankfully it hadn't arrived yet. By the time the tent was down we were dripping, but dry again in seconds thanks to the high winds as we climbed out of reach of the waves. Swells and troughs out at sea came to shore in a boiling mass of white spume. Something was definitely coming. The wind turned the rucksacks into sails, but thankfully the path rolled rather than jerked and stayed away from the edge, falling easily down towards Sennen Cove. The beach was deserted, lifeguards in their hut with the door shut against the sandstorm swirling and eddying inland in a salt-scouring dermal abrasion. Then the rain came, light and mixed with sand at first, then furious, horizontal shards, thundering against waterproofs, painful on exposed skin. Doors were closing, shutters unrolling, Sennen Cove battened down. We ducked into a café and took up the seat by the window, a thin pane of glass between us and the howling beast outside.

Always hungry, we gave in and handed over a cherished note in exchange for mackerel baps and tea. A party of walkers passed by; it was hard to tell in the driving rain if they were backpackers or just deranged. One and the same. By mid-afternoon, the owner wanted to close; we'd been the only customers and she was ready to go. We hoisted our packs and stepped back out into the mouth of the gale.

"So, Land's End then?"

"Nothing better to do."

The end of the land. The start and end of epic journeys. A tourist honeypot, a design disaster, an ecological horror story. Foot-scarred cliff paths led through the clouds to the huge concrete development. Deserted. Late afternoon and even the photographer at the signpost that points the way to John o' Groats had given up and locked his door. We jumped the barriers and took rain-streaked photos on the phone. No welcome committee, no celebration, just two wet people clinging to a post. The shops were closed, the exhibition centre was closed, even Arthur and his knights had abandoned the Arthurian experience for something drier. We stood alone, running with water in a concrete enclave.

"Is that it then?"

As I said it, a double-decker bus pulled into the empty car park. We walked towards it, zombies leaving the post-apocalyptic wasteland. The doors of the open-top coastal cruiser opened. Water was pouring down the steps from the top floor and rushed out as the doors opened.

"Where's the bus heading?" Moth was shouting to be heard above the roaring wind.

"St Ives. It's not bad there. Bloody awful here though."

"Really awful."

Over two hundred and fifty miles of pain, exhaustion, hunger, wild nights and wild weather were behind us. We could get on the bus and head away, back to the familiarity of Wales, to put ourselves on the waiting list for a council house and find a cheap campsite for the winter. Moth held my hand as the bus doors closed.

CHAPTER
SIXTEEN

Searching

We watched the bus drive away from the shelter of the archway entrance to the visitor centre. Sitting on our packs, dripping. Mid-September and it felt as if autumn had arrived. We could have stopped, but we had nothing to lose and everything to walk for. We were free here, battered by the elements, hungry, tired, cold, but free. Free to walk on or not, to stop or not. Not camping out with friends or family, being a burden, becoming an irritation, wearing friendship away to just tolerance. Here we were still in control of our life, of our own outcomes, our own destiny. The water ran from our rucksacks as we put them on our backs. We chose to walk and seized the freedom that came with that choice.

Within a few hundred metres of the Land's End theme park, the wilderness returns. The cliffs are some of the most impressive we'd seen in Cornwall: sheer faces of castellated granite, lashed by seas that hadn't stopped since deep in the Atlantic Ocean, splitting against the first and last headland with unimaginable power. We stood face on to the breathtaking force of nature as immense plumes of sea were driven through the archway of the Armed Knight rock arch just offshore. Two figures alone on a cliff of stone and grass cut bowling-green low by the razor wind. No shelter, no trees, just the prospect of a damp tent. Five pounds twenty, one Mars bar, one bag of rice, one banana and half a bag of wine gums. But it had stopped raining.

The light was going when we hid the tent amongst some rocks, slightly protected from the wind. Two sheets of nylon between us and Canada.

Brief scurries of rain passed, but the sky lifted from the land and rushed away on the morning breeze. We sat on Gwennap Head, our boots off drying in the wind, and shared the Mars bar. We were achy and slow, creaking from the wind and rain of the previous day. Heading east felt like the start of a new journey. Or were we going south, or south-east? We'd been getting closer to the goal, reached it, but now we were just walking, ambling through the day with no real sense of purpose. As we reached Porthgwarra the landscape had already changed. On the north coast, we had come to know a vegetation of low, tough shrubs, grass and thrift, with any trees stooped and gnarled. By comparison Porthgwarra dripped with lush vegetation, trees still stunted but upright and gardens of exotic flowers. We had turned the corner into another country.

In early evening we sat at a picnic bench in a mown field near some houses, considering putting the tent behind some trees. Until the cars came, and it was obviously a car park.

"Maybe something's going on in the village. Where is this?"

"Who knows, haven't looked at the map for a while. Maybe it's bingo night."

We boiled some water, drank tea and shared a banana as the car park filled and people headed away, hats on, carrying blankets.

"Outdoor bingo?"

A Land-Rover pulled up next to us and an old couple got out.

"Wait until this group has gone, then we'll head down." They leant on the truck, watching the scene, obviously not keen on crowds.

"Excuse me, what's going on here, where's everyone going?"

"To the theatre. This is the Minack, the famous outdoor theatre."

"Oh right, didn't realize it was here."

"You're not going to the play then?"

"No, we didn't know. Don't think we could afford it anyway."

"What are you doing, camping?"

"Yeah, camping, walking the coastal path. We've come from Minehead."

"Well, do you want to see this play? I'll get you a ticket but we need to go or we'll miss the start."

We followed the couple through an entrance building and on to the open cliff.

"Goodbye then. You're at the top; we're down there. Good luck with the walk."

222

"Thank you so much. I'll pay you back. What's your name?"

"It's David. Forget it, just enjoy the play."

The cliff tiered down in terraces of seats formed into the natural amphitheatre of the headland and at the bottom was a stage against the backdrop of the sea. In the early 1930s, Rowena Cade decided it would be a great idea to have a theatre at the end of her garden, somewhere to stage plays by the local dramatic society. So she moved half the hillside to create one. So it says in the brochure, but as with all such projects, the gardeners did the work and she instructed and pottered around with a little wheelbarrow, or so the man sitting next to me said, and he would know, as his father was one of the gardeners. Or so he said.

The play unfolded, which wasn't a play, but an opera: Gilbert and Sullivan's *Iolanthe*. It was hard to catch what was going on as dramatic singing swirled around the amphitheatre. From high on the cliffside, we heard the light waft of voices carried away on the wind. As the sea grew dark and the moon rose behind the stage, we were momentarily transported to a magical world where shepherds were sprinkled with fairy dust.

"Where are we going to camp?"

"Wait 'til everyone's gone; it'll have to be in the car park."

We followed the last people up the steps and away from the theatre.

"Oh my word, what are you doing with those big bags?" A man with his hair in a hairnet was hurrying up

223

the hill. I recognized him as one of the actors in the play.

"Walking the coastal path. We're camping."

"Well, where on earth are you going to camp in the darkness?"

"We'll find somewhere."

"Jill, Jill, what are we to do? These poor people need somewhere to camp; we must save them from the tempest."

You think this is a tempest? You should have seen it yesterday.

A fairy bounded up the steps behind us.

"Treen campsite, but hurry, hurry or we'll miss last orders."

We bundled into the back of a van and bumped around for what felt like miles, while the cast of shepherds, innkeepers and fairies chattered loudly.

"How did you forget your words, Gerald? I had to repeat the whole verse to cover for you, I'm almost hoarse."

The fairy gave a weak little cough.

"I didn't forget, I just had to send a text. Anyway, you love the limelight."

The shepherd took his hairnet off and put a beanie on as the van screeched to a banging halt outside a pub.

"Okay, campsite's up the road. Have fun walking! Let's get the beers in." They were gone and we stood on a road in an unknown village in the dark.

"So, why are we here?"

"Surreal." Moth had his head torch on and Paddy in his hand. "This must be a first, I haven't looked at the

224

map all day. Oh look, it even says 'open-air theatre', but Treen's half on half off the map."

We followed the lane to a campsite at its end. Close to midnight and most tents were in darkness; we crept around putting ours up in silence.

"Why are we here? We don't have any money."

"Don't know, we just went with it. Shower now and away early?"

"We'll have to."

Sparrows squabbled in the hedge in the first light of dawn, a soft yellow light giving the broken clouds a luminescent glow. A faint mist was clearing but everything hung heavy with dew, the grass iced with droplets of reflected light. The Channel stretched away, no longer Canada, now France forming the boundary for the tide to rebel against. Sitting on the edge of a picnic table in the sleeping bag, warmer than I'd been all night, I could feel the change of season. At the other end of the campsite a man on a bike with blond dreadlocks piled on his head, wearing layers of washed-out faded cottons, rode from tent to tent checking payment slips tied to guy ropes. He came closer and closer. Nowhere to hide.

"Where's your payment slip?"

"We haven't got one; we got here at midnight. We'll be gone within the hour."

"You can't pitch a tent without paying first — can't you read the signs?"

"I didn't see them, and it was late . . ."

"Camping without paying is space theft. Go and pay now, fifteen pounds."

Space theft? What the . . .?

"We're just packing, we'll pay on the way out."

"I'm watching you." He cycled away, a shell of laid-back hippy cool, but underneath a frustrated box ticker.

It was a perfect campsite; in another life we'd have happily put up a bell tent and camped for a month. But in this life, we jumped the wall and hurried back towards the cliffs.

Cliffs gave way to jumbled rock, tree roots and jungle undergrowth. Sweaty, fly-infested woods were preferable to the open air where the heat was climbing. Not as hot as the searing days on the north coast, but the wind had gone and without it the air was suffocating. We sweated, drank all the water, gathered more from streams, sweated some more. Repeat. The baking jangle of boulders fell to sea level, then rose again, only to fall back. We stayed under the shelter of the trees for as long as we could stand, but the flies became unbearable. We were heading back out to the heat when we saw a woman sitting on the ground, propped against a fallen branch. She was pale, hot and in much worse shape than us.

"Hi, are you okay?"

"I'm good, just resting." She was a large lady, probably in her seventies, with a strong American accent. She got up and leant against a tree. "I've been looking for the house of my old friend John le Carré. I stayed with him when I was younger; we'd spend summers here, just writing, swimming. Great days. I come and walk your path every year, I've searched for

226

him again and again, but I can't seem to remember where the house was."

"But surely you've got great walks in America, much better than here, real wilderness, the Appalachian Trail, the PCT?"

"Yes, but you can never get out of the trees. Walking at home, it's all about the woods."

"People from here fantasize about doing the big American trails."

"That's 'cause we never appreciate what we've got, whichever side of the water you're from. We're the same on that. I'm gonna take this trail uphill; maybe David's up there."

"David? I thought you were looking for John."

"That's his pen-name, silly. Everyone knows his real name's David."

The lady set off, in search of summers long past, always just around the next corner. On a basic level, maybe all of us on the path were the same; perhaps we were all looking for something. Looking back, looking forward, or just looking for something that was missing. Drawn to the edge, a strip of wilderness where we could be free to let the answers come, or not, to find a way of accepting life, our life, whatever that was. Were we searching this narrow margin between the land and sea for another way of being, becoming edgelanders along the way? Stuck between one world and the next. Walking a thin line between tame and wild, lost and found, life and death. At the edge of existence.

"Get a grip, Ray, you're turning into another Cornish sage."

"Maybe that's the answer."

"Thought we were just walking because we've got nothing better to do."

Since Porthcurno, the coast had taken on a different atmosphere, whether it was the effect of the heat on the wet undergrowth, or just the lack of wind. It was hard to tell, but the air hung heavy with a still melancholy. Sitting amongst an outcrop of rock at Carn-du, our first Channel sunset was different too. No golden orb dipping into the sea, just light skimming the water in different tones. We camped in a field and watched ships move across the horizon. The nights were getting colder, much colder. Moth's back and shoulders were stiffening painfully again, only easing with the warmth of the sun.

Soft rain drifted in as we headed into Mousehole, pronounced Mousle, so the woman in the post office said. We found a small, quiet village shutting for the end of summer. We checked the bank account and took the thirty pounds it offered, but held on to the hope that food might be cheaper in Penzance. A tiny old house built of chunks of granite looked out to sea with a "To Let" sign bolted to the front wall. An old lady passing with a bag of shopping saw us looking.

"They want a thousand pounds a month for it. Daft — it's been empty all year. They won't drop the price though, say if they don't get it they'll just turn it into a holiday let. Like all the others, I s'pose. Never been the same since the lifeboat. All the press here, too many outsiders saw the village and wanted to come."

228

On its maiden voyage, just before Christmas 1981, the *Union Star* cargo ship's engines failed just off the coast. The wind was blowing a hurricane force twelve, with waves sixty feet high. The wooden-hulled lifeboat *Solomon Browne* was called out from Mousehole. But after radioing in to say that they had rescued four people from the vessel, neither the crew from the lifeboat, or the *Union Star*, were heard from again. A public appeal resulted in huge donations, creating an argument that raged on as the government attempted to tax the fund while bodies and wreckage were still being found along the coast. The tiny village was worldwide news for weeks, while the villagers were mourning the death of sixteen people, the eight lifeboat crew and eight from the *Union Star*, including the captain's family. On the anniversary of the disaster, the Christmas lights are switched off as an act of remembrance, but there's an air that hangs heavy in the village, as if the locals would like to close their doors to any more intrusion.

Newlyn heaved with harbour industry. The fishing boats of one of the country's largest fishing fleets stood in sandy mud, waiting for the returning tide. Trucks stood on the road waiting to be loaded with fish in plastic crates. Plastic crates stood on the path waiting to be filled with fish. Gulls circled in profusion through streets cloaked in the strong smell of raw fish. We kept walking as Newlyn became Penzance.

Packs full of food, we scoured the outdoor shops for a canister of gas. They didn't have the right one, so we bought two insulation mats for four pounds, then searched the rest of the town for gas, eventually finding one lone can in a dark corner of a hardware store just as it was closing. We bought a pasty from the oldest pasty shop ever, probably, and headed back to the coast through the Bolitho Gardens, a patch of green amongst the concrete. It was early evening and the nearest green after this was miles down a concrete path, beyond Marazion. It was hard to say how far the tide came in; after the storms, the tidal litter covered the sand and over the sea wall to the road above, so camping on the beach was too risky. We settled on a bench in the gardens and waited for it to get dark. A man with wispy grey hair and a full rucksack sat on the bench next to ours.

"Backpackers, are you?"

"Yeah, you?"

"No, I live on the path."

"On the coastal path?" He had a big pack, but it wasn't excessive. "What, in the winter too? How do you keep warm?"

"No, I'm done for the summer now, I'm in this garden tonight, then away on the train tomorrow."

"Where are you heading?"

"Thailand."

"Thailand?"

"Yeah. Always warm, great beaches and the girls are gorgeous."

"Really?"

We left the old man to his night in the garden and followed the walkway, eventually giving up and putting the tent up free-standing on the concrete. The newly

230

added layer of insulation mats under the self-inflating mats was surprisingly comfortable, without a single bump, arid not as cold. Concrete was undoubtedly warmer than sand. Maybe that's why street sleepers stay in the towns. Perhaps a cardboard box behind the bins wasn't such a bad idea for the winter. Or maybe we should go to Thailand. We should have asked him how he paid for the airfare.

Moth stretched out of the tent as dawn broke, moving more easily after a warmer night. We should add "don't get cold" to the already extensive list of things to do to counteract CBD. What had the consultant said just three months ago? "Don't tire yourself, or walk too far, and be careful on the stairs. Don't carry heavy weights, or plan too far ahead." But how could I not look too far ahead, when my whole "ahead" contained him? I couldn't accept it; we were beating it, or if not beating it then at least keeping it at bay. No, the doctor should have said walk every day, do weight-bearing exercise, fight it, keep your mind active, look ahead, fight it. Then if it beats you, when it beats you, you'll know you gave it everything, you didn't lie down in front of the train. Moth took more ibuprofen and we carried on, the sun rising in medieval drama behind the ancient St Michael's Mount. The tide was ebbing quietly away, freeing the mount from its seabound island existence, attaching it again to the mainland by the manmade stone causeway.

The day passed by on the harbour of the mount, racing back across the causeway to beat the tide, then out of Marazion and away from the urban, to

Stackhouse Cove and a tiny grassy promontory above the sea. Oystercatchers on the rocks called all through the night, but it didn't matter; I wanted to feel the nights and the days and every second in-between, to soak up all the moments we could have before the cold realities of winter overtook us.

Over Cudden Point, Land's End was just a memory hidden in blackening cloud. The curve of the Lizard headed away southeast, down through Prussia Cove, once the home of smugglers and coastguards, picture-postcard cottages set in the hillside. Holiday cottages now, half of them empty. I could have lived there, at least for the winter. The rain came, a light coating of drizzle at first, then vertical, heavy-falling stair-rods. Rain that beat our not-waterproofs so hard it was deafening, hurt our heads as it fell, soaked us to the skin. Porthleven finally appeared after what felt like two hours in a power shower, the streets running ankle-deep in water, our feet no longer just wet but actually submerged. The place was deserted. Advertising describes Porthleven as the up-and-coming haven for foodies, with rumours of celebrity chefs on the way. We bought a pasty and sheltered in a shop doorway. Then it really rained. The harbour wall disappeared, then the harbour, then the other side of the road. When it finally eased enough to see our feet we headed out, eventually finding some shelter at the foot of the cliff on the shingle beach of Loe Bar.

The morning brought cold mist, but the rain had gone, leaving the fog on the headland. We could hear it

232

buzzing like wet air around a power line, and walked into the mist expecting to find an electric transformer, but what emerged were men armed with strimmers, whipping down the wet undergrowth. They stopped to let us pass.

"Great job, guys."

"No problem."

The first one took his helmet off to shake free his sun-bleached, shoulder-length hair, then the one with the Australian accent did the same. They could have been in a shampoo advert — just replace the seagulls with parrots and a waterfall. Definitely worth it.

"How come you boys are here doing this?"

"It's winter at home; we get the contract here for your summer, strim the miles, surf the breaks, then home for our summer at the surf school."

"That's a good life."

"It's a great life. No ties, no problems."

The strimming surfers struck up the machines and we carried on through the fog and the coves, Gunwalloe Cove, Church Cove, Poldhu Cove, Polurrian Cove, Mullion Cove. The fog didn't clear; grey headlands, grey sea. We sat in a busy café in Mullion Cove and ordered tea for one with two cups. Exhausted and damp, the attraction of a chair in a dry café was too strong. A man in his twenties waited tables, cleared tables, politely dealt with grumpy customers, cut cakes, swept the floor, helped old ladies to their seats, took payments. We stretched the tea, too cosy to leave. The owner came in.

"What the fuck do you think you're doing? There's two tables out there uncleared. What do I pay you for? You're fucking lazy." The man cleared the tables without complaint. The owner left, followed shortly afterwards by most of the customers. It was a few minutes before closing time when the man came out of the kitchen with two paninis and put them on our table.

"Sorry, mate, we didn't order those."

"I know, but you look like you need them. You'll just need to eat them outside; I'm closing up."

"Sorry, but we can't afford them, we can't take them."

"Yes you can, I'm not charging you."

"You can't do that."

"I can because I'm leaving. He can stuff his job."

We sat outside; he followed us and locked the door, putting the key through the letterbox.

"What are you going to do now?"

"Not sure, but there has to be more than this. I know some guys who strim the path, so I might go to Australia with them."

"Good luck."

The ease with which he'd walked out of his job carried the security of youth. The conviction that anything can be dropped today, safe in the belief that something else can be picked up tomorrow. Does that fade with age, as we look to the horizon and see time running out? He and the strimming surfers made me think of Tom. He should be following the wave to wherever the best surf was, but instead he had become

234

focused on finding work and a flat. Had losing the security of home crushed his dreams? Just another layer of guilt to add to the rest.

The sun went down behind Land's End, catching the sea in rich, early-autumn colours, and we slept for ten hours, dry at last on Predannack Head.

The Lizard National Nature Reserve was created in the 1970s and protects a large part of the peninsula. We walked along the level cliff top, through tracts of rare Cornish heath, full of plants that had Moth in ecstasy. Other walkers of the South West Coast Path talk about miles done in a day, records set, targets met. Our path was getting slower and slower. It could have been the hour we spent examining the rare Autumn Lady's-tresses orchid, or the afternoon trying to photograph one butterfly, or the evening hanging over Kynance Cliffs watching seals in the cove below, but as it got dark we realized we'd probably only covered three miles, so put the tent up around the corner from where we'd taken it down.

In the early light choughs swooped and hovered between the cliffs and the Bellows islet, their red beaks and legs clear against the dark rock. Skylarks rose high overhead, hanging just out of sight, singing endlessly, until they dived back to earth to take a deep breath. A handful of kittiwakes squabbled on the ledges. Shouldn't they have left by now, heading out into the Atlantic? Could the warm weather have confused them? Didn't they realize summer was over?

Reluctantly we dropped down into Kynance Cove and sat on the rocks to boil some water. These rocks, no longer grey blocky granite but now serpentine in hues of dark green and red, a picture-perfect cove of snakeskin rock, calm turquoise water and white sand. Until mid-morning at least. Then they came. Streaming from the hillsides, down every path, every gully. Old people, young people, pre-school children, children that should have been at school, buckets, deckchairs, trollies full of paraphernalia, they all claimed their space by the rocks, then every space up to the tideline, people as confused by the weather as the kittiwakes. A biblical invasion, but what were they searching for? I suspect it was just the last few rays of the summer; if it was anything spiritual they were too late, that wasn't available after ten thirty. We packed the stove away and walked against the tide of humanity. On across open heathland to Lizard Point and the most southerly rocks of the mainland.

The bottom, the very base: any further south involved swimming. Wherever we walked from here would be heading north. Heading up country. A place for choices, for directions taken, photographs, and decisions made. A woman called Phoebe Smith wrote *Extreme Sleeps* about wild camping at every extremity of Britain, north, south, east and west. At the most southerly point she waited until it was dark, unrolled her bivvy bag and had an unsurprisingly bad night's sleep on a ledge above the waves, then up with the lark, or probably the gulls, a quick walk up the coast and back into the car, off to the next extreme rocky outcrop. I wished I was having a nice meal, then unrolling my bivvy without a care, knowing that however wet or cold

I got, it wasn't going to last. But that wasn't our path; it was hers. Ours would turn north and involve making a choice about the winter.

We'd never go back, I knew that. Never walk through the door, drop our bags on the slate floor, feed the cats, cut the grass, walk through the garden on a starry night and see the Plough hanging over the mountains in the north. It was never over the mountains now. It stayed in the north but my perspective had changed; I'd lost my bearings. The country towered above me, a blank empty space containing nothing for us. Only one thing was real, more real to me now than the past that we'd lost or the future we didn't have: if I put one foot in front of another, the path would move me forward and a strip of dirt, often no more than a foot wide, had become home. It wasn't just the chill in the air, the lowering of the sun's horizon, the heaviness of the dew or the lack of urgency in the birds' calls, but something in me was changing season too. I was no longer striving, fighting to change the unchangeable, not clenching in anxiety at the life we'd been unable to hold on to, or angry at an authoritarian system too bureaucratic to see the truth. A new season had crept into me, a softer season of acceptance. Burnt in by the sun, driven in by the storms. I could feel the sky, the earth, the water and revel in being part of the elements without a chasm of pain opening at the thought of the loss of our place within it all. I was a part of the whole. I didn't need to own a patch of land to make that so. I could stand in the wind and I *was* the wind, the rain, the sea; it was all me, and I was nothing within it. The

237

core of me wasn't lost. Translucent, elusive, but there and growing stronger with every headland.

The lighthouse, the southernmost perch on the mainland, twittered, swooped and heaved with hundreds — or thousands — of swallows. As if gravity had forced them down to this point, their last moment of hesitation before they had to take to the sky and commit to a journey south. Were our farm swallows here? Had they spent their summer in the pigsty and were now waiting here with their new family, waiting for that moment when an irresistible force would lift their wings and take them towards the warmth?

Moth stood up stiffly while I held his pack for him to put his arms through. Our eyes went back down to the path and we followed its pull north.

CHAPTER
SEVENTEEN

Cold

When do you accept that someone you love is ill? When a doctor tells you, or when you see it with your own eyes? And if you finally do accept it, what do you do then? Most sane people would instinctively care for them, relieve their pain, ease their suffering. I couldn't do either. I couldn't accept it, so I told myself it simply wasn't true. He could have been in a hostel: dry, safe. Instead we were in a tent on Carrick Luz headland, another Iron Age fort, wind ripping in off the Channel, watching metal detectorists sneaking around in the dark, the Lizard Point lighthouse rhythmically lighting the sea every few seconds. We could have been camping in a friend's garden, close to a hospital and within reach of a bathroom. But we peed in the dark, amongst the stunted blackthorn, wet with the spray caught in the wind and pretending he would never need a doctor. We could have been warm. Instead we were in a tent on a headland in wisp-thin sleeping bags, and it was nearly October.

In the early light, streaks of white stratocumulus clouds raced onshore and a pod of resident dolphins were feeding within sight as we put on our rucksacks and walked.

Sheltering in the Coastguard lookout on Black Head, we read a display about geology, the mind-boggling array of different rock strata that form the Lizard Peninsula. It seemed we'd spent the night on serpentinized peridotite incorporated in gabbros, but neighbouring on to peridotite, gneiss, troctolite, basalt, the Old Lizard Head Series schist faulting with the Meneage melange; it was a foreign language, or geology porn, depending which way your fancy falls. We walked a while chanting the names of rock formations until they all jumbled into one and the path went down into Coverack. Twenty-five pounds in our pocket, stocked up on rice, tuna and mini fudge bars, stuffed with a bowl of chips from the café, we carried on. Basalt, troctolite, gneiss, until we found ourselves inland on a long diversion to miss an obstruction, or landslip, or grumpy farmer, it wasn't clear which. Peridotite, gabbros, the path left the fields and wound through a wood.

Inland, just a short distance inland, and this was not the Cornwall we knew. Lush, warm, sheltered, welcoming. We couldn't afford to stop at the Fat Apples Café, but the name got the better of us, and an arrow pointing to wild camping in a wood had to be followed. We pitched the tent on a grass terrace in the woods. Sheltered from the wind, the trees had grown to full height, woodland birds flitting in the branches and pheasants scratching beneath, leaves beginning to turn to shades of rust and yellow. It was an alien land after the cliffs; a moment of calm in a leafy biome, for only five pounds. We didn't mean to eat in the café, but it was too tempting and we gave in to two forks and a vast plate of vegetarian joy.

"Owner says you're walking. Where're you heading?" Two Australians sat down at our table, followed by two mounds of all-day breakfast. One each. I tried not to breathe too deeply, the smell was so good.

"Not sure now, just going with the weather. What about you?"

"We've camped and done hotels to here. Getting colder though, so B & B all the way for us now. Falmouth next, drop the tent in a charity shop, then I'm going to the hairdresser's, got to get my roots done."

"Wow, luxury. Haven't seen my hair for days."

"You know what, gal, best not to look. Ha, wow, look at all this food. If I ate this much at home I'd be as fat as a pig. On this path all I want to do is eat, eat, eat. It'll have to stop when I get home though."

Was I envious of their mass consumption of food and the prospect of a bed and a bath every night? The food undoubtedly, the constant background hunger was something I'd have happily exchanged for a regular meal, but we could survive without the bath and bed. Although I wouldn't have refused a better sleeping bag. It was hard to leave the sanctuary of the Fat Apples; I could have spent the winter in their wood, using the cold tap in their outside toilet, but we probably wouldn't have been good for business.

Down the hill on the beach in Porthallow is a large carved stone block: the halfway marker to the South West Coast Path: 315 miles done, 315 to go. *Don't walk too far, and be careful on the stairs.* Had Moth really covered 315 miles? Had I? Power-walking superhero Paddy Dillon passes this point on day twenty-four. On our twenty-fourth day we left Tintagel, a lifetime ago, another world. This was our forty-eighth day. By day forty-eight, Paddy's arrived in Poole, taken the slow train home, hung up his boots, been to the pub, bored everyone with walking stories, mown the lawn and is already planning the next trip. At this speed we'd be getting to Poole after they'd turned the Christmas lights on, if we hadn't succumbed to hypothermia in the night or wasted away first.

The tide was in so we took the ferry across Gillan Creek. Hardly a ferry, more a wooden rowing boat through a time warp. Indian-summer warmth hanging over still water; children with fishing nets paddling in their underwear; shepherd's huts on the bank of the river; the ferryman's dog at the helm. Some sort of paradise. Moth was tired so we sat on a bench and soaked up the afternoon sun. Three more ferries to come over the next few days. We really shouldn't have stopped at the Fat Apples; noodles were looking inevitable. We camped at the edge of a turnip field above the Helford River. The wild, exposed landscapes of the north so far behind us now, almost forgotten in the southern atmosphere of domesticated rurality.

The morning was bright, soft early-autumn air hanging damp with dew and cobwebs, a light mist clearing as we pushed through a scrubby copse to a viewpoint overlooking the Helford River and made tea. Yachts drifted out to sea from the syrup-smooth ribbon of dark blue, all heading towards Falmouth through the quiet, fragile tranquillity. The silence was broken by a frantic rustling in the bushes, followed by a Dalmatian screeching to a skidding stop at the edge of the cliff.

"Bloody hell, Buster, SIT." The dog stepped backwards away from the edge looking as shaken as a spotty dog can.

"Oh, morning! Are we disturbing you?" The dog's owner was a Liverpudlian. "We always come to this spot, great view. Every year, but the bloody stupid dog never remembers. What are you doing?"

"Having a cup of tea."

"Bloody good idea."

"Do you want one?"

"Don't mind if I do, make that two, two sugars each." The large man and his wife filled the small ledge.

"There's no milk."

"Oh well, we'll have to manage. You should have camped with the shepherd's huts on the bank, they wouldn't have minded."

"Oh, do you know them?"

"No."

Three squabbling Jack Russells towed another couple on to the viewpoint.

"What's going on here then, a gathering?"

The Liverpudlian jumped in before we could open our mouths.

"We're having a cup of tea. Want one? You'll have to wait 'til we've finished with the cups though. This couple are walking the coastal path."

"Where from, Falmouth?"

"No, Minehead."

"Where's that?"

"Somerset."

"No, you haven't. That's too far."

I handed them two mugs of tea; they drank it.

"Yes, we have."

"No, you haven't."

"We have."

"How come you've got enough time to do that then?"

I heard Moth sigh and raise his eyebrows.

"Because we have no job and we're homeless."

There was a lot of shuffling; the dogs recoiled; the women took a step back.

"Well, we need to be off, thanks for the tea."

"Yeah, us too, thanks for that."

Within seconds they had all gone and Moth leant back on the bench.

"Fancy some more tea?"

"Can't, there's no water left."

We packed the stove away and took the ferry across the Helford River.

Totally mistiming our arrival in Falmouth, it was dark when we hastily put the tent up by Pendennis Castle, too tired to care about the group of teenagers drinking cider on the rocks. They stayed, laughing and drinking, too wrapped up in their hormone-fuelled world to care about us.

"Do you think that's what Tom and Row are doing?"

"Of course, they're students. Well, they were."

"Have we abandoned them? We've talked about losing the house, but not really about you being ill and what it might mean. I've talked to them about everything, always. Every bump and scratch, every little heartache of their lives. But not this, not the biggest thing, not about what effect it could have on us all. It's as if it's too painful to even go there; the elephant in the room. None of us can say it." I turned over to face Moth in the darkness of the tent. "Do you think what's happening to us, our family, will damage them? I can't stand the thought that it's going to cause them lasting scars."

"They don't talk to you about it, because it's you that has the problem, not them. They talk to me. We've talked frankly about it all. It's going to be hard, it is hard, but they're strong. It's changing us all, and if you just try to face it, then maybe we can all cope. There is no elephant. Can't be, we haven't got room."

"Giraffe in the tent then."

"Ray, just go to sleep."

Students had returned to Falmouth University for the autumn term. The town was full of shiny young things, wandering the streets with a sense of studied Bohemian style, returning to the art school with carefully exaggerated nonchalance. Even compared to students we looked as if we'd been on the trail for a very long time. Moth's camouflage trousers were held up in bunches by the belt on its last notch. His black T-shirt was brown with the shape of the rucksack stained into the back, his silver hair had bleached to shocking white and the stubble had become a beard. I'd worn the same pair of socks since St Ives, my short leggings over the long ones, the charity shop jumper growing bigger by the day and a bird's nest on my head. I thought about our Australian friends somewhere in Falmouth getting their highlights done, eating vast meals, and realized I didn't envy them at all. As we walked through the busy streets I was untouched by it, strong and detached, in a way that I couldn't have imagined only two months ago; our path was passing through a different country to theirs.

"Six pounds each? But we're just foot passengers."

"Well, that's what it costs so take it or leave it."

We walked away from the ferry and hung around the harbour trying to find a private boat going over to St Mawes, but there wasn't one to be found, so we went back into town and bought four days' worth of noodles, cutting the food rations so we could afford the ferry. Shouldn't have gone to the Fat Apples.

St Mawes swarmed with cream teas and wasps and the wait for the connecting ferry to Place Creek seemed unending. Dropped on the opposite shore we disappeared into the trees, like rabbits into the brambles, feeling more at home now in the undergrowth than on the street.

The land dropped gradually away towards Greeb Point, smooth flat grass just below the brow, out of sight of the big house above. The moon climbed into a clear sky, just past full, polishing the landscape in tones of grey and silver. Dark, rich, smooth water lapped gently against the wet rock. Taking off our foul clothes,

246

we slipped into the cold sea. As we pushed out from the ledge it eased us back and we had to swim away to hold still for a moment. Then Moth swam further out, diving under before returning.

"You have to come out, you've got to see this."

"I can't. It's too deep."

"No, you have to."

Further from the rock, out into the moonlit water, the cold took a powerful hold.

"Dip under and open your eyes."

"I can't, the salt . . ."

"You can."

I took a deep breath; then, under the water, fighting all my instincts, I opened my eyes. Instead of murky darkness, there were showers of white and silver dancing through the water, each swell sparkling with shattered, iridescent crystals of light. The moon, the source of it all, moving, swaying, refracted through the water to the sand and rock of the seabed. I went up to breathe and at eye level the water fizzed with the same light. Moth took my hand and led me further out. Then down again. The sand deeper below but still in sight, he let me go, his arms stretched wide. Scaled bodies hung barely moving in the water, reflected light shimmering on their skin, the moonlit water embodied. I reached out to one; its smooth coolness flexed slightly away, and then resumed its place among the small shoal. They floated motionless, until their joint sense told them they were too close to shore and as one they moved back to deeper water, stirring the shattered light to sparkling foam.

We left the water, shivering but silent, touched by an almost imperceptible sense of belonging, to sleep between the sea and the sky, dry but salted.

Walking through Portscatho, busy with early autumn visitors — young couples with small children, buckets, wellies and Boden coats — we're unmoved, somehow outside of it all, passing by as if watching someone else's home movie, back into the tunnels of blackthorn and gorse. On Pendower Beach we contemplated eating seaweed, but it would have taken too much gas to cook. The weather was changing, a damp wind was lifting, and the sky in the south and west grew darker. We walked in jumpers and fleeces, the wind carrying a new chill, picking at gaps in clothing, pinching our faces, slapping our rucksacks, chivvying us forward. Keep moving, keep moving. It was early but we were already looking for a spot to camp, impossible as the path was enclosed on a slope amongst spiky shrubs. Finally, resorting to searching off the path, we scrambled through blackthorn and brambles to a field near some abandoned farm buildings. A light drizzle settled over the tent as we cooked noodles, but we were ahead of the rain.

It came in the night, thundering on the flysheet, tugging at the guy ropes. Heavy, pounding rain, a drumroll without conclusion. Fully dressed in the sleeping bags and the blanket stretched over us, we were still cold. The temperatures were dropping dramatically at night, exaggerated by the warmth of the days. By four in the morning we were huddled like

248

dormice in the centre of the tent. Moth slept fitfully, groaning in his sleep. The cold was taking us backwards, down from the highs of Portheras Cove; he was struggling again. The physical endeavour was without doubt his friend, but the cold his worst enemy. I pushed the blanket over him, unrolled the waterproofs over that and he settled into solid sleep. We shouldn't have chosen such useless sleeping bags. Weight over comfort: it should have been the other way around. But we'd needed as little weight as possible and they were so cheap. We couldn't buy any others now; there was only enough money to eat. I lay awake as the wind roared against the flysheet, watching the poles flex with the force of the push, grateful when a thin grey light came and the gusts began to lessen.

The worst of the rain blew by and we walked in heavy drizzle, pulses of horizontal rain passing in squalls on the south-westerly, sheets of grey falling from cloud to sea, a visible cycle of water. Headlands blurred and disappeared. Eyes fixed on the path, focused on the stony, muddy, foot-wide strip, we missed the inland diversion between West and East Portholland and found ourselves on a sea wall that links the two. Buffeted by the wind, trapped against the edge of the land as the sea crashed on to the shingle below, we walked a stone and concrete tightrope between the elements. We finally reached tarmac in front of a row of cottages as a woman stepped out of a doorway.

"Come in, quickly. I don't want to stand here with the door open."

"We're too wet."

"Just drop your stuff on the slates. I watched you coming over the wall. Why didn't you take the diversion? You could have been washed off."

The heat in the house was intense, the pile of dripping plastic quickly turning the room into a sauna. Not a house but a small shop. She ushered us into what would have been the sitting room but was now a tiny tea room. How did we keep ending up in tea rooms, as if someone was waiting with a teapot and a cash register behind every door and acts of kindness had a minimum charge of four pounds twenty? The rain lashed against the window; even the gulls had found a rock to hide behind, so we took the tea. Moth put his head on a cushion by the window and was instantly asleep, his arm rhythmically twitching and his face occasionally tightening into a grimace. The cold and damp were causing him far more pain than he would admit to, but when he slept there was no hiding it. Without the Pregabalin, he was feeling every stab of pain in his shoulder and head, a numbing ache in his leg and a strange nettle-rash sensation running over his skin. Not everything CBD had to offer, not yet, but enough to disturb his sleep and overshadow his days.

Hours passed in the warmth of the room, until the rain eased into fog and we trudged up the slimy path to the broad, high headland of Dodman Point in early evening. We sat at the base of a big granite cross as the fog broke and rushed past in fingers of wet air, breaking to show views south to the Lizard and away into the east, before quickly hiding them from sight. Sheltered from the wind amongst the gorse and stunted trees, an old lookout hut emerged from the fog: a tiny stone building on the site of a tower built to scan the Channel for French ships during the Napoleonic wars. A ruined wall around the building protected the tent as we sat inside the stone hut cooking noodles. Playing house, being tramps, or both. Darkness came early, every scrap of light fading just after seven.

"It must be late September now."

"Really?"

Moth counted the days through the guidebook since we'd last known the date.

"It's nearly October. A few weeks and we'll change the clocks."

"What are we going to do when it's dark at five?"

Back at the cross, lights moved slowly along the horizon; the wind had dropped, letting the night noises come. Gulls floated down on to the cliffs; a group of oystercatchers chattered somewhere on the rocks below. The sea broke against the cliff with a deep background growl. Silently, almost as if it was floating, a small roe deer, grey in the thin moon, passed by, slipping into the undergrowth without the movement of a leaf. We followed her, to sleep, enclosed in the dark green night.

We lay on the concrete by the benches on Gorran Haven quayside and soaked up the retained heat, watching the gulls massing overhead.

"Gorran Haven's not like that, you know, it doesn't have people lying drunk in the streets. The police'll be after you."

I sat up, expecting the big voice to belong to a big man with an anchor tattoo, but was met by an old couple huddled on the bench in anoraks eating chips. The man with the big voice threw one to a gull and three birds landed together in a squabbling group.

"We're not drunk, just soaking up some heat."

"Proper people don't just lie in the street. Are you tramps or something?"

Tramps? Is that what we were now? And we weren't on the street.

"This isn't the street, it's a space to sit and enjoy the view. That's what we're doing. What are you doing?"

"Eating chips." His wife threw another chip to the gulls.

"No, you're not, you're feeding the gulls. Haven't you seen the sign: 'Don't feed the gulls'? You should be careful, never know who's watching."

We picked up our rucksacks and began to head away as he shouted to us:

"Tramp."

Moth turned back and waved.

"Gull feeder."

We carried on through the pretty village towards Mevagissey, the mass of herring gulls ahead a giveaway that we had arrived. They had the sly, pack-hunting look of St Ives' birds, massing on fishing boats and chimneys, hanging around the bins in groups, loitering by the benches. Rashly buying a one-pound cone of chips to share, we clutched it close, one eating, one on lookout. A group of old ladies sat on the bench next to us, a full portion of fish and chips each. We eavesdropped on their conversation.

"I tell you I've lived all over this coast, and I won't go back to St Ives again. Weymouth, I'd move back there, I'd live in Mevagissey again, but never St Ives."

"But you still live in Mevagissey," said a second lady.

A steely-eyed gull stepped sideways towards their bench, nonchalantly looking in the opposite direction.

"Well, when I've left I'll come back, but not St Ives."

"Why are you leaving if you're going to come back?"

The gull turned his back to them, looking longingly out to sea, then continued the sideways shuffle.

"Theoretical, Sheila. *If* I were to move, then I would come back."

"But theoretically, Doris, if you want to come back, why would you want to leave?"

The gull took his moment and, in a flurry of upturned chips, he was gone, battered fish in his grasp.

"Bloody seagulls! That's why I'm leaving Mevagissey. It's the same as St Ives."

"Oh Doris, what a mess, but if it's the same as St Ives then why are you coming back?"

"Sheila . . ."

We pitched the tent on Black Head, near the memorial to the poet A. L. Rowse, with its inscription: "This was the land of my content". Content in mind, if not in body, we ate noodles while fat gulls stuffed with chips settled on the rock ledges.

"Strange, they've never been interested in noodles."

"They're not that stupid."

★ ★ ★

The area north of St Austell is the land of the china clay pits. The very fine clay, kaolin, has been mined locally since the mid eighteenth century, when William Cookworthy developed a process by which impurities could be removed from the clay. The industry grew around the production of fine porcelain china, but went on to export clay across the world for use in everything from teacups to toothpaste. When the copper and tin mines ran out or closed, the clay pits carried on growing. Unfortunately, for every tonne of clay produced a further five tonnes of waste is also created. This has mounded up across this central belt of Cornwall into what locals affectionately call the Cornish Alps, but to any untrained eye would be spoil heaps. Apparently there are lots of opportunities to be had when faced with a big white hole in the ground. You could let it naturalize: fill with murky green water and grow scrub around, then call it a heritage trail; or you could create another Eden and fill it with plants from across the world, plastic biomes and millions of visitors at twenty-five pounds a pop. You could of course put all that spoil back into the hole and relandscape it, but that would be just too obvious, and no tourist is going to pay to walk over a meadow with a leaflet that says, "You'd never know it, but this used to be a mine."

Charlestown, previously West Polmear, remains a picturesque harbour, built, oddly enough, by Charles Rashleigh, who wasn't even slightly egotistical and changed the population from nine lobster-pot-weaving, pipe-whittling fishermen to three thousand warehouse workers filling cargo ships with clay, quicker than you can say "kaolin poultice anyone?" But the tens of thousands of tonnes of clay moved out of the local harbours each year during the nineteenth century was as nothing compared with the millions of tonnes in the twentieth. Now Charlestown is a picturesque harbour, thriving on its heritage and a favourite haunt of Ross Poldark.

As we approached Par the world became white, a fine dust covering the land like talcum powder. Funnelled around the outside of the clay-processing plant, between the high wire perimeter fence and the railway line, the path passed through a village and then on to a beach backed by the warehouse and chimneys of the clay works on one side and a sprawling caravan park on the other, and everywhere white. White trees, white path, white beach, white dog walkers. We passed through the cluster of pubs and cafés in Polkerris, ignoring the smell of food, and up into the autumn glow of the mature trees on the hillside, glad to have returned to a world of colour.

We lay in the tent with the flaps open on the flat grass of Gribbin Head and watched the shipping and the stars pass us by. We were in the land of the Rashleighs, the wealthy family who have owned the Menabilly estate since the dissolution of the monasteries. Where Daphne du Maurier was a tenant and dreamt of Manderley, we lay homeless and penniless under the stars. We had lost everything except our children and each other, but we had the wet grass and the rhythm of the sea on the rocks.

Could we survive on that? We knew the answer, but to give up on this and return to the world didn't seem like the answer either.

Following the path of gentle hillsides, woods in yellow and orange, rocky shores and the gulls, always the gulls, we came to Fowey. The village had grown alongside a natural harbour on a deep estuary, the narrow streets and multi-coloured houses threading up a steep hillside. It is apparently home to some of the highest-value housing in the south-west, and looking at the yachts still moored here in early autumn, the money had obviously come by sea. Another tea room, another pot of hot water and a chance to charge the phone; we'd forgotten we had it and hadn't looked at it for days.

"Row'll give me hell for not charging the phone." But when it came back to life, among the mass of texts from the kids, there was a missed call from an old school friend, Polly. Last time we'd spoken was just after we'd moved out; I found the idea of calling for a catch-up now too painful. "Oh yes, still homeless, still dying, how are you?"

We took the money from the bank, bought a loaf of bread and a tin of soup, and caught the passenger ferry across the river to Polruan, a smaller, reduced, mirror image of Fowey. We sat on the quay and watched sparks flying from a welder repairing a boat in the boatyard on the opposite side of the slipway. Our path was becoming smoother, less jagged, less tossed by the storms, more a flow of slow-running water over tide-rippled sand. We had changed with the path,

256

become stronger, calmer, our passage quieter. A cormorant flew by low on the water, heading out to sea. The sky was grey, not threatening rain, just grey sky merging into grey sea. The sparks continued to fly from behind the boat. I imagined the welder had *Flashdance* playing on his headphones, but it was more likely to be Pirate FM.

We made the steep climb out of the village, above Lantic Bay to Pencarrow Head, sheltering the tent behind some gorse, watching the lights of ships coming out of Plymouth in the far distance.

The morning returned as a slice of palest yellow between layers of grey. A bird lifted from below the line of the cliff, silhouetting a large wingspan against the lightening sky. Coasting on the wind, it tilted its grey back to show a pale, barred underside, before swooping at such velocity that it was gone in a breath. The rabbits had scattered and small birds fell silent.

An old man walked slowly across the headland towards us. Slightly scruffy, his clothes dirty, walking with a walking pole and a cut hazel rod, slowly getting closer until he stopped. And when he opened his mouth words rolled out in smooth globular balls of clotted cream.

"Did you see her, the peregrine? She's been here for a few weeks, beautiful in" she. Not been here before she 'aven't, no she's new. Have you seen her before, I "aven't?"

"We only got here last night, so it's the first time we've seen her. Magnificent."

"Jus' passin', are you? I've lived here all my life. Got a shed in the woods I 'ave, keep some chickens, cut some timber. She is beautiful in' she."

"Yes, beautiful."

"You going east are you? They all go that way. You'll go to Rame Head and Bigbury and Bolt Tail. They say I could have that glau, glauc, thing with my eyes, say I might go blind, say I've eaten too many biscuits."

"Glaucoma."

"Is it, is that it? I come here every day I can, got to remember it see, for when I can't see it."

"It's a stunning sight to remember."

"I'm glad she's come, she's a special thing, beautiful in' she."

"She is, beautiful."

The light grew, prising the sky and the sea apart. Had I seen enough things? When I could no longer see them, would I remember them, and would just the memory be enough to fill me up and make me whole? He walked away, slowly back the way he came. Could anyone ever have enough memories?

The phone rang, harsh, insistent, interrupting.

"Where are you?"

"Still on the south coast. Why, what's the matter, Polly?"

"Look, you can't stay there for the winter. I've got a shed — used to be the meat-cutting room. They've put a bathroom in it, but it's still lined with plastic. You can have it for a bit if you want. You'd have to finish the work off, though."

258

"I don't know . . ."

"It's up to you, take it or leave it."

The tent backed into the gorse, facing east, towards the path we had yet to follow. Undiscovered coves, headland on headland we had yet to cross, sunrises to walk into, sunsets to sleep beneath, weather to marvel at, cold still to be endured. But the cold we were feeling now would be nothing compared with the winter to come, when storms would lash this coast, meaning we would have to move inland. But where to? Polly lived in the middle of the country, in a place we barely knew; what would we do there, what future could that hold for us anyway? The decision seemed an impossible one to make.

We left the tent where it was and explored along the coast to Lantivet Bay. To the granite landmark obelisk painted white, and the lookout cottage tucked into the cliff. We ate rice and tuna and went down the steep scramble to Lantic Bay, beach-combing along the seaweed line. The peregrine tilted her wings and curved around Pencarrow for three mornings. We needed shelter, we needed warmth, we needed money. We could try to restart a life in the normal world, or we could face the winter on the path. Moth needed warmth.

Some wrong decisions are easy to spot and easy to rectify: you get on the wrong train; you get off at the next stop. Others you don't know are wrong until it's too late to step back.

"Hi, Row. Could you lend us forty pounds for the train?"

"I haven't got forty, but I can send twenty."

"Tom, can you send us twenty pounds for the train?"

"Yeah, okay, but I think it's a mistake. In my gut it feels like a mistake."

PART FIVE

Choices

Everybody needs beauty as well as bread.

The Yosemite, John Muir

CHAPTER
EIGHTEEN

Sheep

Dislocated, disconnected, uprooted. As far away from the coast as we could be. As rain lashed against the corrugated roof of the disused meat-packing shed, we erected the tent in the middle of the floor and huddled in the familiarity. We were lost; what peace of mind we had found was quickly retreating.

Our rucksacks sat forlornly in the corner, propping up a piece of peeling plastic wall covering. Although someone had lived in it temporarily it still felt like a processing room. A wood burner had been placed too near the plastic and caused it to melt and curl; moss grew in the windows; insulation hung from open rafters; an industrial strip light flickered on the stained ceiling. But it had a roof and we were grateful for that.

Polly was so glad we were there, so glad she could help. No, she didn't want rent, but if we could help with the building and on the farm, that would work out fine. If Moth could just start by plasterboarding and plastering the building out? We'd been friends through teenage crises and adult anxieties. It could work; we'd be helping each other out.

★ ★ ★

I followed the hedgerow to the wood at the top of the hill, lost in the foreign landscape of middle England. Crows circled overhead, lifting in the cold, late October air. A buzzard glided by, following the air currents downhill, its plaintive call stretching across the valley. The large cones of a fallen larch tree scattered the ground, grass and nettles growing up through the long-dead branches; a pheasant took off from the undergrowth, disturbed from its safety, clattering wings flapping away with a cry of alarm. I now came to this place whenever I could get away from Polly's farm. Intensely grateful for a roof, but hollow inside, an emptiness had crept over me. My days had no meaning, just a repetition of toil with no purpose for us, other than to keep warm and dry. I was alone among friends. Homelessness had taught me that however much people think they want to help you, when you enter their home, you quickly become a cuckoo in their nest, a guest that outstays their welcome. Or their usefulness. But here we were useful, for a while yet at least.

When Moth took the rucksack off and stopped walking, the stiffness returned and the neurological pain increased; he was sleeping twelve hours a night and struggling to move in the mornings. We revisited the consultant, and explained how much better Moth had been when he was walking, how his symptoms had almost gone, until he was cold.

"Well, you've just made it worse, accelerated your own decline; you should be resting, occasional gentle walks, not too far, and be careful on the stairs."

264

"But couldn't the constant hard repetitive movement be helping? Maybe the extra oxygen being forced through the body can in some way halt the process, slow the build-up of tau protein? Or it's causing something else to happen, some other beneficial reaction?"

"Absolutely not. You're just in denial; it's natural — most people go through this phase."

We walked whenever we could, but it didn't have the same effect as hours of repetitive motion with a weight on his back. We went to the gym, but that left him in agony for days. He sat on an exercise bike; the steady, repetitive action helped a little, but not enough and a cramping slowness began to take hold, punctuated sporadically by a tremor in his arm.

Resting wasn't an option; we were earning the roof over our heads through manual labour. Slowly, painstakingly, Moth plasterboarded the shed walls, moving his shoulders in a way that caused him endless pain. He laid a tiled floor. He built a concrete block wall, freezing in the cold. Working four hours a day was as much as he could manage, finding every movement harder and harder.

Winter came with force, biting cold, temperatures dropping below freezing, ground hard as a stone and six inches of snow. It was moments like this when I was grateful that we were not out in the tent. We had a roof and a stove which gave us heat, even if we did need to cut wood to power it.

We spent Christmas with Moth's brother, sleeping on his floor, comfort, warmth and happy families, trying to pretend nothing had happened and life was the same as it had always been. Late December saw us back in Polly's woods, cutting fallen trees into sections to be chopped into logs. Days were spent clearing brush and undergrowth, creating vast mounds of timber, then, when darkness came, going back to the shed, Moth lying on the floor crippled in pain. I restored a range cooker to go into the shed, knocked down a partition wall, timber-lined the entrance room, cleaned holiday lets, and worked in the laundry. We paid no rent, just electric, but we had no money. I needed to find work, but I needed to be with Moth too; he was exhausted, getting weaker. However glad we were for the roof that Polly had provided, the physical price Moth was paying for that luxury was high.

"You can't go on like this, it's killing you."

"But we've got a roof and I'm grateful for that."

Spring came and the woodland floor burst into life, carpets of previously hidden bluebells lit the top of the hill like a blue crown. A fallow deer walked across the fallen larch, her delicate legs carrying her strongly over the trunk, out of the wood to graze in the field at dusk. We watched her covertly, for fear she would end her days in the freezer. She was alone, beautiful, free and our secret.

With spring came the lambing. We watched the hundreds of ewes in vast corrugated barns for signs of the start of labour: unsettled ewes trying to find a space alone, pawing the ground, lying on their side, necks straining, their heads to the sky. Then wet, wriggling, instant life. A time of excitement, hope and fresh starts. But I felt outside of it all, an empty shell, going through the motions. Spraying lambs' navels with iodine to prevent infection. Cleaning out the mothering pens, bedding them down with clean straw. Familiar actions from a familiar life, but one I no longer lived. I wasn't living my life; I was just existing in someone else's.

Everything we'd ever worked for or towards in our long years together was gone. Our first home, a tiny Victorian terraced house that looked across a road on to a wood, where we'd returned after work every night to start work again on its restoration. Rolling in stripped wallpaper on Sunday afternoons, pointing chimney stacks at two in the morning, dreaming of buying a place with a bit of land where we could be free of the nine to five. Selling that house and piling all the money into our dream. Even that was lost, the memories drained, worthless, because it was all gone. I was grateful we'd had the life we had, a place some people aspire to all their lives and never achieve. But we'd worked so hard to get it, to make it happen; all our time, energy and ambition had been sucked into it. It was everything. When our friends were on foreign holidays, we were reroofing the barn. The kids went to the beach with other families because we were digging ditches to lay drainage pipes. It had taken everything and now the whole thirty years had gone. What now? What the fuck now?

I missed my home for the memories of family life, the closed, safe sense of security, for knowing where I would sleep next week, next year, for the decades it represented. But now I missed something else just as much. I woke in the nights to the hot dust smell of the baked path, or the citrus tang of a salt-laden rainstorm on molten earth. Alive with the anticipation of following a buzzard as it swept through silent, dappled woodland to bright, open headlands, filled with the hope of a future just beyond the next combe. Waking to a night filled with the call of gulls on the wind through racing skies and the view to an infinite horizon, lifting me up and beckoning me on to endless possibility. But then the room would come into focus in the darkness, and with it a realization of the hollow truth. I was living someone else's life while Moth slowly died. Time ran backwards, the past became the future, things that had been became anticipated events, memories ran in fluid streams, transforming into rivers yet to come. In the darkness, I began to believe the doctors and accept that I had been in denial, to realize that their words could be true. No matter how much I fought it, he would die, and I would somehow have to live without him. I was spiralling down. It was no comfort that books suggested I was in a normal state of pre-bereavement grieving. I was haunted by ghosts of Moth that stalked his living days. Spiralling down.

We searched the area, trying to find somewhere to rent, but nothing had changed; we dragged our credit history wherever we went. I looked for work, but in such a rural area there was nothing that paid more than enough to cover the petrol costs to get to the job. And who wants a fifty-year-old woman whose work history for the last twenty years has been self-employment? It didn't count that I'd been a farmer, plumber, builder, electrician, gardener, decorator, designer, accountant, tree surgeon, and run a holiday let. I had neither a piece of paper or an ex-employer to prove it. I would have to retrain. But even then, who would want to employ a fifty-year-old newly qualified woman when they could have the equivalent twenty-three-year-old? Without a job and an income, we would never be able to find a home independently. Spiralling, spiralling down.

Moth was a trained master plasterer; the action of skimming over plasterboard wasn't something new to his body, rather a skill he'd returned to often throughout his life, a muscle memory. But his body screamed as if he'd never lifted a trowel before. I couldn't help him; the ability to create a perfect glass finish isn't something you can pick up in a few lessons. The mornings became harder; I was lifting him from the bed, helping him to move reluctant limbs until slowly, by lunchtime, he was ready to start. He crawled through the work, turning the meat-packing room into a comfortable, habitable space. It just needed the plumbing to be altered for the restored Rayburn range cooker, and decorating, and then it would be complete. We craved the security that staying in the shed would provide, yet at the same time we needed something more: we needed a future over which we had some control.

"Sometimes, Ray, I wake up and I can't remember what I'm supposed to do. It's as if my body's forgetting how to function. I have to tell myself I should eat or drink or go to the bathroom, because I should, not because I want to. Is this it, am I dying now?"

It was late April, the swallows were returning, the lambs were growing strong on the hillside. In the dense wood, behind the fallen larch, I glimpsed the fallow deer, no longer alone, but with four tiny frail legs next to hers. Reluctant to leave the safety of the trees she slipped back into the darkness. Seagulls massed raucous over a late-ploughed field, clustering more tightly than they did on the coast. My thoughts drifted south, as they always did when I had a moment alone. The gulls would be busy now. Rearing their young on cliffs and rooftops, hanging out in the harbours waiting for pasties.

Early on a May morning, Polly rushed into the shed.

"Found you some work if you want it." Of course I wanted it. "The shearing team need a wrapper; do you think you can do it?"

"Of course." I had no idea if I could do it. Wrapping our few fleeces after they had been shorn was one thing. Wrapping for a team of three competition-standard shearers, who could each shear a ewe in under four minutes, was quite another.

The pick-up truck pulled up outside the shed at six in the morning, towing a rattling trailer made up of confusing strips of boarding and metal. I sat in the rear seat amid a tangle of tools, grease-covered clothing, sandwich boxes and a black dog, hot and panting. We collected other shearers on the way to the farm where

270

they had been contracted to remove the fleeces from over eight hundred ewes.

"Take us about two days if it goes well."

The ramshackle farmhouse held an old couple in ripped clothes, cotton aprons and trousers held up with baler twine. The old man, stooped and arthritic, led us out of the farmyard to a dip scooped from the hillside. Within the dip was a vast expanse of corrugated metal, a state-of-the-art barn, racked with quad bikes, tractors and farm equipment. I'd never looked at eight hundred sheep in an enclosed space before. They went on and on, filling over half of the barn, the collecting yard behind and out into the field. Gordon, the team leader, reversed the trailer into the barn and began unfolding the boarding/metal contraption. It consisted of a ramp, which would usher the sheep to the top of the trailer and then into a half-metre-wide trailer-length dead end, called the race. Three doors opened from the race on to a platform where the shearers stood, each hanging their own set of shearing equipment above their door. The electricity was connected to the small motors that powered the shearing heads. They all removed their boots and put on thick leather moccasins, soaked with dark lanolin. I stood below the waist-high platform, behind me a metal frame, from which a two-metre-long woven plastic sack was hung, to be filled with fleeces. By eight o'clock we were set and ready to go.

Each shearer opened his door, grabbed a ewe by the fleece and rolled her on to the platform, shutting the door behind her. The pull cord fed power to the shearing head and they began. The ewe on her haunches as the wool separated down the belly first, and then around the head and neck. On to her side, held between legs, and smooth, long strokes down the flank and back; then the other side. Pull the power cord and release the ewe, who would turn and leap from the trailer to a pen created to hold the clipped sheep: thin, white, fleeceless, heads huge on their naked bodies.

As the first fleece dropped on to the platform my day began. My aim was to roll the fleece, bind it into a tight bundle and put it into the sack. Flip the fleece on to its clean side, head end facing me, fold the leg sides into the back, roll it tight keeping it about a foot wide, take the last piece from the rump end and tuck it into the previous bind to create a tight ball. Stuff it into the sack. Clear the platform of debris with the flat edge of a stick. The moment the fleece had dropped, the shearer had already turned to take the next ewe from the race, so the wrapping had to take place on a small space to the side of the next ewe. Too close and the platform was a mass of tangled wool, wrapped around the feet of the kicking ewe. Times three.

The first few of the day were difficult, everyone shearing at roughly the same speed, and I ran from one to the next. But as the morning progressed so the time per ewe began to vary and I fell into a rhythm. When the sack was stuffed full, I took an eight-inch-long wooden peg from a bucket, driving it through both sides of the top of the sack twice to form a closure. Four of those and the sack was closed tight and one of

272

the shearers jumped down and helped me drag it to the side of the barn.

Having left the shed at six, the morning was long, with a break at ten thirty and then lunch at one. The afternoon felt longer, with a break at four before carrying on until seven. At the end of the day the farmer brought out the last pen of sheep. The rams. Muscular Texel beasts. When sitting on their haunches, they were nearly the size of the smaller shearer. Once that was done, we finished the turn-out of the sheep: the clipped ones to one field, those yet to be shorn to another. Then the drive back. I crawled into the plastic shed just after eight.

"How was it?"

"Yeah, it was fine. More than I've ever done before, but I'm okay."

I stood in the shower as green lanolin slime washed down the drain. I ate a bowl of soup and was asleep by nine. I woke in the night, my arms pulsing in pain, got up and took a handful of ibuprofen and went back to sleep lying on my back with my arms propped on pillows, until the alarm blasted out at five thirty.

Repeat.

Some holdings we visited were small, family-run farms, three generations on a couple of hundred acres, deep in the rolling moorlands. Others were vastly intimidating industrial units with thousands of ewes. The tight-knit group of shearers rarely spoke to me, confining themselves to discussions about equipment and sheep breeds. But I watched; I didn't really need to talk. Days ran into weeks, with only wet days off, during a warm, dry early summer. The Rayburn was plumbed in, the decorating done, blinds hung. I talked with Polly, rebuilding some of the friendship we had shared when we were young. Days when our relationship wasn't stained by time and events. It could never be the same. I was now an unpaid employee, a tenant, a recipient of her brand of philanthropy, grateful, obedient, and always aware of my position. She was a landlady with a tenant who paid no rent, an employer of a worker who earned no wages, possessor of a life that represented everything her friend had lost. She was in control. On rare occasions, she invited me round to the farmhouse and we sat in the garden on the hillside and watched the stars. The plough held its place in the north, while everything around it changed.

"The shed's looking great, better than I hoped. Stay as long as you like, stay forever if you want."

A home, a place to be, a platform to rebuild from. Was this real? Could it work?

There was a rapid scramble as everyone tried to capture the ewe before she left the platform. This happened at least five times a day; the ewes in the race would become so pressed together in their attempts to escape that when one was pulled through the door others would force their way out behind her, leap across the platform and away into the already shorn sheep. This would mean precious time lost in trying to separate her out again.

The huge Leicester/Suffolk cross ewes were producing massive, deep, loosely connected fleeces, taking half as many as usual to fill the sacks. As Gordon pulled the ewe through the door, two more burst out, swirling the vast fleeces into a half-woven soup of wool and green sludge. No! One turned and leapt into the air next to my head; instinctively I grabbed her wool and hung on. The barn floor, which began the start of each day dry and clean, was wet with lanolin and dung, and she began to run, towing me behind her until my foot wedged into a patch of broken concrete and we both rolled into a puddle of slime, two heads and six feet encased in green.

"You're shearing that one, Gordon, I ain't touching that."

"Fuck, time for a break, I think."

I washed my hands and hair under a standpipe before opening my flask of tea.

"You hung on, I'll give you that." Did my greenness make me one of the gang? Was Gordon actually talking to me? "Done a good job of the old meat shed; I like it, like the floor."

"Have you looked at it?"

"Yeah, Polly showed me round — you were out. No, it'll do me fine."

"Do you fine?"

"It's all I need really, since the wife left. Back to a bachelor pad. The rent's steep for what it is, but it's handy, where I need to be."

I drank the tea, while he told me about moving into the shed, *stay forever if you want* echoing in my ears.

"It's got no planning permission, you know."

"All the better — no Council Tax."

★ ★ ★

When I got back, Moth was finishing some plastering around the Rayburn flue pipe; installed now, shining chrome and cream enamel. "Why am I not surprised? They've got to make money where they can, I suppose. I wonder when she was going to tell us? After the shearing, I expect. We need to make a plan."

"I know, but what?" I looked at Moth, stiff and hunched, hardly able to raise his hands above his shoulders, plastering with a small trowel, as close to the wall as he could be. What plan could we possibly make?

"I've been thinking a lot these last two months while you've been away. I obviously can't go back to physical work, but most of my life's been spent in the environment; I've got so many skills that I could pass on. So, maybe I could teach. Perhaps I could go to uni and get a degree, then train to be a teacher. Start again. We could get cheap student digs."

"But do you think you could manage it? What if you get worse? You're already much worse than when we came here. I thought I was the one in denial."

"And what if I don't? I've been on the internet. I could do a degree in Cornwall — there's a campus that's part of Plymouth University; then teacher training somewhere else. It's not too late to apply; they've still got vacancies. Maybe my brain needs a jolt. What if I force myself? Look how much better I was physically when I forced myself to walk; it could work for my brain. I need to try."

"Why didn't you say?"

276

"Because you were back with your friends; I thought you were happy."

"Really? Well, yes, it's been comforting in some ways to be with people we know so well. But even if it had gone on indefinitely it would've been hard to find a way to create a new life here."

Moth made an application, had a Skype interview, and was accepted. We applied for student finance — fortunately our credit history didn't prevent us receiving the reliable fixed income it would provide. Two of us could live on one student loan until I found work; we'd lived on less. We'd wait and see what happened about the packing shed before we made a firm decision. To give up the security of a roof and voluntarily step back out into the abyss of homelessness seemed like an unnatural move.

The summer warmed into early July. Ewes that hadn't had their fleeces removed earlier were starting to suffer from maggots. Flies lay their eggs on the dirty wool of sheep, usually around the back end; the eggs hatch into maggots that wriggle through the wool to the skin, burrowing in, causing the wool to lift off and creating raw, infected sores. If left too long they get under the skin and into the spinal area, eventually killing the sheep. Picking patches of maggots out of the last fleece of the season, I dropped the last green handful of wool, skin and fish bait on to the floor. Two and a half months of work were over. We went to the pub and Gordon handed out the season's earnings. The one and only payment, but I had fifteen hundred pounds in my hands. A fortune compared to the day in Bude when we had only eleven pounds to last a week.

We locked it into a metal tin under the bed and I carried on working in the laundry and cleaning holiday lets. Moth was in so much pain that he was considering returning to the Pregabalin. Was going to uni a stupid idea? He seemed to be deteriorating so quickly. Maybe if we held on, Gordon might not move into the shed, maybe he'd got it wrong. We said nothing to Polly about the uni application, unsure if Moth would be able to do it anyway. Until one hot afternoon in Polly's kitchen, as she leant against the work-top, arms folded, worried, explaining that she desperately needed to find extra income for the farm, as finances were tight.

I could understand that; farm finances are precarious at the best of times, and I could see she was struggling with something she wanted to say. I had to say it for her. Now was the moment. If we were to make a forward move in our lives, it had to be now. I took a deep breath and told her about Moth's uni application, mentally leaping from the cliff edge, spreading my arms into freefall.

"Gordon said you'd showed him around the shed, so if his rent will help, we'll go as soon as we can."

We packed our things, taxed and insured the van, put enough money for a deposit and a month's rent into the bank and handed back the keys. We wouldn't be able to rent anywhere yet as we needed to wait for the student loan to come through in late September. We had over two months with nowhere to go and Moth's health was at its lowest point so far. With two hundred

278

pounds left in our pockets we loaded the van and said our goodbyes. But I could already feel the wind in my hair.

We drove away, homelessness ahead of us again, but this time we knew where we were going.

PART SIX

Edgelanders

Meet me there, where the sea meets the sky,
Lost but finally free.

Inscription on memorial bench, Mên-y-grib Point

CHAPTER
NINETEEN

Alive

The wind licked warm air in from the Channel. This time we had chosen to stand on the sand with the salt in our hair. Blue water lapped against our feet, the water of life rising on unstoppable tides, climbing, irresistible. Not yet, for now we were above it, breathing, alive. Homeless still, but this time with a possible end date.

We got off the ferry from Poole and took a photograph of the marker post with its familiar white acorn: 630 miles from South Haven Point to Minehead. In a different life, one in which we'd miraculously survived a winter of wild camping, this could have been our finish line. Instead, we were starting at the end point, and heading back west to Polruan, walking towards the point where our path had abruptly ended almost a year ago. Only 250 miles left to complete; an infinity of steps that might never be taken. The steel sculpture of a compass and sails marked the end of the Coast Path, blue against a blue sky, a beginning at the end.

Moth hunched under the weight of his pack, muscles receding against the incoming tau. Confusion washing over him in waves, falling quietly like a sandcastle in the water running before the tide. The start of the mental decline that accompanies CBD. Salt water lapped against my legs, rising, syrup-warm, clinging. Drawn here by the sweat and tears of the previous year, markers of the salt path we had followed, pulling us back to the sea where we could feel each grain of sand as it ebbed away. So quickly, the parapets becoming tide-rippled seabed.

Beyond the stifling dunes, we stepped on to the path of trodden sea grasses and heather. Our eyes focused on the sea, waves of relief bringing salt streams dripping from the overhang of my face. After months of inland confinement, drowning in a place that didn't hold us, returning to the cocoon of an untouchable horizon gripped me with a spasm of joy. We peeled away from the heat to the shelter of the trees and the path of short open grass that funnelled a pilgrimage of people to the white arches and stacks of Old Harry Rocks and the cliff edge. Swallows dived in the hot air, snatching insects as they hovered over low, scrubby gorse, rich in yellow flowers. Breathing deeply and turning away from the massed photographers, we faced into the wind, towards the path as it unfurled west along the white chalk band of the Jurassic Coast.

Starting at Old Harry, the World Heritage Site runs for ninety-five miles along the south coast to Orcombe Point near Exmouth. This is an area of coastal erosion, where exposed rocks display over 185 million years of the earth's history, stretching through the Triassic,

Jurassic and Cretaceous periods. Within the stone and mud are the fossilized remains of creatures and plants, from tree ferns to insects, molluscs to mammals, some even found with the remains of their last meal preserved inside them. Rocks span the journey from salt to soil, catching life in motion, holding it still into eternity.

My feet refound the short, wind-cropped grass, the sun, the wind, the salt on my lips, the familiarity of the unknown soothing the way, the magnetic pull of the path drawing me onward. Whatever the outcome, this felt right. We camped on Ballard Down, watching the lights of Swanage stretch across the bay, glittering reflections from the black water.

"Have we done the right thing?" Moth had taken four painkillers and sat on a rock while I rubbed his shoulders with a Chinese pain-relief gel we'd found in a herbal shop. It smelt like boiled cabbage and didn't work, but it felt like we were doing something.

"How can it be wrong? We'll pay for a room with money we've earned, you're going to retrain, and I'll pick up some work somehow. If not I'll retrain for something too. But we'll have somewhere to live that's ours, not living on others' goodwill."

"Yeah, I know, that's obvious. I meant coming back on the trail."

"It's the most right thing we've ever done."

"Good. That's what I hoped you'd say."

We settled into a warm night in brand-new three-season sleeping bags. We'd sacrificed fifty pounds and space in the rucksack for these. We could manage without plates or a spare torch, but warmth was essential.

Compared to the start of the north coast, the south was easy; occasional steps going steeply down and then drastically back up again, followed by long stretches of easy going across bracken- and gorse-covered slopes. This was why we had wanted to start our journey this way round originally, before discovering that we'd have to read the guidebooks back to front. Reading it in reverse seemed less important now; we were so familiar with Paddy's writing that even backwards we understood his meaning. Red deer grazed quietly above the path near Dancing Ledge, while rock climbers hung from the cliffs below, each seemingly unaware of the other's world. We walked between the two, invisible to both, our only traces those of Moth's left leg, heavy and awkward, leaving uneven footprints in the dust.

Dark massing clouds rolled in clusters across the evening sky as we camped on a grass ledge on the slopes of St Aldhelm's Head. The currents meet in the waters below the head, clashing in a foaming mass of boiling water. Small boats heading towards Poole attempted one by one to navigate their way through the irregular waves, pushing forwards only to be driven back over and over. A fishing boat approached the area, taking a wide arc out to sea to avoid the confluence, reaching the other side long before the others who were still struggling through the watery mayhem. The light faded into tones of grey and silver. Before darkness completely engulfed us, a slight movement caught my eye on the path and a wide black body came out of the gloom, the white stripe of his badger face shining in the twilight. Two metres away he stopped dead, his regular evening path barred by the tent; time stood still, frozen for minutes or seconds, as all three of us stared into the darkness, unsure what to do. The badger slowly turned and retreated into the bracken, to find another route. We stared long after he'd gone, enchanted by this wild moment imprinted on the dusk.

The next morning, small boats were still trying to cross the mess of tides, under the careful watch of two old men in a coastguard hut.

"Please could we fill our water bottles?"

"That'll be a pound a bottle."

"Oh. I think we'll manage."

"Don't go taking photographs round here."

Was photography banned? That was a bit extreme; I knew we were getting close to the military zones, but thought they were only training areas.

"Crumbling rocks, see. Man came up here a few weeks ago, stepping back to take a selfie, over he goes. Next time we saw him it was down there on the beach."

Moth and his lazy leg stepped a metre further from the edge.

We filled the bottles for free at a spring at the base of West Hill and began a slow, slow walk up Houns-tout Cliff towards the Kimmeridge Ledges, where rock climbers hung in effortless patterns of Lycra and chalk bags. When we were twenty, we'd spent every spare weekend rock climbing on the crags of the Peak District, but watching the supple bodies swinging across the rock face it seemed as if I was remembering someone else's life; however hard I tried I couldn't recall how that ease of movement felt.

"We were never that good."

"I'm sure we were; they've just got better kit than we had."

But that was a different life, long gone, and it seemed that now we were walking slowly out of our current existence into an unknown life where all we could hope for was insidious decay. In another millennium, someone would discover fossilized hikers in the mudstone. Last known meal: noodles. The creeping shadow of our future was taking shape, but I hung on to the memory of Portheras Cove, the tent aloft over Moth's head, and hoped.

The heat soared as we walked through wheat fields. The dust from early combine harvesters cloaked our packs, hair and clothes in soil and chaff. The year since we'd left our land could be measured by the dirt we'd accumulated, and the rare days we'd been clean. Muddy from the path, green from the sheep, dusty from plaster. Dirt had become a normal part of our life. Emerging from the cloud, sunlight glinted from a car park in Gaulter Gap. This eastern part of the south coast is softer, more populated than the north, where the luxury of washing our heads under a tap by the toilet block and dropping our packs on the grass by an ice-cream van had been just a dream. The pleasure of finding water whenever we needed it couldn't be underrated, but already we were finding ourselves looking for the more rugged, wild and isolated spots.

A woman lay on the grass with a hat over her face, a huge rucksack by her feet.

"Hello, are you a backpacker? There aren't many of us around." She sat up and took her sunglasses off: our age and a backpacker, a rare sight. Then it went dark. A vast black shape moved in front of the sun; it could have been an eclipse, but slowly the silhouette of two ice creams emerged from its sides and it sat down.

"Bugger me, are you backpackers? Don't see backpackers, do we, Ju? Well, tell a lie, we saw two near Swanage, going t'other way. Said they'd come from Minehead. Didn't believe 'em, did we, Ju? Looked too clean. Then those other two, but they were just out for the weekend so they don't really count, do they? We've come from Poole. Well, Bournemouth really. We were going to get the bus to the ferry then we thought well no, might as well walk, then we got here like and they've got ice creams, bloody marvellous. Are you camping? We're just camping where we end up. Just washed our feet at the toilet block. Bloody stink, my feet do."

"Dave, slow down."

"What? Just telling them what we're doing and stuff like that."

"Yeah, we're wild camping too."

"Thought so. We camped on the side of St Aldhelm's last night. Did you come through that dust? Couldn't see a bloody thing, could we, Ju? God that was good; I'm going to have another one of them, me."

The sun came out as he headed back to the van. We looked at each other; then we felt in the pack for the purse. We liked them immediately and Dave's enthusiasm was catching. We rashly bought two ice lollies, and lay on the grass chatting, which consisted mainly of us listening and dozing, until the sun began to dip below Tyneham Cap. We left them in the car park drinking coffee and headed away to find somewhere to put the tent.

The hillside ahead looked really promising, until we passed a nodding donkey oil pump and came to a six-metre-high razor-wire fence that announced the start of the Lulworth Ranges, where the army hide in the undergrowth ambushing rusty retired tanks, which run all the way to Lulworth, miles to the west. A large sign states no camping, fires, drinking, running, photographs or unnecessary breathing, but it was the weekend so the path was open. We could have gone back and camped in the car park, but would inevitably have been thrown off, or we could try to make it up Tyneham Cap before it got dark, put the tent somewhere out of sight and hope not to get shot. We went through the bolted gate and carried on. Moth had sat in the car park for too long, enough time for his muscles to stiffen and refuse to go far. So we camped halfway up the hill, where we were out of sight of the village and could be away early enough to avoid being ambushed by squaddies camouflaged as sheep.

290

The night wasn't as quiet as we'd hoped. I woke to a strange clicking, wheezing sound, first around the tent and then moving towards the cliff. I held my breath waiting for the tent flaps to be ripped open and polished leather boots to appear outside, but the noise faded away, the boots didn't come and Moth, snug in his new sleeping bag, carried on snoring. Morning broke and we left early, before anyone could know we were there. Then, as we broke over the ridge of Tyneham Cap, Dave and Julie were sitting at a picnic bench drinking coffee.

"You're up early, aren't you? Bloody hell, we've only just got the coffee on. What did you think to those deer last night? Got out for a pee and I thought crikey, they're having a great show. All round your tent they were, deer, probably twenty of them, round your tent for ages they were, then they came over here and down into that scrub on the side of the cliff. Bloody amazing, they were."

"I heard a weird noise, but we didn't see them."

"Missed something there, you did. I thought they were roe deer, but that wouldn't be right, they're usually solitary, unless they're starting to get together for the rut, early for that though. Anyway, they were deer and they went over into the scrub, hiding for the day and stuff like that I expect. Red deer, maybe that's what they were, but it was dark."

Julie sat quietly drinking her coffee, only occasionally interrupting Dave's rapid conversation, but smilingly content to let the big-hearted man talk on.

We left them packing their tent away and followed the path in the fresh morning air, down to Worbarrow Tout, past the village of Tyneham, which was requisitioned by the army in 1943. Locals accuse them of failing to give it back, although technically, since the army placed a compulsory purchase order on the land and buildings after the war, it belonged to them. However, the villagers were still displaced, all sense of home lost as the military used their history, their memories, as target practice. Strangely enough, limited public access, a lack of intensive farming and the occasional blasting by small-arms fire has allowed wildlife and vegetation to thrive throughout the ranges. A form of khaki conservation that no one expected to be the outcome when the villagers left their homes as part of the war effort.

The cliffs of Worbarrow and Mupe Bay dazzled white against the sea, Mediterranean-turquoise in the early sun. The steep rise of Flower's Barrow was a shocking reminder of the true nature of the coastal path. Dry and crisp in the heat, the slippery grass rose to a degree that would have been easier to crawl than walk. We finally gasped on to the top, stunned by views that opened to the north through the rolling hills and valleys of Dorset and west along the white chalk cliffs towards Lulworth. As steep as Flower's Barrow had been up, Bindon Hill was going down. We could have taken a gentle stroll across the ridge and a slow descent into Lulworth Cove, but missed it and headed down the steep path to Mupe Bay, stopping thankfully halfway down to allow a large family to pass on their way up.

Armed with picnic baskets, blankets, cool boxes and dogs they filed past: young aunties having a "lashings of ginger beer" time with fitter nieces and nephews, then harassed mums and dads with collapsible chairs, dogs knocking slower children off their feet, teenage grandchildren grumbling into mobile phones and finally grandparents, stopping to pant at every chance: "Remind me why we do this every year?" They passed as our crunching descent carried on, knee joints losing years of use with every step. At the bottom, we paused on a ledge to look down on huge fossilized growths in the rocks below: four-feet-wide swellings with a depression in the centre, like giant, freshly squeezed acne. Apparently, according to Paddy, this isn't the fossil of a teenage troll, but the remains of conifers that grew 135 million years ago, in their original soil.

Aching, tired and feeling every step of our walk through time, we stopped at the end of the army ranges to take our boots off. The toenail that had healed over in the winter had again burst out of the side of my toe. I bound it up with tape and hoped it would stay in, before walking through the cobbles at the base of the curved cliffs of Lulworth Cove. White rock cliffs interlaced with black, scattering the cove with a smooth mix of black and white pebbles. Iconically picturesque, the cove is probably one of the most photographed spots on the South West Coast Path, and inevitably heaved with tourists. But as the sun began to drop and the cliffs picked up the muted hues of the late-afternoon sun, their photographs would have been worth the crush. We picked up a leaflet in the village and tried to discern if we were moving from the Cretaceous to the Jurassic period, but gave up and bought chocolate bars and hot water instead. We left the village in early evening and followed the coast of stacks and pinnacles to the vast rock arch of Durdle Door. Dusk was falling over the white rollercoaster when we finally pitched the tent beyond Swyre Head and I watched the last of the light transform the cliffs into blue and pink, warmed not just by the three-season bag, but by the sound of gulls and oystercatchers chattering through the night. A sense of calm washed through me that I hadn't felt since watching the peregrine on Pencarrow Head and I fell into a long, restful sleep for the first time in weeks.

The drama of the high white cliffs came to an end as the path descended to sea level and a shack selling breakfasts. The morning had been bright and clear, but the sky was darkening, a growing purple hue creeping in beyond the Isle of Portland, highlighting the island with exaggerated brightness. Portland isn't really an island but a bulge of land that hangs out in the sea, attached to the mainland by a thread of shingle and road. One day that too will erode and it will truly become an island. Virtually out of food, we shared a sausage sandwich and a pot of hot water, desperate not to dip into the luxury of the cash still in the rucksack, but unable to resist the smell of breakfast. A group of divers squelched up from the beach, like penguins in drysuits with flippers in hand. The one nearest the shack peeled off the drysuit to reveal another, very feminine-shaped wetsuit underneath, removing her neoprene balaclava to set her long dark hair free in the rising wind. As she struggled to release herself from the black, body-hugging skin, the elderly fishermen on the next table fell silent. By the time she finally rolled it down over her thighs to reveal a perfect body in a red bikini, they were close to slithering from the bench in a state of self-transcendent ecstasy.

"Bloody hell, love, you should cover yourself up, you'll catch your death."

She looked up at Dave, seemingly oblivious to the effect she was having by standing dripping, almost naked in front of the fishermen, who were now nearly catatonic.

"Why, thanks, I will."

Her breathy tones were more than one of the old men could bear; he put his head in his hands and started rocking. His group of friends poured him a cup of water, and handed it to him.

"Take your heart pill, Doug, and look the other way."

"It's all right, mate, if you pass out I can do CPR." Dave and Julie sat on the other side of the picnic bench. They'd followed our path since leaving Tyneham Cap, only diverting to take a different route into Lulworth Cove, always just a mile or so behind. "Bloody hell, old men, eh? Don't want to get old, me, angina and diabetes, arthritis and stuff like that. No, I'm just going to keep walking, then we'll be all right, won't we, Ju?"

"Hopefully."

"We all hope for that." Moth gave me a look that said, "Don't say it." To anyone else he appeared to be just laughing and drinking tea. We left Dave and Julie eating massive fried breakfasts, never expecting to see them again.

The path was gentle and low level between trees and high hedges. Disturbed by the wind, the gorse seeds rattled in their pods and blackthorn branches clattered. Walking beneath their canopy we didn't see the purple hue spreading east, or the wall of water approaching from the sea. Without warning the sky opened and a vertical flood hit us, turning the dusty path into a treacherous soup. Hard rain spears drove into our faces, so hard we could barely see where we were going. Suddenly my feet had no hold and I watched them fly into the air in slow motion as the world spun like a gyroscope. The sky was in front, then below, and the hedge came from nowhere. I stopped spinning and tried to stand, but was pinned into a blackthorn shrub by dozens of barbs. Eventually back on my feet, Moth pulled them out one by one, leaving a throbbing red pincushion of hands and legs. The not-waterproof was even less waterproof and I was covered head to toe in black mud. We trudged on through Osmington Mills and dozens of people sheltering under garden umbrellas. The sun returned as quickly as the rain had come, spreading across Weymouth Bay, drying the mud until it cracked like crazy paving and fell off. The puncture wounds throbbed remarkably. We pulled out the last bits of thorn and followed the evening lights into town, intending to get some supplies and camp on the beach if we couldn't find anywhere else. That was our intention, but we should have known that for us the best plan was to have no plan.

Weymouth was by far the biggest urban area we'd seen on the path since Newquay, a year earlier. We bought an ice cream near the statue of George III and wandered through the town amongst the bustle of the first week of the summer holidays; families heading out for dinner, tired kids that should have been in bed, mothers-in-law and sons-in-law who didn't care if they never saw each other again. I could feel a weird sensation growing in my gut, as if my stomach was shrinking to the size of a pea and then rapidly expanding to a football. Maybe I was just tired, or I'd strained myself when I fell over, or I was hungry. The swelling and shrinking got faster and I was burning hot, then with one fiery spasm I retched up the ice cream and what was left of the morning's sausage sandwich. After half an hour my stomach had resorted to producing a strangely frothy green bile, but the retching didn't stop. Moth found a taxi and asked the driver to take us to a campsite.

"No point, mate, they're all full."

We sat on a bench on the beach, and the retching went on. After two hours I couldn't walk anywhere and was drifting between sleep and heaving.

"Can you walk? I've found us a B & B."

I hadn't even realized that Moth had left my side.

"We can't; it'll take everything we've got left."

"We can; it's done."

There was a lift in the tiny hotel, and a bed and a toilet, and for about thirty-six hours that's all I saw. I

297

lay on the bed and threw up in the toilet bowl and staggered between the two, drifting in and out of sleep. Then I was sick some more. Then I slept. It was about five in the morning when I realized it wasn't the same day, this was actually our second night in the hotel. I shook Moth awake.

"What are we doing here? We can't pay for this."

"It's okay, it's all paid for, go back to sleep."

I slept and dreamt of green ice creams.

The next morning I ventured out of the room to sit in the dining room and eat dry toast with barely the energy to lift it to my mouth.

"Are you better? You don't look it." A huge, familiar figure dropped himself down on a seat opposite. Dave. "Moth told us about the blackthorn. Mind you, I've not heard of it giving people sickness though. Arthritis, yes. We're off round Portland today. Quite like Weymouth, me, we've done some shopping, tried to do some washing but it won't dry so we've bought new socks and T-shirts, went to a museum, even got me into an art gallery, didn't you, Ju? Not for long though. So we're round Portland. Two days for us, I think, so won't see you again after this."

"What are you doing here? I don't know if it was the blackthorn. Might have been the ice cream."

"Nowhere else to go, was there? Campsites were all full, police wouldn't let us camp on the beach, so we're trapped here too, the only place with vacancies. I like Weymouth though, me."

After breakfast, we waved them off, larger than life with vast rucksacks and walking poles, totally out of place among the holidaymakers. Sad to say goodbye to them again.

The seafront would have the character of any ordinary English seaside town if it weren't for the stunning Georgian buildings; once the domain of royalty and aristocracy, venue for grand parties held by the holidaying wealth of the nation, now home to hotels and guest houses, cafés and trinket vendors. The beach, which would have been a place for the discreet and delicate to promenade under their parasols taking in the health-giving sea air, was now rammed full with deckchairs, inflatables, chips and herring gulls, pink flesh and arguing families. I'm not sure if George III was standing on his plinth horrified by what the place had become, or wishing there'd been blow-up dinosaurs and flip-flops when he was here. I sat on a bench with my head on Moth's knee and slept for an hour, then slept on the beach until the street lights came on.

"You won't be able to sleep here, you know. Soon as it gets dark the police'll move you off. Better to head out of town."

Two men stood on the sand, loaded down with rucksacks and carrier bags. They were as dirty as us, darkly tanned, hair pushed under hats. Backpackers possibly; homeless maybe. No, not backpackers, looking at the multi-pack boxes of food in the bags. Nor homeless, with that much food.

"Do you live here then?"

"No, out of town. Where are you heading?"

"Not sure." Moth was on his feet, but I didn't have the will to get up. "Campsites are all full, Ray's been ill, food poisoning maybe, so we can't walk on far today."

The older of the two looked down at me. His face relaxed a little, easing open the wrinkles to expose the white skin beneath, a face that had spent a long time in the elements, months squinting against the sun and wind. He sat down, but didn't let go of the bags. There was something in the way his clothes hung loose, something in the tight grip of his hand on the carrier bag.

"Hi, I'm John. So, what are you, backpackers then?" Something, too, in the way his grey hair curled from beneath the tattered woollen hat.

"Well, yes."

"That's a good decision, when you've got nowhere to go, to just keep moving. It's the staying still that drags people down. Yeah, there's plenty here that stay still for too long — they've given in and accepted that the streets are their home."

"How did you know? Are you an aid worker or something?"

"No, you give yourselves away. Lying there, propped on your rucksack with your arms still through the straps. A backpacker would have taken it off, but not you; what's in that pack's too important to you to let it go in town."

"Really?"

"Come with us, if you like. We live outside of town; you'll be able to camp there. Just for tonight though. It's quite a way, but we've got a van."

Rashly, or instinctively, we trusted them. Moth helped me to my feet, and we followed them to a van parked in the street. We lay on blankets in the back as the van left the street lights and headed away from the sea, into country lanes and darkness. I dozed on and off for half an hour, maybe more, until the van stopped on gravel. Getting out, we found ourselves in a woodland car park, huge pines rattling overhead in a stiff wind.

We followed John and Gav down woodland tracks in the darkness, heading deep into the forest by only the faint light of the moon. The trees thinned slightly and more light crossed the pine-needle path. Ahead of us, only faintly illuminated by low-powered battery lights, shapes emerged from between the trees. Tents, tarpaulins, shelters made from fallen branches. A village of forest dwellers, quietly sitting together, chatting, cooking food. John showed us a patch where we could put the tent, then we sat with them as Gav emptied the carrier bags from what had been their twice weekly shopping run. As the others took their purchases and went to their beds, John sat and told us about their home.

"Couldn't live in a town; when the countryside's in your bones you can't stay in those places, sucks the life out of you."

He was a farm worker, had been all his life. He'd lived in a tied cottage on the land where he worked, but when the farm was sold, the houses were split off from the land and bought as second homes; he became homeless. He found other work, but the jobs never came with a house and his wages couldn't cover an expensive rural rent. That's when he first camped in the wood. Soon, others joined him, until their camp grew into a fluid village of people that came and went as the need arose.

"At the most there's about thirty of us if everyone turns up at once, but usually we're about eighteen, give or take."

Most of them worked: part-time, insecure jobs, low wages, seasonal living that made it difficult to secure a rented home.

"But we can live here, keep a little self-respect. Some leave when things are good, come back when they go wrong. We keep it clean; we're not substance dependents like many on the streets, just country people; the countryside's our home but we've been priced out."

They kept their lives hidden, never lighting fires for fear of the smoke giving them away. In winter they used gas heaters and thick duvets, laying pine branches down to keep the mud at bay. In summer the life was easier; they slept under the tree canopy on warm nights with the smell of the pine all around.

"I'm sure some people know we're here, but we're careful not to be seen in a group; there's a few ways in and out. Don't know how much longer we'll be here for, though. There's talk of them clear-felling the forest; the purists want to return it to indigenous heath, like it would have been in Thomas Hardy's day. Thought they had forests then; didn't he write that book about forests? *Woodlanders*, that's it. They can't seem to see the beauty in what we have now."

"They were deciduous woodlands though, before the forestry plantations." I'd loved that book too.

"But the pines have been here for so long. They're as much a part of the landscape now as the old woods are. I know it's too dark for much life in here, but there's buzzards, they nest here every year, and foxes, badgers, woodcock, and sloe worms and adders in the heath at the edge and in the clearings. Where will the buzzards go? It's their home. It's our home."

We slept in the darkness of the tent, listening to the rush of wind through the branches, but warm and protected on the soft pine-needle bed.

The next morning John dropped us at Ferrybridge, on his way to work.

"Come back if you need somewhere. Well, this year anyway; after that there might not be a wood."

"Hope you find somewhere else if that's the case. Take care."

"You too."

As John drove away in the van, we stood on the pavement and looked down the long strip of road connecting the Isle of Portland to the mainland. It seemed to stretch on endlessly.

"Shall we miss Portland? Just take a slow few days along Chesil? I'm absolutely drained."

"Course. Not as if we're on a purist mission, is it?"

Chesil Beach isn't a beach at all, but a fifteen-metre-high, eighteen-mile-long bank of pebbles, running from the Isle of Portland in the east to beyond West Bay in the west. Believed to have been formed during a period of rising sea levels, this stretch of stones honed perfectly round through millennia of movement by the force of the sea is known as a barrier beach, or a tombolo. The pebbles are fist-sized near Portland, but only the size of a grape at West Bay, possibly showing that they were picked up from two separate pebble beds and then deposited here by the rising sea at the point of the breaking waves. Inland of the bank is the Fleet Lagoon, a tidal lagoon, cut off from the sea but still subject to its ebb and flow, as Portland is to the mainland. At Ferrybridge in the east, where the sea pushes in, the waters of the lagoon are saline, but at its western end, where freshwater streams feed in, the salinity is reduced by half. A vast area of land and sea in motion together, a never-ending partnership in which each of the couple loses and gains in equal measure, but neither can exist without the other.

It was easy walking alongside the lagoon, hazy sunlight and post-sickness frailty making the day dreamlike. Tiny huts scattered the landward side of the pebble bank and occasional rowing boats were pulled up beside them. A long stretch of wire fence topped by crows bordered the path, over fifty silent black birds perched a metre apart along the edge of an arable field. We paused, not wanting to pass the sentinel. In the Welsh mythological tale, the *Mabinogion*, the crow is the bringer of death, but also the form taken by those with magical powers, allowing them to escape from danger. In other cultures, they're believed to be a harbinger of change. Or just black birds, very weirdly lined up on a fence. Two steps further and they took off in a black, cawing cloud.

"Good job we're not superstitious then." Moth walked on, laughing, his outline shimmering in the heat haze from the dry ground, his footprints firm in the dust.

The path wound through reed beds and rifle ranges, coming out on to a single-track road and a collection of sheds painted in flaking blues and greens, peeling in the hot salt air. On a wooden plank bench in the shade of the shed sat three old men, gnarled, wizened and flaking like the paint, in vests, straw hats, baggy cotton drill trousers and bare feet. Oh no, more soothsayers. One spoke:

"Where're you heading?"

"West."

"That's a long way."

"Yep."

"There's a hotel, further on, beyond the swans."

The scrub hedge and dusty arable land carried on, flat and easy, our legs falling into a metronome of motion without thought. A white haze gathered in the crook of the lagoon, and cleared into a flock of white swans, over a hundred swimming, preening and landing.

"I thought he meant metaphorically, as in: 'you'll walk with a tortoise'; I wasn't expecting actual swans."

"Yeah, me too, this day's getting more surreal as it passes."

And beyond the swans was a hotel, Moonfleet Manor, from Falkner's tale of smuggling and dirty deeds.

"Let's go and have a look. I read the book when I was young; didn't know it was a real place."

We sat in the garden with hot water and one teabag and imagined moonlit nights and dastardly goings-on for most of the afternoon. Before we left I went to the toilets for a moment of luxurious flushing. As I came out of one cubicle, Julie came out of the other.

"What? Even more surreal."

We washed our hands in the hot water, smothering our sunburn in fantastic-smelling hand cream, as if we were old friends who'd known each other all our lives.

We walked on quietly together, through the syrupy air of the perfectly still evening. The sun was setting, lighting the sky in late July tones of gentle southern colour. The land ahead turned blue in the falling shadows and the lagoon fell silent, birdlife fading away as the water receded without wave or motion, leaving only channelled streams in the muddy sand. A small boat made its way back to the shore, a black shadow weaving quietly along rivulets of molten sky, disappearing as mud and stone blended together in the low rays of the last reflected light. A mist began to lift as the air turned silver and night blue, the reeds becoming dark silhouettes against the line of the pebble bank and the dimming sky. We pitched the tents amongst the marsh grasses, hearing only the evening calls of the wading birds and the rustle of seed heads in the breeze.

We continued together through the next day and camped near West Bexington, on the shingle ridge of the beach. Mackerel fishermen dotted the shore, the lights of their lanterns swinging through the night and the rattle of the ever-moving pebbles eerily punctuating the darkness. At first light they packed and left, buckets brimming with fish.

As we took the tent down the first of the tent poles broke, splitting through the plastic sleeve where it connected to the alloy ferrule. Dave rooted through his immense pack, reappearing with a pair of pliers, a small saw and a roll of duct tape. We cut through the broken plastic, bound the split and carried on.

We left Dave and Julie in West Bay to catch the bus for their return home. As we hugged them goodbye, we knew that this time really was the last. It had been a relief to share the path with them, a happy distraction from our own lives, and the sunlight was just a little dimmer without them. We bought a roll of duct tape and walked on, looking back over our shoulders for miles, expecting them to reappear.

Below Thorncombe Beacon in a cold south-westerly wind we squatted to examine the tent poles. The ends of almost all of the plastic tubes were beginning to split; we were merely days or a high wind away from the tent becoming useless. It was almost dark by the time we had carefully bound each end with tape and forced the now fat poles through the too narrow sleeves, easing each one gently into position.

"It should hold — just hope we never have to put it up in a hurry." I rubbed boiled-cabbage back rub on

Moth's shoulders as the wind increased and we packed everything loose into the rucksacks in case the duct tape didn't work.

It held, but first light brought rain squalling in on a strong wind, pushing us downhill and onwards, onwards, roaring through a maize field, clattering the tall stems before it blew past, agitated and eager to be gone as quickly as it came, leaving behind a dense, cloying mist. We walked slowly up Golden Cap in a cloud so thick there was no sign of why it was called Golden, but as the highest point on the south coast it had to be celebrated.

The trig point stood among clumps of broom, with other paths leading off in every direction — it was impossible to see where to. Our home in Wales had been deep in mountainous countryside and whenever we had a moment spare, we walked in the hills. The children were pre-school when they climbed their first mountain, but as they grew older it often took some imagination to encourage them to be out in the cold on an arduous walk. Whenever we reached a trig point Moth would jump on and plank for a photo, lying on his stomach on the column and pretending to fly, anything to cheer up kids who were ready to give in. It became a family tradition, so the sight of the Golden Cap trig point was too appealing, CBD or not.

"Do you think you can do it without hurting yourself?"

He dropped his pack down and putting his hands over the top of the column hoisted himself on. I waited for the cry of pain, the inevitable self-rebuke for having been so silly. It didn't come. He spread his arms and flew into the clouds, free and floating, for all the world as if he would live forever. I ran around taking photos as if it was the first time he'd flown, or the last.

"Maybe it's the cabbage rub."

His face was clear, he wasn't even hiding pain, and he was laughing. In the fog-bound heather we hugged and jumped, laughing, kissing, shouting. Was this possible? From the point of not being able to get out of bed, back to strong and in control of his limbs in just under two weeks. This shouldn't be possible. But it was. I should have noticed that I was no longer seeing the drag in his footprints, but it hadn't registered.

"Maybe it's because we had a rest in Weymouth. Maybe my body's adjusted quicker, like acclimatizing to altitude."

"But how? How can the stiffness have receded so quickly? On the north coast it took weeks."

"I've no idea; I knew it was feeling easier over the last couple of days, but I didn't dare hope."

"Do you think it could be something to do with oxygen? I know we thought it before, because the path makes you breathe so deeply. That huge wash of oxygen — can it somehow affect the brain? It can't be, though. If it was that simple, the hospital would just hand out oxygen tanks."

"I don't know. It's obviously got something to do with heavy endurance exercise. It must cause some sort of reaction that we don't understand. I don't know how it works, I just feel great." We jumped and danced in the fog of Golden Cap.

"Be careful on the stairs."

"Don't plan too far ahead."

"We don't need to — we've got Paddy for that. Even if everything he says is backwards."

CHAPTER
TWENTY

Accepting

Living with a death sentence, having no idea when it will be enacted, is to straddle a void. Every word or gesture, every breath of wind or drop of rain matters to a painful degree. For now we had moved outside of that. Moth was on death row, but he'd been granted the right to appeal. He knew CBD hadn't miraculously disappeared, but somehow, for a while, it was held at bay. While we had space to think clearly, when death wasn't hanging around the tent like a malevolent stalker, a thing to fear, Moth felt he had to say it.

"When it does come, the end, I want you to have me cremated."

There had been a spot in the back field of our farm, near the hedge with a view to the mountains, where we said we'd be buried, in the days when we thought it would be our home forever. But now there was no field, no religion, no place where he felt he could safely be left.

"Because I want you to keep me in a box somewhere, then when you die the kids can put you in, give us a shake and send us on our way. Together. It's bothered me more than anything else, the thought of us being apart. They can let us go on the coast, in the wind, and we'll find the horizon together."

I hung on to him, too choked to speak. It had been said; death had been acknowledged. He would fight, but eventually he'd lose. Moth had been strong enough to see this from the start; now I was calm enough to know it was true and let it be. We lay in the tent at the edge of Lyme Regis, on a patch of grass between the lobster pots and the chalets, and let death in. And life came with it. The jagged, shattered, lost fragments of our lives slowly, mercurially drawn back together.

Leaving the sea, we entered the woods, our packs weighed down with fossilized ammonites from the beach, relics of other lives, other millennia, from a time when we were fish. The trees closed behind us and we entered the Undercliff: an eerie, damp British jungle, created on Christmas Eve 1839, when eight million tonnes of soil slipped towards the sea leaving a huge chasm. Sheep, rabbits, a tea room and an area known as goat island were taken with it. A field of wheat slipped intact, and was harvested the following summer. Left alone, the slip has naturalized into seven miles of ferns, ivy and trees that dripped and oozed with water in the steady rain. A land changed forever in a moment, and now caught in it. Wild and untouched plants have grown in their own way, taking their own form, free to gnarl and twist and seed at will. The path is the only way in or out and it weaved on for eight miles before we finally emerged into the light.

Our strength seeming to increase by the day, we were in cruise control and the miles slipped easily by. Seaton and Beer were gone in the flash of a 1950s' time warp and we stopped on the beach at Branscombe to make food, nestling the stove on the shingle beach. Branscombe is still part of the Jurassic Coast, still within the World Heritage Site, yet in 2007 when the MSC *Napoli* ran into difficulties in the Channel, rather than take her to the much closer Falmouth Harbour, it was decided by the powers that be that the vast container ship should be taken to Portland. Inevitably she didn't make it and ended up a mile off the beach at Branscombe, an area of great importance for wintering sea birds and endangered seabed marine life. The ship began to list and flotsam washed up on the shore. Perfume, wine and BMW motorbikes. Hard as they tried, the authorities couldn't stop the scavengers, who were later said to have only been "helping in the clean-up operation". As we walked the beach, there was no sign of what had occurred seven years before, but when we left we did spot the shiny chrome of a motorbike in the shed behind the café. We camped on a perfectly flat mown field, which in 1935 had been given to the community by Mr Cornish. The common close to the field was a swathe of low undergrowth and we sat on a bench under silver birch trees, overlooking the lights of Sidmouth below. A badger walked quietly past, disappearing along one of the many intersecting paths through the bracken. Totally oblivious to the smell of people who hadn't seen a shower for days he disappeared into the green, only to quickly reappear down another path. Moments later he popped out of a further path only to end up back where he started from. He was either very fast or there were a few of them running through the bracken. Looking at the tracks in the heavy dew of the following morning, it seemed as if badgers hunt in packs. But it was a great thing that Mr Cornish and others like him had created safe havens for wildlife and walkers; they both needed sanctuary on this coast.

Since leaving Dorset and walking into south Devon, not only had the cliffs turned red, but there appeared to be a caravan park around every corner and finding somewhere to camp was becoming increasingly difficult. Leaving Budleigh Salterton in the dying light it seemed almost impossible. Darkness fell as we followed the path, trapped between high hedges and an impassable wire fence that bounded a golf course.

"Told you we should have gone back down to the beach."

"No, it was too close to the town."

"Better that than this — there's just nowhere."

We came to the top of a hill, gorse and brambles at shoulder height on both sides of the narrow path. Below us, the lights of Exmouth spread away into the distance, but in the foreground a grid of roads and stadium lighting marked a vast holiday park, resembling more closely a prison camp than somewhere you would choose to go for a holiday. There was nothing else for it; we climbed over the fence on to the golf course. The sixteenth hole was made for camping. Perfectly flat with a velvet-short sward of grass and a bench. Ideal. It was pitch dark, interrupted only by the glow from the lights below. The golf course stretched out inland, but to the seaward side, the undergrowth mounded up between us and the path six feet below, just enough to block us from the view of any early-morning dog walkers. If we were gone before the first golfers came, we'd be fine.

The tent poles fell out of the sack with the usual clatter. There was no need to be quiet; we were at least a mile from the nearest habitation — unless there was a house hidden somewhere in the gorse, which seemed unlikely. Anyway, we'd had no problems with people on the whole of the path — crumbling cliffs, man-eating ants, over-friendly dogs, but never humans. All the same, a rustle in the undergrowth made us feel uneasy. We stood silently, frozen to the spot. It could be just a badger or a fox; there'd been plenty of those and they gave us no cause for alarm. We heard the rustle again, a few metres to the left. The noise was circling around the perimeter fence, in the undergrowth, not on the path. Maybe it was a deer, perhaps a little muntjac? Was that a head and shoulders that sprang up, then disappeared? We crouched down below the thorn bushes. Then we saw him. A black figure, clinging to the fence, looking over the golf course, pale hair catching the lights from below. There was no other sound as he stood there; hopefully he was alone, but there could be others, hiding, waiting. We stayed low, knees locking, trying not to breathe loudly. He moved around, back to the right. Was he heading away, following a small path that cut inland? We waited forever, until we couldn't squat any longer and had to stand. With a start the man shot up out of the gorse two metres in front of us and fell backwards through the bushes. We heard him scrambling around, and then running off down the path. Would he come back? Would he come back alone? We daren't put the tent up and sat on the bench expecting him to reappear with back-up at any minute.

By midnight we gave up and pitched the tent, cold and wet from the rising dew. Too tired to make food we ate a fudge bar, but hadn't fallen asleep when we heard a deep rumbling like distant thunder. Not just a sound, but a sensation that rose through the ground. Was he coming back with an army? We lay still, waiting for voices that didn't come. Getting out of the tent into the starlit night there wasn't a sound, not a movement, except for a small boat that moved into the bay, its light swinging rhythmically across the cliffs.

Before six the next morning we packed the tent away and sat on the bench to make tea. The sun was rising, bathing the red cliffs in rich rust colours and lighting the sixteenth hole. Other than the disturbed dew it was impossible to tell we'd camped there. We'd mastered wild camping, turning "leave no trace" into a fine art. A man in the distance was walking his dog across the course, meandering between the holes, but undeniably making his way across to us. Eventually he walked on to the sixteenth green.

"Hello. Beautiful spot for a sunrise, isn't it?" Moth as usual ploughed straight in with his charm offensive. The man looked at us and grunted, two dogs running around his feet as he walked around the green, clearly

316

checking for damage to his grass. But there was none; we'd carefully removed any loose earth as we'd withdrawn each tent peg.

"You'll be off when you've had your breakfast then?"

"Yes of course, just came up for the sunrise."

He grunted and walked away, his white hair catching the morning rays. We watched him go with relief as the water boiled for a second cup of tea.

We headed down towards the holiday camp and very soon the source of the rumbling was obvious. A large earth slip had occurred only a couple of hundred metres away. A long stretch of red earth and stones had slid into the water and now boiled around the base of the cliff in a rust-coloured stew. The whole stretch of land between the golf course and Straight Point looked as vulnerable as the section that had gone. At any moment the holiday park might have less grass to cut and our friend with white hair could have more to worry about than the movement of a few grains of soil.

Through the regimented rows of caravans and chalets, down the long pavement walk into Exmouth and before we knew it the Jurassic Coast was behind us. We bought rice, tuna and chocolate bars and caught the ferry across the River Exe to Starcross. Leaving the jetty, the path followed the road and then wove in and out between the railway line and patches of scrub and concrete. We finally wandered out on to Dawlish Warren and camped behind the visitor centre on the nature reserve as it was getting dark.

"Just looking at the map, we've got another thirty miles of this. Built-up areas, railway line, seafront.

There'll be nowhere to camp. What do you reckon if we blow the last of the cash and get the train, then the bus to Brixham? Back into open countryside and we'll be fine. It's that or we could find ourselves in a doorway somewhere and we don't need to do that." Moth was thumbing backwards and forwards through a section of the guidebook.

I thought about our restless night on the golf course and realized that our nerves probably wouldn't take many more nights like that.

"Okay. Feels weird to miss another chunk, but maybe we'll come back one day and do this and Portland."

"Don't think it matters. It's not a pilgrimage. Is it?"

We got off the bus in Brixham and wound our way back on to the coast at Sharkham Point. Life was back to normal. Rucksacks full of rice and noodles, thirty pounds in our pockets and my nose red and peeling. It was August, peak tourist season, and people were everywhere on a very popular stretch of coast. The route to Plymouth would pass through busy towns and bustling seafronts and would entail at least five ferries. Having caught the train, we now wouldn't be able to afford anything except ferry tickets for the next week.

"Well, here's a thought. We've just dawdled along since we started again and it's been fairly easy." If you say so, Moth. "What if we were to up the pace a bit? Get through this section and over the last ferry as quickly as we can. We don't know how much the ferries will cost, so at least this way they'll be behind us and we'll know what cash we have left to buy food."

"What do you mean, up the pace?"

"Well, try and keep up with Paddy."

"You are kidding me."

"We could do it."

"Preferred you when you were ill."

Man Sands, Long Sands, Scabbacombe Sands, Ivy Cove, Pudcombe Cove, Kelly's Cove, Newfoundland Cove, oh look a herring gull, Mill Bay Cove, ferry, Compass Cove, Combe Point, sleep. The rain whipped in, foaming froth around the base of the Dancing Beggars rocks off the headland, easing to drizzle as we took the tent down.

Moth looked at the map.

"It's going to be a big one today. Do you think you can do it?"

"Do I think I can do it? You're the one that's ill. But this is mad; we could do a few ferries then just wait it out until we get more money."

"Then it'll be the same next week, daren't eat because we don't know how much the ferries are going to cost. Let's get it over with, and then we'll know where we stand. There's a great beach after Plymouth; we can hang out there for a week if you like."

"Yes, I like. So are we going to walk then or what?" What was going on? Stronger, energy levels rising, mind clearing. But I didn't dare hope; there'd come a point when we stopped, then we'd see how he really was.

We sat in the reed beds between the main road and the Slapton Ley nature reserve: a long shingle bar separating a mile and a half of freshwater lake from the

319

salt water of the Channel. An information board at the head of the lake offered the chance to see a profusion of wildlife, including grebes and otters. One mangy-looking heron stood passively rocking on one leg, and a few sparrows squabbled in the reed heads, but definitely no grebes or otters. Maybe the wildlife was clustered on the other shore, away from the constant stream of traffic passing along the main road that topped the shingle bank.

In Beesands we stopped to enjoy a moment of virtual eating outside the pub, as a young couple tucked into piled plates of fish and salad, half a bakery of crusty bread and a dessert ballooning with cream and chocolate. We held our breath as the path narrowed on a rocky ledge around Start Point, but as the drizzle lifted away to leave a clear evening we could see all the way back to the Isle of Portland, or thought we could, almost. At Prawle Point we tucked the tent into a dip out of the wind and heated up some rice and tuna.

"Could really have eaten that food at the pub."

"You probably couldn't even if you had it. My appetite's disappeared."

"Mine too really; it just looked great."

The next morning should have stimulated an appetite, with a whole section of the coast being named after the contents of a butcher's shop. Gammon Head, Ham Stone, Pig's Nose, ferry. Salcombe. We walked through the town quickly, trying hard not to look at food and on around the rocky, exposed Bolt Head. We pitched the tent, finally, on Bolt Tail and watched the lights of ships heading into Plymouth.

The heat increased as we took the ferry across the estuary from Bantham to Bigbury-on-Sea. The aura emanating from us smelt faintly like a dead animal. The family already sitting in the small wooden ferry shuffled ever further down towards the ferryman as we chugged across the estuary. By the time we reached the other side of the short crossing, the other passengers were so close to the ferryman at the rear that the front of the boat was starting to rise out of the water. We gave up on our race through the ferries and leapt into the sea, my parched skin sucking up the cool water, layers of grime and sweat washing away on the tide. We swam in circles, floating on the gentle waves until all we smelt of was ozone and salt. Our filthy clothes soaked in a rock pool while we dried in the sun. My hair, which had taken the winter to recover, had resumed its bird's-nest form and my skin, which had slowly shed the layers of cracked dryness, was rapidly returning to a leathery state that seemed to move separately to the muscles underneath.

Then onwards as the afternoon cooled. Refreshed, invigorated, our wet clothes hanging from our rucksacks. As the light began to fade we stood on Beacon Point and watched the sun dip behind the rippling inland horizon of Dartmoor, before dropping down towards the crossing point of Erme Mouth. The tide was going out but the water was too high to cross, so we sat under the trees and ate the last of the rice. Darkness fell and slowly a moon began to rise, glinting on the receding water. We could have waited until mid-morning and crossed then, but we walked out into the thigh-deep river, picking our way slowly across by moonlight, a tawny owl calling from the trees along the bank. We camped in a field beyond the wood and listened to the owl as he moved up and down the riverbank.

The morning came in waves of rain, soft and floating through, muslin curtains of water stroking my face in the breeze. We shook the tent and rolled it, knowing it would be saturated when it came out later. Conversation petered out as we fell into our own thoughts, walking on in silence through the drizzle. Plymouth stretched ahead and it felt like a barrier, a huge urban doorway through which we would pass into an unknown future. Just a few days to the west of Plymouth lay Polruan and the end of our trail. The next two ferry crossings had become a symbol of the final leg of our journey. The path had given us certainty, a sense of security that came with knowing that tomorrow and the next day and the next we would pack up the tent, put one foot in front of the other and walk. I was afraid and, although it was unsaid, I knew Moth was too. Not just of an unknown future in a strange place, among people we had yet to meet, or of financial difficulties yet to come, or the practicalities of starting again. But a much bigger, more-resounding fear than that. When eventually we had to stop walking, as we would have to in order to start living back in the world, what would happen to Moth? The question followed us like a flock of gulls that could smell our tuna. We camped above Wembury, not wanting to go around the corner and allow Plymouth into view.

At Mount Batten, we faced more everyday questions. The sort that had become the normal problems of our life. Should we take the ferry across to the Barbican for three pounds and then from the ferry terminal there take the long crossing to Cawsand for eight pounds, or the short one to Mount Edgcumbe for three? Or keep the money in the purse and take the long hike of five or six miles through the city and hope we reached the ferry point before the last crossing? Cawsand was nearer to the open headland so easier to find somewhere to camp, but would cost more. However, although it was cheaper, passing through Mount Edgcumbe Country Park in the evening would mean encountering the inevitable patrols of the deer park and would probably result in us hiking in the dark to find somewhere to camp. Or if we walked through the city to save the crossing fare and didn't reach the ferry terminal before the last ferry, having to find somewhere to sleep in the city. Too many choices. We had fifteen pounds left, one pack of noodles and half a tube of wine gums. We opted to cross to the Barbican, then the connecting ferry to Mount Edgcumbe and have time in between to spend the remaining nine pounds on food to last for the next two days.

We got off the ferry and wandered through the arty, wealthy area of Plymouth, finally finding a shop that sold food that wasn't already on a plate, bought what we could and wandered back to the ferry with half an hour to spare before the last crossing. We waited on the metal walkway with a group of others and ate bread rolls and bananas. The ferry didn't come. The people in the queue started to get twitchy. It still didn't come. Finally a ferry pulled in and we all drifted towards it, but the ferryman pulled the barrier across.

"No, I'm not going to Mount Edgcumbe. There won't be another one going there 'til tomorrow."

"Well, where is it? We've waited for an hour."

"Stuck on a sandbank. Misjudged the tide, di'n' he. He's going nowhere tonight."

The others in the queue marched away, grumbling about long bus rides and taxi fares, but we just stood on the bouncing metal gangplank.

"Well, that's shit."

"Fudge bar?" Moth sat down on his rucksack.

"So, what now? Remind me why we've never made plans before. Oh I know, because they always end up like this." I could feel a flush of panic; it was not a place I wanted to be.

"Tour of Plymouth then? Nothing better to do."

"I thought we'd always be able to avoid sleeping in a town. Too many people about — anything could happen."

"Let's just have a walk around; it'll kill a few hours anyway."

Leaving the well-heeled Barbican, full of tourists and night-outers, chatting, laughing, fuelled by pre-party drinks, we wandered aimlessly, finding ourselves in the centre of the city as the street lights were coming on. Past the shopping centre, then on through the university buildings.

324

"Next month I'll be part of that uni; now I'm walking through it without enough money to catch the bus."

"You're going to be a student; we still won't have enough money to catch the bus."

As darkness fell, under the underpass a homeless person was bedding down on the concrete, arranging his cardboard and sleeping bag. Decent bag; I wondered where he'd got it from. Much better quality than the ones we'd had last year, yet he looked as if he'd been out for a long time.

"Got any money, mate? Just need some food for the night. Haven't eaten today."

"Haven't got any, I'm sorry." I could feel Moth's mind searching the contents of the food bag. "I've got some bread and a tin of tuna though."

"Thanks, mate, that's dead generous of you."

We left the archway, went back out to the open pathways and sat on a bench watching people as they rushed through their lives. A man came and sat on the bench opposite and stared at us. I tried to focus my eyes elsewhere, but he kept staring. In his late forties or fifties — it was hard to tell; time spent on the streets ages people in a way that doesn't happen on the sofa in front of the television. A grubby pair of cargo trousers, generic trainers, a ripped fleece over a hoodie gave him away, but the brand new Carhartt baseball cap was an incongruity that I couldn't place. Maybe he was looking at us with the same thoughts.

"Can't make you out. What you doing here?" He got up and walked across the paving to sit on our bench. I

325

felt a slight sense of fear, and it was hard to grasp why. Was it coming from an irrational anxiety in my other life, the one in which I myself hadn't been homeless? Or was it because we were now in a city and being approached by anyone was making me jumpy? "Are you hikers? You look like it, but then there's something about you that tells me there's more going on here."

"Homeless hikers. Just here for the night." Moth didn't seem to feel threatened at all.

"The hiking homeless — I like that. Well, you won't be alone tonight; there's quite a few of us around. Where're you going to sleep? Got to be careful not to crowd anyone's spot. They can get a bit touchy about that. I'm Colin. Fancy a beer?"

"Haven't got any money, sorry."

"No, I've got a beer; want one?"

Moth took the can, taking a drink then passing it over.

"Only got these 'cause my daughter came by today. It's my birthday; she gave me the beers and this hat, nice, very nice."

"You've got a family and you don't live with them?"

"No, well, yeah, had it all, wife, kids, house. Then it all just fell apart. Embarrassment to them now."

We sat in silence. What was there to say? He didn't have to explain to us how easy it is for a life to fall apart. A younger man walked across the open paving, beanie hat pulled low on his face, a ripped parka hanging loose.

"Oh fuck, here we go, careful what you say. G'day, Dean my man, how are ya?"

Dean was younger, a swagger in his manner, yet his thin, hollow-cheeked appearance showed that his life was a struggle.

"Drinking already, man, without me?"

"Yeah, well, it's my birthday. Present, weren't they."

Dean took the remaining can, clearly his by right.

"Drinking with strangers instead of me, man, that's not the way. Who the fuck are you anyway?"

"Don't worry, man, they're the hiking homeless, just on their way now, aren't you?"

"Drinking with strangers, man, what the fuck?"

The man in the underpass rolled his cardboard, put it under his arm and walked away down the tunnel. Dean pressed his face hard up against Colin, who was gesturing us away with his hand.

"Fuck off, you two, don't know why you're hanging around here anyway."

We walked away slowly, though inside I wanted to run. By the time we were fifty metres away they were fighting on the bench.

"Feel like that was our fault and we've abandoned him." I'd wanted to leave, but now I felt responsible.

"It's nobody's fault. You could tell by the way Colin reacted. It's probably the same every night."

We wandered through the city, invisible to the evening revellers, heading towards the Hoe in the hope of finding a quiet spot. But every side street or bench seemed to have a resident already. Either in a sleeping bag, curled under a blanket, or just foetal on the ground, trying to hold in some warmth. Official figures in the autumn of 2014 put the number of rough sleepers in Plymouth at thirteen. If that was true, as in Newquay, we met them all that night and some.

We found a patch of grass by Smeaton's Tower and unrolled the mattresses and sleeping bags at the most hidden edge, not daring to put the tent up as it would be far too obvious. It didn't get dark, the street lights giving a permanent twilight. I felt exposed, vulnerable, as I never had on the path. The wild rawness of nature had never made me nervous, but here in the land of densely packed humanity I felt fear for the first time in my homeless life, every footstep, raised voice or car door making me jolt with adrenalin.

As light started to break we packed the sleeping bags away and sat on a bench to boil some water, relieved that the night was over.

"How can they live like this? It's exhausting."

"Like everything else, I suppose; they just get used to it."

Wandering the empty streets as the light lifted into day, we saw bodies emerging from piles of rags and stretching into the daylight. Life went on; the same routines to be played out again and again.

Passing a cash machine, we stopped to check the account, unsure what day it was, whether there would be money there or not, and gratefully took the thirty pounds it offered. We found a café that was open and sat at the window sharing a sausage sandwich, watching the morning city start to move. Between the bohemian shop owners and restaurant workers, a man shuffled down the narrow street with his hood up, barely hiding

328

his bruised face. Moth bought another sandwich and had it wrapped to go.

"Colin," he called towards the man in the street, who stopped moving, and turned around hesitantly.

"Oh jeez, it's only you, man. Don't normally come down this end, but had to get out of Dean's way last night. He's a bit fuelled-up just now. Got no brakes, that one."

"Are you all right? You look a mess. Here, I bought you a sandwich."

"What? You bought me a sandwich? Fuck, thanks. Oh, sausage, my favourite."

"We're off to catch the ferry. Take care, mate."

"And you, homeless hikers. I might do that myself one day: just go for a hike. Yeah, one day."

CHAPTER
TWENTY-ONE

Salted

The tent rattled and shook in the strong wind whipping around Penlee Point and into Plymouth Sound. Below the stone wall of Queen Adelaide's Chapel, the gale caught us full on. We should have had more concern for the frailty of the duct-tape-encased tent poles, but after Plymouth we were happy to be back at the edge. Devon behind us now, we were back in Cornwall and so close to the finish line of Polruan. The fabric flapped and the poles creaked as we watched a giant boat of lights sailing out of the sound, floating in a pool of glowing yellow. In another life we had been passengers on that ferry, sailing overnight to Santander in northern Spain. The children were small, we were in our early thirties and life appeared to be falling into place. The lights grew smaller, fainter, until finally they disappeared. Our old life had sailed away, and we let it go, turning our eyes to the west with a fizz of hope.

At Rame Head the wind lifted from the sea on both sides, colliding in a Mohican of air, sending the gulls into a spin before jetting them away at high speed. Banks of white cloud raced through, leaving patches of blue sea spray and the endless sands of Whitsand Bay spreading before us. There were only a few days of walking left, time to stop and rest, to be still, a quiet moment before the start of a new life. The rocky hillside of bracken, blackthorn and gorse fell in a steep incline to the sea, and scattered intermittently along the miles of its length were sheds and chalets balanced on platforms cut from the slope. An old man passed us through a thicket of thorn trees, so we stopped to remark on them.

"This is so unusual, all these shacks, spread out like that; we've seen nothing like it on the whole path."

"They were plots given to people between the wars. The local farmer rented them out on peppercorn rents and people just came, cutting platforms on the cliff, putting up tents and shacks. Then after the Second World War, others came who'd lost their homes in the bombing of Plymouth. That's how my family came here, and they just stayed; well, why wouldn't you? They've passed down through generations, been added to and stabilized over the years. The Council own the land now. They tried to throw us off, but we won the right to stay. Much bigger rent now though. Nearly all holiday homes of course, like everywhere else."

The path wound on through the undergrowth until we found our way down to the beach and dropped our packs on the rocks. The cliff climbed high behind, an endless expanse of sand spreading west and a pale blue sea crashing into white foam, the noise blocking out every sound. There is a quote, thought to be by Icelandic author Thorbergur Thordarson, which goes: "When the surf was high, the sound of the sea was one continuous roar, heavy, deep, dark, sombre, with all kinds of variation, and at its height you felt it also came from the very earth beneath your feet." This was the Icelandic sea, part of that same body of water that wraps the northern hemisphere in one continuous, deafening roar, making the earth tremble beneath my feet.

"We'll find somewhere above the high-tide line; looks promising to the west."

It wasn't worth trying to shout above the noise, so we walked silently across the sands, my thoughts drifting back to the shacks on the cliff and the families who came here looking out to sea, looking for space, shattered from the war, picking up timber and saws to build a shelter and start a new life. How can there be so few individuals who understand the need for people to have a space of their own? Does it take a time of crisis for us to see the plight of the homeless? Must they be escaping a war zone to be in need? As a people can we only respond to need if we perceive it to be valid? If the homeless of our own country were gathered in a refugee camp, or rode the seas in boats of desperation, would we open our arms to them? Our native homeless don't fit that mould; we prefer to think their plight is self-induced and their numbers few, yet over 280,000 households in the UK claim to have no home and the percentage of those who arrive at that state because of some kind of addiction is small. If they — we — all stood together, men, women, children, we would look very different to one man alone in a shop doorway, addicted to anything that gives him a means of escape.

How would we be viewed then? Two hundred and eighty thousand? More, less? The true numbers are unknown. Refugees from western civilization, cut adrift from life in a boat that rarely finds a harbour.

"Can you imagine if Plymouth Council gave Colin a patch on the cliff?"

"Or us?"

"I'd build a shed on a ledge. I think I'd stay there forever."

It was difficult to say where the high-tide line was; different levels of sea debris showed that the sea battered into this bay without restraint, stopping only when it was ready. We scrambled up a small rocky spit of land and found a relatively flat patch in the undergrowth, pitching the tent facing across the Channel, and took a deep breath.

When daylight came we went to the beach and walked its full extent and back again. When the tide was fully out we foraged for seaweeds, adding slimy shreds to noodles to make a foamy green pan of slippery food. It's slime-to-taste value didn't equate and so we stuck to bladderwrack, steaming it with tins of tuna and gristly limpets popped off the rocks straight into the pan. Groups of oystercatchers gathered to run together along the flat sand, rhythmically dipping their heads in an orange-booted line dance. We swam in the frothing incoming tide, surfing in on powerful waves of salt water that could have touched the shores of Iceland, Spain or America, a roaring broil that may have travelled thousands of miles or just two. We lay on our backs on hot sand and baked in the sun. Salt-crusted, preserved. Later, in the darkness of the green dome I felt his hand brush against my thigh, and with it the same electric pulse of need there had always been. Silence descended; everything stopped; I didn't move, afraid to ignite a want that wouldn't be satisfied, or lose a hope I'd held on to forever. He hesitated for a long moment, his hand stretching hot against my cold skin, a moment that hung between us in an unanswered question.

Days passed. Clouds moved in from the south-west, white rolling cumuli disappearing inland. Winds changed direction: damp and light from the west; dry and cooling from the east; colder from the north-west, carrying hints of another season soon behind; then gently from the south, summer not quite yet spent. The heat reflected off the flat rocks, less jagged than those that surrounded them in the cove. We dried clothes on them, sat the stove flat on them to cook limpets, cracked an egg on them in the hope that it might fry, but when it didn't, scraped it up and scrambled it, picking out bits of sand and grit. We lay on them, crisping to leathery brown. Bodies that fourteen months earlier were hunched and tired, soft and pale, were now lean and tanned, with a refound muscularity that we'd thought lost forever. Our hair was fried and falling out, our nails broken, clothes worn to a thread, but we were alive. Not just breathing through the thirty thousand or so days between life and death, but knowing each minute as it passed, swirling around in an exploration of time. The rock gave back the heat as it followed the arc of the sun, gulls called in differing tones as the tide left the shore and then returned, my hands wrinkled with age and my thighs changed to a new shape with passing miles, but when he pulled me to him and kissed me with an urgency that wasn't in doubt, with a fervour that wouldn't fail, time turned. I was ten million minutes and nineteen years ago, I was in the bus stop about to go back to his house, knowing his parents weren't home, I was a mother of toddlers stealing moments in a walk-in wardrobe, we were us, every second of us, a long-marinated stew of life's ingredients. We were everything we wanted to be and everything we didn't. And we were free, free to be all those things, and stronger because of them. Skin on longed-for skin, life could wait, time could wait, death could wait. This second in the millions of seconds was the only one, the only one that we could live in. I was home, there was nothing left to search for, he was my home.

Days passed. Heavy driving rain came from the west in banks of purple angry cloud; forked lightning danced across the sea; light rain drifted from the south in gentle cloaks of dampness falling from impenetrable grey skies. Dark black nights were lit by endless pinpoints of light, sparking with shooting stars in profusion, the late summer Perseids, meteor showers from another world. We gathered water from a stream gushing down the rock face after the rain, drinking at will, washing salt from dried throats and skin. Fat black dung beetles scurried around the low vegetation and common blue butterflies dusted the air as the sun returned, bringing a cooler, gentler warmth than before. Ever conscious that Moth shouldn't be still for too long, we walked and swam through the days, but we were rested. Strong but peaceful, held at the ocean's edge, out of time, closer to it than ever before. A dog walker came twice a day and peered down at us from the path above. We had been there for over a week, our food supplies had run out, limpets had lost their appeal and it was time to move on.

The path wound gently on and off the road until it hit the concrete surrounding Tregantle Fort. Built in the nineteenth century to ward off the French, it became a gas school during the Second World War, preparing soldiers for the horrors of gas attacks. We took deep breaths of crystal-clean air and walked on, ever grateful not to have lived through that time. Beyond the tiny village of Portwrinkle the cliffs became craggier, steeper and gnarled, more Cornish, thick with undergrowth. Scrambling through the gorse and over a broken fence as the wind picked up and heavy banks of cloud began to build, we found a relatively flat patch in a field on the highest, most exposed spot there could have been. There was no best way to pitch the tent in a wind that spiralled in every direction. We huddled and crossed our fingers as rain lashed in on gale-force winds, ripping against the thin synthetic fabric and duct-taped poles, pushing at the side of the tent in a deafening growl of wild power. We lay awake, waiting for the poles to break as they distorted into weird elliptical angles. But they held, and as dawn came the wind died and we slept until the sun was bright through

336

racing clouds. The tent had ridden the storm, battered, bent, but not broken.

Coves of blue, green and black slipped by, the colours of Cornwall, always lit by the line of white water breaking at the base of the black cliffs. The end was so close we could almost see it. Soon we would be back on Pencarrow Head, and then we would have to begin the search for student accommodation in the hope that the security of a student loan would override our dismal credit rating. And if we failed?

The path dropped down into Looe, a fishing village split in two by the river, its narrow streets filled with tourists. We squeezed awkwardly through bus trips of old ladies and children crying over lost ice creams. Cutting up an alleyway in the hope of avoiding the crush, we came to a dead end at a tiny three-tabled café. The red-haired Polish waitress brought us a pot of tea for one, with two cups.

"They're very big packs for people your age. Where are you going?"

"West on the coastal path."

"And where have you come from? Lots of walkers come through; usually they start in Seaton, did you?"

Moth looked over and raised his eyebrows: was that Seaton four miles east, or one of the many other Seatons on the south coast? They were starting to blur.

"No, Poole in Dorset."

"But that's another county."

"That's right, with Devon in between."

"And where are you sleeping, in guest houses?"

"No, in the tent, wild camping."

"That's the most amazing thing I've heard. And you've walked all that way, and you're so old. I must tell my friend — she's always saying she wants to do something adventurous but she has no money. I'll tell her about you. Old people, just walking and sleeping in a tent, that's an inspiration."

"Not so old."

We walked out of the village, dirty, threadbare, but strangely lighter. Inspirational? What a warming thought. A young woman on the opposite pavement waved to us and ran over the road, her red hair blowing wildly in the gusting wind.

"My friend phoned me. She said run out and see the old people with big rucksacks. Are you really sleeping in a tent? How far have you walked?" Obviously the friend of the girl at the café must have shared the same box of hair dye.

"From Poole, but last year from Minehead to Polruan. In a day or two we'll have finished the whole path."

"The whole path? How long is this path?"

"Six hundred and thirty miles, but we've missed about forty of them. One day we'll go back and do the bits we've missed, but not this year."

"That's amazing. I want to do something big and life-changing like that, but it's scary, it puts me off."

"Scary? You've come to a foreign country to work — how can going for a walk be scary compared with that?"

"A group of us came together, just a gap-year sort of thing. No, what you're doing is an expedition, an adventure, a trial. It's what I want; I want to know what I can do. Gap-year work hasn't given me what I need. I need something, something inside."

"Then you must do it. If you feel you have a question, you must answer it. Do it before you go home."

"I will, I will, and when I do I'll be thinking of you. Old people walking."

The path rose steeply up a series of endless steps with wide blue views, back across Portnadler Bay to St George's Island and beyond. We sat at the top, struggling to catch our breath.

"Are we really getting old? How many times have people said that to us now?" I tried to run my fingers through my hair, but they got stuck in the tangle.

"Well, we're not young, are we? Think I need oxygen."

"You know what I mean."

"So what if we are? Who cares? Not as if we haven't lived, is it? Anyway, what was all that 'you must answer your inner question' rubbish?"

"It's not rubbish. If we hadn't done this there'd always have been things we wouldn't have known, a part of ourselves we wouldn't have found, resilience we didn't know we had. Like the court case. If we hadn't tried to defend ourselves we'd be plagued by what if? So we lost — at least we found the truth, and we're here now knowing we did everything we could and we still couldn't stop it, so no regrets. If we hadn't walked this path, we'd have waited for a council house, hidden ourselves away and given in. Who knows how far you would have deteriorated? We'd be bitter, angry and muttering 'what if' into our milky tea. Or we could just have let it all go and found ourselves on the streets, lost like Colin. Most people go through their whole lives without answering their own questions: What am I, what do I have within me? The big stuff. What a waste."

"All right, Yoda, I was only joking."

"What do you think I'd look like with red hair?"

"Please don't."

The headland eased forward; mid-afternoon and there was a cooler chill in the air. Not the damp feel of approaching rain, but the softening, cooling suggestion of late August when the heat changes and there's a smell of dewy nights and cobwebbed mornings to come. The end of the trail was near, just a day away. Moth would begin his degree in less than three weeks; we would have to find a room in a shared house somewhere, although the thought of a room in a house full of teenagers made me shrivel a little inside. I'd already done that and thankfully they grew up. The only alternative was to hope for a long-term pitch on a campsite that was keeping its toilet block open for the winter. I tried not to think about it but took out Paddy Dillon and stroked the familiar, comforting plastic cover. Minehead to Polruan was bound by an elastic hair band, as was Poole to Looe, only two meagre pages remained free, untrodden. Very soon all the pages of *The South West Coast Path: Minehead to South Haven Point* would be held tight by a frayed black elastic band; there would be nowhere left to go but into the future, whatever that was.

Down steps, like all the steps, steep and merciless to the little cove of Talland Bay, the path winding its way between the benches of a café on the edge of a holiday park. We dropped our packs and found a teabag to dip into yet another scrounged pot of hot water.

"Bugger, the car won't start, again."

A small, delicate woman with a strong northern accent sat down on the bench next to us. "It's only just back from the garage and it's gone again — always does when you're in some nowhere land like this. Oh, sorry, not from the caravans, are you?"

"No, we're just passing on the coastal path."

"Oh, coastal path, should have noticed the rucksacks. The days will be getting shorter soon — where are you heading for? Home soon, I would have thought; not all the way at this time of year, surely?"

"Just heading west. We don't actually have a home to go back to." Moth had stopped pretending we'd sold our house, and was telling the truth to anyone who asked, amusing himself with the reactions. I tightened the straps on my pack, preparing to leave, which was the normal process after Moth had told people we were homeless, and wild camping. Normally they became uncomfortable and we set off.

"So you're actually homeless?"

"Yep, that's us." I put my pack on ready to go.

Amazingly, the woman didn't flinch.

"Come inside the café — it's chilly out here. I'll get some coffees, and you can tell me more about your trail."

"What about the car?"

"Sick of the damn thing. I'll get a taxi."

The café was warm, dry and full of the smell of seaweed and sweet chilli sauce, with views out to sea across beds of bladder-wrack. Over hot mugs of coffee Moth spun a story of golden summers spent under canvas, of changing weather unfolding around two people living wild in nature. Of a narrow path alongside the busy world, but as separate from it as if it were in another dimension. The woman, Anna, sat mesmerized, caught by his stories, spellbound as people always are. He could have been reading from *Beowulf*.

"And now it's the end of the summer, where are you going to go?"

"We have to stop. I'm going to uni next month, so we'll have to find somewhere to stay."

"What, as a student? At your age?"

"A late start, I know, but a fresh one hopefully."

"Do old people get student loans?"

"Yes, although I could be dead before I've paid it back."

Anna sat quietly for a moment, looking from Moth, to me, then back again.

"Look, I have a flat in Polruan. My tenants are moving out tomorrow but I haven't advertised it yet; I was going to do the photos when they'd gone." Moth went very still on the seat next to me. "You could rent it. If you want. It'd be perfect for you: the coastal path runs past the front door."

Was this real, could it actually be happening? Stay calm, keep breathing.

"You'd let us rent, even after we've told you our situation?"

"Yes, of course. If you're a student and you're getting a loan or grant or whatever, I'm sure that'll be enough to cover the rent. It's only a small place; it's not much."

"Do you really mean that?"

"Yes." Anna laughed "I like you, so why not?" Her taxi came and she left the café, waving. "See you tomorrow night."

We clutched the napkin with the address scribbled on it. Our address.

The shock of something going right is almost as powerful as when it goes wrong. We stared at each other not knowing what to say, as if by speaking we might wake from a dream and it wouldn't be real. Then together we ran out of the café and leapt and shrieked in the bladderwrack beds. The young Costa Rican café owner came out to join us and we danced in a circle like children.

"Why are we dancing?"

"Because we have a roof."

"Is this a great thing?"

"The greatest."

"Then we should dance more."

We would have passed through Polperro as the lights were coming on in the pub, but that night we ran in and bought two beers, one each. We had the deposit and first month's rent. We had noodles in the pack and a student loan coming in a few weeks. And a roof. Could life be any better than that?

We pitched our tent one final time, crouched amidst scrub on the cliffside, with a view out of the door across the Channel. The coast to the east stretched away into the darkness: I couldn't see it but I could feel its presence. Our long path was nearly over, littered with the past that we had dragged with us. The cool, damp wind wet my face and I knew that, at last, I could turn away and look to the west and a future less than a day's walk away.

"It can't be a coincidence that we'll be living where our path ends. Not just now, but last year too. It has to be fate."

"I'll give you that — it is weird. But I'll stick with coincidence."

We closed the tent flap against the southerly wind for the last time. I was exhilarated by the sudden, unexpected end to our homeless life, but what would happen when I woke up and wasn't putting my rucksack on to walk for another day on the cliffs? What would I be, who would I be? I didn't know, but it was all right not to; the past was on another headland and I was happy to leave it there. I could at last look to the future with hope.

We packed the tent in bright sunlight, carefully folding the duct-taped poles, and turned the page on Paddy, slipping the last page under the hair band. There were no more loose pages. The last rollercoaster took us up and down in an eddying climax of hills, combes and coves. A white painted landmark pointed down to a perfect, short-grassed platform. The ideal spot that we always looked for at seven in the evening, but as usual we found it at midday.

Not a person in sight, except for a man on the grass lip above the rocks. He was dressed as if he was on safari in the 1950s: stone-coloured long shorts and matching gilet, with a wide-brimmed hat. Standing looking out to sea, his left hand in his pocket, his right outstretched holding a rope that appeared to have a rock on the end. Occasionally he took a step forward and the rock followed along the short, wind-mown grass. We watched him for ten minutes as he moved three metres forward, one small step at a time.

"Can't resist it, I've got to see what he's doing."

As we got closer it became obvious it wasn't a rock.

"Hello there. Nice day for walking your tortoise." It had been well over a year since our encounter in the woods on the second day of our walk from Minehead; we had long since dismissed the prophecy that we would "walk with a tortoise". Yet here, attached to a customized dog harness, as we neared the end of our journey, was that very thing. A tortoise, taking bites of grass and herby undergrowth, then moving on, one slow step after another.

"Lettuce."

"What?"

"Her name's Lettuce."

We all took a step forward.

"What are you doing with it — her — up here?"

The man looked at the lead in his hand and then at us as if we were stupid, as if what he was doing was the most obvious thing in the world.

"I'm taking her for a walk."

"For a walk? She likes a long walk, does she? Not sure you need the lead, though, she's not really going to run away in a hurry."

In unison we took another step.

"Don't let her deceive you; she looks slow, but if I turn my head, puff, she's gone. Then I have to get the lettuce out and sit and wait; eventually she'll smell it and come to it, but it can take hours." He lifted the flap of his pocket to show us the little gem lettuce inside.

"So that's why you call her Lettuce. Wouldn't it be easier to just put her in the garden?"

The man rolled his eyes as we took another step forward.

"You can't do that. She needs to get out and stretch her legs. I can't confine her; she's a wild animal. I bring her here every day."

"Right."

We climbed up the next headland before either of us dared to speak.

"What?"

"Don't even try to tell me that was a coincidence."

When we'd stopped laughing and turned around, Lantivet Bay was below us, and beyond that the familiar sight of Pencarrow Head. We walked painfully slowly, stopping to look around every few minutes, excited to get to the end but willing it not to come.

That night, not some disconnected night in some possible future, but that night we would unpack our rucksacks and unroll our sleeping bags on an unknown floor. Over the next few weeks we would sell off most of our remaining possessions to pay for a hire van to move what little we needed to Polruan. Moth would begin a degree without any real hope of surviving to the end of it. I would look for a job and start writing. And out of thin air, out of loss and pain and fear, we would be as happy as we were when we were twenty.

When it couldn't be delayed any longer we walked over Pencarrow Head. Our homeless trail was over. We sat on a bench overlooking Lantic Bay, our rucksacks propped together, and shared the last of a pack of wine gums. The peregrine swooped close by, following the line of the cliff down towards the bay before soaring back up and out of sight.

A figure appeared out of the gorse, wearing the same coat and hat he had a year ago, walking with the same stick.

"She's been back a week now. She'd gone same day you were las' year. Knew you were comin', told them all you were comin', that she were bringin' you back. It's a sign, i'n' it."

He headed slowly away to the road as the sun began to drop on the horizon and the mist lifted in the hollows.

We hadn't been afforded the luxury of time for the shockwaves from our past to play out and then — as in any good nature-redemption story — to go off into the wilderness to refind our way in life. Bad things had hit

347

us in the face like a tidal wave and would have washed us away if we hadn't found ourselves on the path. Our journey had drained us of every emotion, sapped our strength and our will. But then, like the windblown trees along our route, we had been re-formed by the elements into a new shape that could ride out whatever storms came over the bright new sea. I thought about the two teenagers wrapped up in the essence of each other, of a passion that had lasted for most of my life, of heavy rain and burning sun, of a peregrine soaring free on the thermals of the cliff edge, of two molecules that were held together by little more than an electrical charge, a charge that had been strong enough to form a powerful bond, but a bond that one day soon might break. At last I understood what homelessness had done for me. It had taken every material thing that I had and left me stripped bare, a blank page at the end of a partly written book. It had also given me a choice, either to leave that page blank or to keep writing the story with hope. I chose hope.

I had no idea what the future would bring, how it would be shaped by the months spent living wild on the Coast Path. All I knew was that we were lightly salted blackberries hanging in the last of the summer sun, and this perfect moment was the only one we needed.

Acknowledgements

Huge thanks to two amazing people: my incredible agent Jennifer Christie from Graham Maw Christie and my talented editor Fiona Crosby of Michael Joseph. Without these two visionary women this book might not have made it into print. Also Jane Graham Maw, for her help and hospitality. I can't thank Richenda Todd enough for her meticulous copy-editing, she was a pleasure to work with, and Angela Harding, whose artistic skills have created this beautiful cover. I'm also incredibly lucky to be working with the many other wonderful people at Michael Joseph; their enthusiasm is uplifting.

For all their patience and generosity as we sofa-surfed through their lives, I'll always be indebted to Adi and Cara, Sue and Steve, Janette and of course Polly. Sorry to all of you — for loitering too long in your bathrooms and using all the teabags.

We met many helpful, interesting and thoughtful people on our journey, many of whom are untraceable, but they know who they are. A special thanks to Dave and Julie for their continuing friendship, and Anna, who gave us the thing we needed most — a roof.

However, there's one friend we made on the path without whom we couldn't have made the journey. His foresight, wisdom and judgement made impossible days possible and encouraged us through the hardest moments. Without the friend in our pocket, Paddy Dillon, we might not have made it to the end of the path. In the writing of this book, I've found that he's just as enthusiastic and reliable in real life as he is on the page.

But, most importantly, all the love to my children Tom and Rowan; thanks for believing that I could walk 630 miles and write a book, when I didn't believe it myself. And of course Moth. Kind, persistent, inspirational Moth. Love of my life. Thank you.

MOTHER SHIP

Francesca Segal

They are the furthest from me, and the furthest from one another that they have ever been. I do not recognise them. They are otherworldly in their strangeness, and oceanic in their beauty . . . After her identical twin girls are born ten weeks prematurely, Francesca Segal finds herself sitting vigil in the "mother ship" of neonatal intensive care. Her gripping diary of those months brings to tender, evocative life the fresh challenges she and her babies face every day, while she makes a temporary life among a band of fearless mothers who take care not only of their children but also of one another. *Mother Ship* is a hymn to the sustaining power of women's friendships, and a loving celebration of the two small girls — and their mother — who defy the odds.

LOOK WHAT YOU MADE ME DO

Helen Walmsley-Johnson

Helen Walmsley-Johnson's first husband controlled her life, from the people she saw to what was in her bank account. He alienated her from friends and family and even their three daughters. Eventually he threw her out, and she painfully began to rebuild her life. Then, divorced and in her early forties, she met Franc. For ten years she would be in his thrall, even when he too was telling her what to wear, what to eat, even what to think. This is Helen's candid memoir of how she was trapped by a smiling abuser, not once but twice. It is a vital guide to recognizing, understanding and surviving this sinister form of abuse and its often terrible legacy — and an account of how one woman found the courage to walk away.